Steel Spine, Iron Will

By Rod Lewin

❖

Boomerang Books
Dallas, Texas

To Tommy
Best Regards!
Rod Lewin

Library of Congress Catalog Card Number 91-78105
ISBN 0-9632031-0-X

———————— ❖ ————————

Boomerang Books
P.O. Box 280781
Dallas, Texas 75228

Printed in the United States of America by
Taylor Publishing Company

This book is dedicated to Barbara.

Her love, dedication, devotion and attention to me after the plane crash were the primary forces which initially motivated me to get back on my feet. She will always be a part of me, and I am thankful for the time we shared together.

❖

ACKNOWLEDGMENTS

Writing a book is a complex task. Publishing one would not be possible without the advice and assistance of many people. I cannot begin to thank every person who either took part in the story or assisted with the writing and publishing of it.

However, I feel I must mention the following people.

First, I would like to thank Evelyn Oppenheimer, whose encouragement and support after initially reading the manuscript, gave me the inspiration to continue with the project. She is a great lady and a fine author, and I have the deepest respect for her.

Helen Lance is more than just a publishing consultant. When I approached Taylor Publishing Company to produce this book, Helen was my first line of communication with them. She has been my advisor throughout the production process. I could not have done it without her.

Scott Harmon volunteered to spend many hours editing the copy and content, and painstakingly converted my Australian verbiage and stilted paragraphing into a more readable and enjoyable style.

All my friends and colleagues at my airline deserve a special mention. Their enthusiasm about this project, and their advance orders for the book, helped me with much of the initial production costs. They are a fine group of people, and I am proud to work with them.

My mother, Marj, and my father, Bob, have been unwavering in their support for me throughout my life, but particularly during the events described in the book, and indeed, with the book itself. Their generosity, tolerance, understanding and love have been a constant source of strength to me.

Finally there is my wife, Cindy. Her patience, strength, and constant gentle nagging have seen us through this project (and our lives in general). She is an extremely talented graphic artist, and the covers of this book are her work. She is my mate; the best I could ever ask for.

INTRODUCTION

This story is true. I have, however, taken certain liberties with the names of some of the people involved in my hospital life to protect their privacy.

I have depicted as descriptively as possible the trauma I suffered as a result of becoming a paraplegic. There will be many people reading this book who can understand from first-hand knowledge what a debilitating condition any form of major paralysis is to learn to cope with.

No hope of recovery was given by the surgeons who operated on me. They were convinced that the nerve damage caused by fragments of crushed vertebrae was so extensive as to preclude any return of normal feeling or movement to my lower abdomen and legs.

There is absolutely no doubt in my mind that, despite their gloomy prognosis, nothing helped me more than a fierce and unrelenting determination to prove to the world and myself that I could win this battle against my own body. I am totally convinced that the old phrase 'mind over matter' is our greatest ally against almost any affliction known to man.

I must also confess that this determination, which became evident only after initial bouts of bitterness, depression and self-pity, was generated by an indomitable yearning to fly again.

All anyone needs in life is a goal, and the will to reach it.

R.J.L.

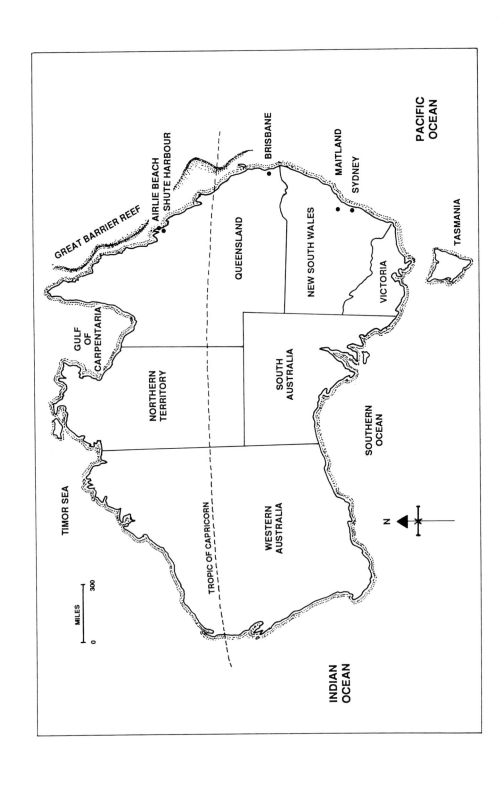

1

A cold, drizzling rain fell from the low, rolling layer of gunmetal colored stratus cloud as I eased the little Piper Warrior out on to the single, narrow, asphalt-surfaced runway at the National Aviation Academy about one hundred and fifty miles north of Sydney, Australia.

Although I had reservations about taking off with an overcast layer at one thousand feet, I was elated at having just heard the results of my written examinations for my Commercial Pilot's License. I had passed, and this was to be my last solo exercise before the 'big' one; the check ride with the Academy's Chief Flying Instructor, who held the power to make or break my future flying career.

There was no control tower at this small country airfield, so as I methodically completed my pre-takeoff checklist, I smoothly pushed the T-bar throttle all the way forward to the stop, releasing the brakes at the same time, and watched as the tachometer rose to the 2700 r.p.m. mark. The trainer leapt forward with the enthusiasm of a wallowing hippo and about fifteen seconds later we were almost at the sixty-five knots needed to break ground and fly. I eased the control wheel back slightly, the nose of the Warrior came up, and then we were airborne, struggling for the safety of altitude.

I lowered the nose to build climbing speed to about seventy-five knots and brought the throttle back slightly to maintain 2500 r.p.m. on the tachometer, then turned toward the designated training area about ten miles east of the academy complex and leveled off to cruise just below the ragged gray ceiling. Raindrops hit the windshield, instantly disappearing in the blast from the small propeller.

The last solo exercise! All the hard work was behind me now. After my check ride tomorrow, I could relax with the rest of the boys in my flight. We would probably go into town, quaff one or six 'stubbies' of beer at the local pub, and top them off with a celebration dinner at the Chinese restaurant a couple of doors down.

That was our idea of a good time on a limited budget (or any budget for that matter) in Smalltown, New South Wales. But right now it did not matter what town it was. Soon we would all be going our separate ways after spending eight rigorous, grueling months together, four to a room, under military type conditions and discipline.

Several months into the course, I had been elected Academy Captain, responsible for the general welfare and discipline of the entire student body of one hundred and twenty-five cadets. Most of them were several years younger than I. Many were just out of high school. They looked upon my old age of twenty-nine as having one foot in the grave, and consequently sought my paternal advice on all matters ranging from sex to sky-diving.

The only event most of them did not approve of was the mandatory morning drill session. Part of my role as Academy Captain of a quasi-military style institution was that of drill instructor. I definitely did not win any popularity contest when I had to roust them out of bed at five a.m. for room and uniform inspection, followed by a couple of hours of marching around the parade ground, rain or shine, to work up an appetite for breakfast.

Then, several hours in the classroom followed studying basic navigation, engines, principles of flight and meteorology before they got down to the really important stuff — the flying — in the afternoon, weather permitting!

But on this dull gray morning, all that was behind me now, and all I had to do was shoot some simulated engine failures and perform some basic airwork to polish myself up for the big show tomorrow. I approached the training area and looked all around to assure myself that I was not going to collide with one of my colleagues who was also in the area. Then I began my first engine failure routine.

I climbed to the very base of the overcast, until wisps of dirty scud swirled around my tiny machine. Then I deliberately closed the throttle and felt the familiar knot of tension curl in my stomach as the roar of the engine died and the propeller slowed to windmill in the airflow. I performed my emergency engine failure routine required to re-start the engine in the event of a real failure, and then selected a grassy field, reasonably flat and free from trees, and commenced my glide down. I lowered the flaps for slower speed and steeper approach one stage at a time, until I was sure I was going to make the meadow I had chosen.

At three hundred feet above the ground, I pushed the throttle all the way forward again and was relieved to hear the roar of the engine once more as I raised the nose to climb attitude and retracted the flaps.

I climbed the Warrior back to just below the cloud base at one thousand one hundred feet. It was the 19th day of September and the chill of winter still hovered in the air.

I zipped my navy blue uniform jacket higher towards my throat, as I shivered in the cool cockpit. I reached down to the lower panel and pulled the cabin heat knob out.

It did not occur to my enthusiastic but inexperienced mind to afford the same luxury to the engine carburetor, even though there was a control right next to the throttle quadrant for that very purpose. (Piston-engine airplane carburetors are notorious for icing up in a variety of atmospheric conditions, causing the engine to fail from fuel starvation.)

The second engine failure routine went just like the first, and as I applied power to climb away from undesirable proximity to the ground, I had convinced myself that I could acquit myself admirably tomorrow when John Forrest, the Chief Instructor, deliberately pulled the throttle and failed the engine somewhere over 'tiger country,' as we called the heavily wooded mountainous areas surrounding our little community.

Just to be absolutely certain I had the routine down pat, I thought, I would perform one more engine failure, choosing a different field this time. I closed the throttle for the third time, selected another paddock below and to my left, and with a perfect glide speed and attitude, coasted down to one hundred feet above the ground.

As the uneven grassy surface rose to greet me, I rammed the throttle home to the full power position, raising the nose and retracting the flaps at the same time. The Warrior sank further towards the ground as the flaps came up, robbing her of some precious lift, but then we were climbing away as the engine roared to noisy life. Without warning, however, it coughed once, sputtered twice, and instantly and irrevocably died!

I could not believe it, but my limited survival instincts took over and the emergency shut-down procedures which I had just been practising a few moments before were performed without my mind being conscious of directing them. We were still in a shallow climb with the airspeed rapidly bleeding off when I became aware of the line of trees looming ahead.

I checked the airspeed again and noted that the aircraft was still enough above the stall speed (the speed at which the wings can no longer generate lift to support the aircraft) to glide over the trees and into the beautiful, flat, green meadow which I could now see beyond.

"Come on," I silently pleaded. "Just a little bit more. Just a few feet further."

Then we were over the treetops — just barely — and I knew we were going to make it as I nosed her down, quivering on the edge of the stall, towards the meadow. Too late, much too late, I sensed rather than saw the horrible danger just ahead.

The windmilling propeller slashed into the high tension power lines with enough residual revolutions to completely sever the first cable. Thirty thousand volts of blue spark and flame crackled all around me like a bolt of sapphire lightning. The little aircraft plunged into the rest of the wires and the screeching sound of tearing, tortured aluminum filled my ears. I knew I was going to die!

We simply stopped flying in mid-air as the cables arrested all forward movement. My uncomprehending mind ridiculously compared this sensation to that of landing on an aircraft carrier. Then we were plummeting earthward — straight down with no forward movement at all.

My brain raced with a million thoughts. I cannot honestly remember my life flashing before my stunned eyes, but I sure did cram a lot of long-ago memories into a very few seconds.

The ground raced towards me and above the pounding of my heart I heard the grinding, wrenching noises of impact. The propeller and engine buried themselves deep into the soft earth. The wings tore free. The gas tanks inside them, weakened and torn by the power lines, ruptured and spilled 100 octane gasoline all round, saturating the ground and the wrecked aircraft.

Severed power lines lay on the ground arcing blue fire, exposing thousands of naked volts to the high octane fuel only feet away and creeping closer by the second.

I was going to burn!

Just one tiny spark and I would become engulfed in flame. I would be a fireball!

Blood on the windshield! Blood on my jacket and shirt and tie! Coppery taste in my mouth. I put my hand to my face. Wet and warm and sticky. I stared at my crimson hand and for the first time realized that I had remained conscious throughout the entire nightmare. At first, I thought that I had punctured a lung because of the blood in my mouth. Then, I discovered that it was oozing from my nose. The impact had thrown my face against the side of the canopy, breaking my nose and rupturing the blood vessels inside it.

I gazed around the wrecked cockpit. All the important fuel and electrical switches had been turned off, including the radio and main battery switch. I did not remember touching any of them. I must have subconsciously gone through the entire pre-impact checklist.

I had to get out!

Any second now, that leaking gasoline was going to reach the arcing cables and that would be the end of it. I probably would not even hear or see the explosion. I reached across the cockpit to the door on the right side of the aircraft, unlocked the safety latch, and attempted to drag myself out.

Nothing happened!

I tried again. I thought my legs must be pinned beneath me somehow. I looked down and saw that they were in their normal position on the rudder pedals. A wave of nausea swept over me. Once more I tried — with all my strength this time — to move to the right. A tremendous pain, the like of which I had never known before in my life, struck me like a physical blow.

I screamed! The pain doubled, if that was possible, and I passed out.

When I regained consciousness a few moments later, I looked up to find a curious farmer, no doubt the owner of the field into which I had crashed uninvited, standing beside the wreck. The first thing I remembered seeing was the smouldering cigarette butt hanging between his thin and dirty lips.

"Can I do somethin' for yer?" he asked laconically.

My eyes bulged as they focused on that cigarette which was now between his bony fingers, about to be flicked onto the volatile earth.

"Christ!" I gasped through the pain. ". . . only thing you can do is get the HELL away from here with that cigarette . . . get to phone . . . call ambulance and fire brigade . . . GET 'em here . . . quickly!"

He ambled off without a reply, and I wondered if he would bother to call anybody at all.

Meanwhile, I thought, with reasonable coherence under the circumstances, I still have to get out of here. The only way I could be sure of getting some assistance was to call for it myself. That meant re-activating the battery and the radio, and all I needed was one little spark from either of those components as I closed the switch and pressed the transmit button on the microphone, and I would be barbecued!

It had to be done.

I closed my eyes as I flipped the master switch on. The wrecked and twisted panel came alive. No spark! The radio switch. No spark. Now for the big one. I gingerly pressed the mike button and scrunched down in my seat, expecting to be instantly blown to eternity. No spark! Instead, the crackle of the carrier wave hissed through the speaker.

"Mayday! Mayday! Mayday! . . . Charlie November Romeo. Piper Warrior . . . Charlie November Romeo . . . crashed one zero miles east of

Cessnock . . . five miles south of Maitland airport. Plane destroyed . . . pilot badly injured . . . severed power lines . . . ruptures fuel tanks . . . need immediate assistance. Repeat, need urgent and immediate assistance. Somebody, please reply!"

I released the button and slumped lower in the broken seat, perspiring from the pain, the shock and the terror of fire. A few moments later, a reply crackled through the speaker. The voice was hesitant and disbelieving. I recognized it immediately as belonging to my friend and fellow student, Paul Howard.

"Charlie November Romeo, this is Charlie November Lima. Is that you, Rod? Tell me you're kidding!"

I closed my eyes and hit the mike button again. ". . . wish I was kidding, Paul," I replied, clenching my teeth against a red mist of pain.

"I'm serious. I'm trapped in this wreck, . . . fuel all around . . . can't move . . . don't know why. Hit the panic button for me!"

"Sure thing. Right away. And I'll head back to base and get help from the boys there. We'll be back with you in no time, buddy. Just hang on tight."

"Thanks, mate." I replied, barely able to speak by this time.

I waited until I heard him relay the Mayday call to the nearest Flight Service Station, then I shut down the power for the second time and once again struggled, with increasing pain and panic, to get out of the stricken aircraft.

I do not remember passing out. I came to as I was being bodily manhandled out of the wreck. Opening my eyes, I focused on a blurred sea of strange faces looking down on me as they lifted me off the broken right wing. They carried me with their arms linked under my body from my shoulders to my ankles, with one other gently supporting my throbbing head.

The pain in my back was unbearable! One of the men supporting my lower spine stumbled on the lumpy ground and in his effort to recover, his arms jerked into my back. I screamed! Just before I passed out again, my befuddled brain recorded images of several police cars with flashing lights, the ambulance into which I was being gently lowered, and before they closed the rear doors, the rugged, bearded face of Chris Bull, my flying instructor at the academy.

I will never forget that ambulance ride over the rutted paddock and rough country road to the small community hospital in the town of Maitland. Although they had pumped me full of some pain-killing drug before we began the journey, I still felt every single tiny bump and pothole on that second-longest ride of my life. The longest was yet to come!

They wheeled me into the casualty and emergency ward. Blurred impressions of men and women in white gowns. A huge x-ray machine. Doctors whispering. Fragments of conversation . . . "Nothing we can do for him here. . . . Spine crushed. Paralyzed from waist down." Oh God! No. Please, no. Not that! "Need to get him to Sydney Spinal Unit. Best neuro-surgeons in the country." Oh dear Lord! Please. Not paralyzed!

Strong overhead light gleaming on the sharp point of a six feet long hypodermic needle. Watched as it disappeared somewhere inside my right elbow. Faces swimming. Another ambulance, barely recognizable. More bouncing along a rock-strewn desert track. Doors open. More faces. Gray overcast. White aeroplane. Two engines. Good! Don't like one engine. Cargo doors. Red Cross. Pretty face hovering above. Going round and round.

Vague idea that I was being strapped down from my chest to my feet. I became aware of the familiar smells of an aircraft, then through a red haze induced by pain and morphine, saw two faces gazing down at me. One was that same pretty face I seemed to remember from a hundred years ago, as they lifted me out of the ambulance into the aircraft. The other was Chris Bull.

By now the shock was well and truly setting in, and the pain did not seem to be quite so bad. Somebody closed the aircraft doors and I felt vibration flow through my broken body as the engines started. The moment we moved, I knew that the pain was not really going away. It was going to stay with me forever!

The engine note rose to an almost unbearable level and we rolled down the short runway. My second takeoff that day, I remember thinking as I lay there half-conscious. Not exactly the way I had planned it.

The irritating thrum of unsynchronized propellers at take-off power pulsed through my brain and body, and I mentally begged the pilot to equalize the r.p.m.s of the engines. As though he had read my thoughts, the noise eased to a steady and rhythmic roar and I fell into dazed and drugged torpor. I had the ridiculous idea that this was all a terrible dream. I had not really taken off on that fateful flight at all. I was still in bed and any second I would wake, get dressed, have some breakfast and go out to my aeroplane for my final sequence. Then another part of my brain said, "Oh, it was your final sequence, all right. And it has already happened and . . . "

Then, in the only part of this nightmare that seemed to take no time at all, we were touching down. I am sure that it was probably the best landing that pilot had ever accomplished, but my back did not think so. It screamed in protesting agony as the wheels hit the runway at Sydney International Airport, then we were taxiing into the Air Ambulance Headquarters. About two weeks later, it seemed, the doors were opened and my strapped-down body was lifted into bright white light. The only clear recollection of that moment was the huge red and yellow air conditioning ducts running around the high arched ceiling of the hangar.

Then they were rolling me into another ambulance for this, the longest ride of my life. I have no idea exactly how long it took to drive the ten or twelve miles from Sydney Airport to Royal North Shore Hospital. All I know is that every bump, every stop, every turn, every skid on old tramlines, was transmitted directly from the wheels to my spine by some invisible cable. The entire ride consisted solely of unbearable pain, groaning, passing out, and waking to more pain.

Finally, I fell into a deeper state of black and thankful oblivion. From somewhere deep in my sub-conscious, I could hear voices whispering around me. Time no longer had any meaning and I had no earthly idea how long I had been lying there. I do remember my entire body being passed through a huge round open-ended cylinder which was rotated around me several times. Much later, I discovered that this was a huge x-ray device which took pictures of my entire skeletal structure from all angles. I was to visit the thing several times during the months ahead.

A male voice was speaking quietly. I could not see him, but his words were sharp and clear, despite my drugged condition. " . . . and the prognosis is quite good, really. Of course, he will be a paraplegic, but under the circumstances, he is an incredibly fortunate young man."

I heard only one word. PARAPLEGIC!!! NO!! Fortunate? Paraplegic? Please God, NO! Not that!! Then I was being wheeled off to some other part of the hospital.

Double glass doors. Clusters of blinding white lights directly over a long table covered in white. Lots of little steel trolleys littered with gleaming surgical instruments. Some kind of electronic machine with a radar screen. Hundreds of hands reaching for me, transferring me from my mobile stretcher to the table. Turning me ever so slowly on to my stomach. I opened my mouth to scream again. No sound came out. My face was turned to the left side. No pillow under my head. Rubbery odor. Mask over my nose and mouth. Strange sensation. Pain subsiding. Consciousness sliding away. I'm dying. It's so wonderful. No more pain! No more . . .

❖

2

Consciousness came and went, interspersed with broken, blurred images appearing, then disappearing, before my aching eyes. A billowing green wall closed in on me. Fragments of pale gold sunlight flickered on that wafting wall. Voices murmured outside my closed prison. Strange people came and went, subjecting me to painful examinations and injections; I did not know what or why. I floated on a bed of soft pillows that seemed to rotate around my battered body.

Finally, I became aware that I was actually awake and still alive, though in what condition, I had no idea. A dull, aching throb in my lower spine reminded me why I was here. I tried to rise and the agony returned, forcing a groan from my very sore and swollen lips.

The green curtain was pulled aside to reveal a nursing sister and two wardsmen, all dressed in crisp, starched white uniforms. They immediately began fussing over and around me with pillows, bed pans and other assorted hospital necessities, and an examination of myself revealed that I was permanently attached to the bed by various tubes and appendages. One of these, I was quick and horrified to observe, protruded from my lower stomach — my bladder, I was later shocked to discover.

I gazed around the ward exposed by the open curtain and found that I had three room-mates; two of them younger and the third a lot older than I. At this point, my interest in the outside world rapidly waned as the sister instructed the wardsmen to tilt the bed, roll me on my side and place more pillows under my back.

I supposed that this was an effort to make me more comfortable, but the only effect was to bring another wave of pain and anguish washing over me. I let them know in the only way I knew how. I screamed — very loudly. Instinctively I tried to pull away from them. I could twist my upper body, but was horrified to discover — for the second time — that from my hips down, there was no response to any commands my brain sent in that direction.

It is impossible to describe to a person with normal movement, the feeling of utter futility, dejection and abject terror when one discovers that he is paralyzed. Between rushes of nausea, I began the self-pity, thoughts of the bleak future, the senseless stupidity of it all; the "Oh God, why me!" syndrome, which was to last for many weeks.

Not a pretty sight!

I yelled at them to leave me alone and to go find a doctor who could tell me when I could get out of this place.

The sister called off the two wardsmen, then she replaced the curtain around the bed and left me to stew in anxiety and fear for what seemed like hours. I was just dozing off when the curtain was once again pulled aside to reveal the same sister, this time accompanied by a kindly looking man, stocky with wavy blond hair and twinkling blue eyes and a dimpled smile. I guessed he was about fifty. He wore a smart gray business suit and certainly was not my idea of the doctor he turned out to be.

The sister, speaking to me directly for the first time, introduced him as Doctor John Yeoman, adding with the first hint of compassion I had so far observed, that he was the finest neurosurgeon in the entire country.

Dr. Yeoman extended his perfectly manicured right hand, took mine and shook it firmly.

"Good morning Rod," he said cheerfully. "I guess I don't have to tell you that you are a very lucky young man. You could have — indeed, you should have — died in that crash. Fortunately we got to you in time. Late last night, we operated on your lower spine. We . . ."

I interrupted him rudely and, rather more harshly than I had intended, said, "Look Doc. Please don't give me the run-around. Just tell me in plain language. When will I be able to fly again?"

He sighed, turned to his companion and said, "Sister Wang, please leave us alone for a few moments. I will call you if I need you."

Sister Wang — that was the first time I had heard her name — nodded, turned and left, pulling the curtain closed behind her.

I was too apprehensive of what I was going to hear to say any more, so I lay there and waited for the bad news.

"All right, Rod. I'll give it to you straight," he said. "Please interrupt me if I say anything you do not understand. I will make it as plain as possible."

"You had severe compression of your lower spine as a result of the crash. In other words, all your lumbar vertebrae, which took the entire force of the fall, were smashed and the bone splinters from them fragmented like an exploding hand grenade and entered your spinal cord. These bone splinters are what caused the major damage. What we have done is to open your back, surgically remove all the smashed vertebrae and as many of the bone fragments as possible from your spinal cord, and reinforce the remainder of your spine with what is called a Harrington rod, connected to your tail bone below, and the upper portion of your spine, which was not damaged.

"We then taped your spinal cord, which sends all your brain signals to the various parts of your body, to the Harrington rod. The damage caused to your spinal cord by the bone splinters is what has initiated the paralysis — and also the pain — of which you are now aware."

I lay there in silence for a few moments, trying to absorb what he had told me. Then I mustered up the courage to ask the big question.

"All right. If you have repaired the damage, how long will it be before I can walk again?"

He raised his hands and shoulders defensively and replied in a guarded tone, "I am afraid it is not quite that simple, Rod."

"The injury to your spinal cord is substantial," he went on.

"It will take some considerable time before we know if we have been able to reverse the result of the damage. I cannot say, at this stage . . ."

"Oh come ON Doc," I interrupted again, becoming frantic by this time at the implications of what he was saying — or not saying.

"Say what you mean, for God's sake. Tell me if I am going to walk again or not!"

He shrugged and raised his hands again in resignation and said, "Rod, I honestly don't know. Despite the operation we have performed to remove the vertebrae and the splinters, all indications at this stage seem to be that the damage is permanent. Your spinal cord is not severed. Therefore, in theory, you should regain some movement in your legs. However, if you do walk again, it will probably be necessary for us to fit you with calipers and crutches. Your muscles will atrophy with lack of use and you will not have the capability to walk again unaided."

I must have been holding my breath for the entire time he was speaking. I let it go in one long sigh, and covered my face with my right arm. I did not want him to see that I was crying.

He put his hand on my shoulder and squeezed it gently.

"The one thing you must remember is that in a case like this, half the battle is in your head. You must never give up hope."

"I will be by to see you as often as I can. We shall want to x-ray you again in a week or two, depending on how you are feeling."

I ignored him and kept my face covered. He turned and strode out of the small enclosure that was to be my prison for many long months. I did not see him again for a week.

Sounds outside the bed curtain seemed to be a million miles away. I lay there and cried for a long time. The pain in my back was killing me again, and eventually I had to emerge from my shell of self-pity to call the duty nurse for something to relieve the agony.

Sister Wang came back, saw my condition, and knew instinctively what to give me. She injected me with some kind of sedative and the next thing I remembered was waking in the dead of the longest night I have ever known. The curtain had been pulled back and I could see light in the corridor outside the open door. The voices of the night staff drifted in to me. Normal people out there. Talking, drinking coffee, passing the long night vigil with their workmates, then finishing their shift and WALK-ING out of the building. There were millions of people outside this room, and they were all walking, and I was stuck here alone, never able to do anything by myself again. From now on I would have to depend on somebody else for everything I wanted to do, every place I wanted to go, and I would NEVER BE ABLE TO WALK OR FLY AGAIN!

I lay awake all that long and lonely night, wallowing in self-pity and writhing in unrelenting agony. At least, the top half of me was writhing. No matter how I tried to move to relieve the pain, my body from the hips down would not function, and the pain would not cease.

That was the first time in my life — but not the last time in that bloody hospital — that I sincerely wished that I had died in the crash. My entire life — all my dreams and ambitions and hopes for the future — had collapsed around me. I was a paraplegic forever.

The night dragged on and on. Several times my anguished cries became so loud that the duty nurse had to come and calm me down with another sedative. I must have been driving them and every one of the other patients in the room crazy, but I did not care. I was too involved in my own terrible nightmare.

Finally, as the dawn light began angling through the single tall window of the room, creeping towards my bed, I dozed off into a fitful sleep. The last thing I remembered was one of the night staff drawing the curtain around the bed so that the sunlight would not waken me again.

I awoke about mid-afternoon. The burning hell of the night before had subsided to mere agony. The curtain was drawn back to reveal a hive of activity. The other three occupants of the room were wide awake and being attended by various nurses and relatives.

The fellow in the bed on my left was sitting up — or rather, propped up and people who turned out to be his mother, father and younger brother were standing around talking and joking with him.

Nobody had realized that I was awake yet, so I lay there and listened to their conversation; and my self-pity and anger at the world of the night before was quickly replaced by a fervent gratitude that I was not as badly off as my neighbor.

His name was Mark. He was eighteen years old and he was a quadriplegic. He was paralyzed from the neck down! He could just barely nod and shake his head. He could not speak or move a single muscle of his body.

He had been at a college dance. He had stumbled and toppled backwards over a railing surrounding a landing at the top of a small flight of steps, fallen five feet, landed on his head, broken his neck and severed his spinal cord.

Finish. The end.

Death would have been kinder, and he said so many times during the course of my stay there. Often in the coming weeks I would wake, not to my own screaming as on that first dreadful night, but to Mark's, begging for one of the nurses to give him an overdose of something to put him out of his misery.

Eighteen years old! No!! I had no right to be bitter at the world.

I was turned toward his bed and his father caught my eye. He came to me and put out his hand.

"I'm David. Mark's father. And this is Helen, my wife, and over there is Steven, Mark's younger brother."

They were all in remarkably good spirits under the circumstances, and I could not help being affected by their friendship and kindness to me.

David told me all about Mark's injury. It had happened two days prior to his eighteenth birthday, which he had spent sitting in the same position he was in now. He had been there six weeks. His every move, his every physical need had to be performed by either his parents or the nursing staff. There was absolutely no hope that he would ever move again, and his family was having their house altered to allow for Mark and his wheelchair: A big and expensive job. When it was completed, Mark could go home. There was nothing more that anyone could do for him here, apart from helping him to adjust mentally to his new life.

Sister Wang came in while David was talking. She excused us, drew the curtain around my bed, and proceeded with what was to become a horrible and humiliating routine. She called a wardsman who mercilessly rolled me on my right side and placed a bedpan under my useless hips. They then left for a few minutes and waited for the result of the previous night's concoction they had force-fed me to take its course. They had it down to a fine art, too. I suppose it kept their schedule nice and orderly having everyone go at the same time. God, it was awful!

From that first day on, I fought it every way I knew how. I threatened, cajoled, pleaded and screamed at them to leave me alone to have my bowel movements in peace. I told them I could look after myself. Finally, they left the bedpan on the bed. It was my first big challenge. I quickly realized that it was not going to be as easy as they made it look.

Eventually however, with my back screaming blue murder as I tried to roll, and my hips and legs refusing to budge, I got the damn thing under me fortunately in the right position. The rest was easy.

The second night, the pain was almost as bad as the first. I know I woke Mark and the other two patients. No matter how hard I tried to control my urge to cry out, every few minutes, a shock wave of agony would surge through me, causing a bellow that brought one of the nurses running. But, as with the night before, I eventually fell into a restless and uncomfortable sleep which was punctuated with recurrent nightmares of the crash.

When I woke on the third morning, the pain had once again receded. The curtain was still drawn around the bed, but I was not alone. Even before I opened my eyes, I could sense her presence. A familiar scent reminded me of things long past and I thought I was dreaming once more.

I opened my bleary eyes and there she was; a vision of loveliness from my past, sitting beside the bed watching me. Long, black hair, shiny as a crow's wing; big, bright glistening brown eyes; nose and cheeks with just a hint of her Pitcairn and Norfolk Island heritage, and that lop-sided smile revealing the flashing, perfect white teeth I remembered from long ago.

Barbara!

The smiling face and the instant recollection of wonderful memories conjured up by her name brought me to instant and total awareness.

"Barb!!"

I cried her name out loud and tried to sit up. She stood, leaned forward, and pushed me gently back to the pillow. Her perfume wafted over me and my heart pounded and my pulse ran wild.

She sat on the edge of the bed and took my hand. I winced as the bed shifted under her, causing a spasm of pain. She immediately returned to the chair, drew it closer, and once more gripped my hand.

"Barb," I repeated. "Is it really you? God, it's so good to see you!"

"Hi handsome," she replied, flashing that brilliant, infectious smile.

"Of course it's me. Who else were you expecting? And who else would trek all the way across Sydney in the dead of night to get here in time so you wouldn't wake up alone again? I only heard about it a few hours ago. Paul called me. Another fine mess you have got yourself into!"

Memories of all our wonderful times together came rushing, surging back through me. I began to cry. I could not stand her seeing me like this. All the incredible, crazy things we did together, we could never do again. Not now. Not ever!

She read my mind, as she always could.

"O.K. Baldy," she said, irreverently referring to my thinning scalp.

"You've been here two days. That's enough time to wallow in self-pity. One look around this room should be enough to tell you that you're not as bad off as some. I have seen Doctor Yeoman and he has told me all about your injuries. I don't care what he says. You are going to walk out of this hospital. I am going to spend every spare minute of my valuable time right here in this room, to make sure that there is not a moment of your day, awake or asleep, that you are not trying to get out of that bed and walk. You always would use any excuse to do as little as possible, you lazy bum."

I looked at her through stinging eyes. This girl did have a way of making me stop feeling sorry for myself! She was right, of course. I damn well had to get my act together and start working on recovering the use of my legs. Nobody else could do it for me. As usual, it was Barbara who managed to point out the obvious to me. I wiped my eyes with my free hand, returned her squeeze with the other, and dragged myself up to a semi-sitting position, for the first time ignoring the pain.

"So what have you been doing the last couple of years?" I asked, trying to change the subject.

"Are you still with QANTAS? How is your Mum?"

"She's fine. As a matter of fact, she is coming by this afternoon to take a look at you. She agrees with me that this is all a big act of yours to get some attention. As for QANTAS, I am still on the fourth floor. Been promoted to senior marketing programmer. I was going to London in a couple of weeks on an advertising campaign. I told my boss it will have to wait for a while because something more important has come up. He was not very impressed, of course. Too bad! You know me. The lame and sick always have come first. I just can't help it."

As she spoke I gazed into her smiling eyes, recalling all the good times we had shared between the time we had met on that February day and the time we had reluctantly parted, each of us realizing that we had met too soon; that neither of us was yet ready for total commitment to the other.

I could never forget that day. It was the fifteenth day of February. I was flying, as a flight attendant with QANTAS, on the return leg of a short trip to Auckland, New Zealand. She had been sitting in my zone on the 747. I could not stay away from her and kept returning to her seat to offer her the very best service any passenger on QANTAS had ever received. She was very shy at first, convinced that I was just trying to pick her up.

Of course, she was absolutely right! But it was a little more serious than that. I was struck at first sight by her unusual beauty. She wore a cream slack suit which was a perfect contrast to her coal black hair. She had a huge bouquet of red roses carefully placed on the empty seat next to her. I told her that she would not be allowed to take them through Customs as the Agricultural Inspectors would confiscate them. She did not care and wanted to hold on to them as long as possible.

She told me she had been living in New Zealand for two years, but wanted to return to Sydney and had chosen to arrive in time for her brother's twenty-first birthday party on the following evening.

Just before the big 747 landed, I mustered up the courage to ask if I could see her again, perhaps the evening after her brother's party. She refused at first, but finally agreed, I think to stop my constant visits to her seat, which were beginning to draw attention from other passengers who were wondering why they were not receiving similar excellent service.

Two nights later, I took her out and we wined and dined and began a wonderful relationship which was to become sometimes tempestuous and frustrating, and sometimes the most splendid and loving affair I had ever experienced.

The weeks passed and our feelings grew stronger but always there was a shadow of foreboding hovering over us. My job with QANTAS took me away sometimes for weeks at a time. Barbara was a girl who needed constant love and attention. She could not stand being left alone for such long periods. Eventually she asked me to resign and find a job on the ground where I could be home all the time. This led to constant bickering and finally, though our love and friendship was stronger than ever, we — or rather I — decided we had to part. We both cried a million tears on that final night, but the next morning, I took off on a three week trip. I knew she would not be there when I returned.

I tried calling every day I was away. There was never any answer. When I got home, I learned from her mother that she had left the country and gone on an extended cruise. She finally did call me when she returned. We remained firm friends and dated from time to time. She had, under my influence, applied to QANTAS for a position on the ground in marketing, a job for which she was ideally suited, with her unique personality.

She had been accepted and was doing exceptionally well. She had also begun dating one of her co-workers. One day on a lunch date, she reluctantly told me that she could no longer see me. She said that although we would always be close, she could not continue dating, as it simply hurt too much to see me on a casual basis.

I agreed with her. It was affecting me in the same way and I had been absolutely miserable while she was away. I had time and time again tried to tell myself that she meant more to me than my job, and that I simply must get a ground job and ask her to marry me.

When it came down to losing her, though, I still could not quit flying. I let her walk away on that last day, knowing that this was my final chance; that I would probably never see her again.

I got home that afternoon, restless and miserable, not knowing what to do with the rest of my life. I had admitted to myself for some time that I did not really want to be a flight steward forever.

I wanted to fly. I wanted to be a pilot! That was what had been nagging at my insides all this time. I was flying on those big, beautiful airplanes, watching the fellows up front have all the fun, while I was down the back serving tea and coffee.

I wanted to fly!

I knew this was the only thing that was going to save me from the misery of missing Barbara.

Instead of frittering my money away on buying junk overseas, as I usually did, I began saving earnestly. I stopped drinking, which I had begun to do seriously, like many of the flight crews did on layovers on long trips, mostly out of boredom.

There was an Academy of flight training about one hundred miles north of Sydney. I enrolled in a class beginning the following March. That gave me almost a year to save the necessary fourteen thousand dollars; a lot of money on my salary.

I did not see Barbara. Instead, I called her mother and brother many times in the following months. I wanted to stay close to the family as it made me feel close to Barb even though I had lost touch with her.

The weeks and months rolled by and then it was Christmas. I went home to Brisbane to spend the holiday season with my own parents; something I had not done for many years. I corresponded with them regularly by mail, of course, but I rarely had the opportunity to go home.

I had not told them about my plans to resign from QANTAS and commence commercial pilot training, so I broke the news to them at Christmas. My dear mother, in her own inimitable style, told me she could not understand my wanting to leave a nice, safe, secure job with QANTAS to join the ranks of the unemployed pilots in the country.

My father, on the other hand, agreed completely with my decision, as he had always wanted to fly himself but had never found the money or the opportunity to do so.

Several days after Christmas, I returned to Sydney and enjoyed the last few weeks of jet-setting around the world.

February came, and I reluctantly handed my resignation in to my supervisor in the Cabin Crew Department, giving him four weeks notice.

I returned from my last trip to London via Singapore, where I took the opportunity to buy one last swag of inexpensive junk in Change Alley before I went home. I got off the 747 for the last time, took a cab to my apartment on the beach at Clovelly, packed the clothes I would need for the next eight months into my battered old suitcase plastered with thousands of airline and hotel stickers, and lugged it down to the bus stop. (I had sold my car to help raise the money I needed for the flying course.) Half an hour later, I was heading north.

No regrets. No fanfare or farewell party or drinks with my pals from eight years with QANTAS. And not a word to Barbara. I called her mother Nellie, said good-bye and told her to give Barb my love. She knew how deeply I meant it. She had always wanted me to be her son-in-law.

During the next few months, I was studying so hard that I had little time to think about Barb. The course was extremely intensive. Up at five a.m. every day, classroom academics on the many subjects that had to be completed, then flying every afternoon, weather permitting.

No time to go to Sydney on weekends. We got as far as the local pub or maybe sometimes we visited one — or several — of the many vineyards in the Hunter Valley. Our airfield was conveniently situated right in the heart of one of the finest wine producing areas in the country, which we at the academy considered to be very fortuitous indeed!

Time passed quickly. I grew to know and like my new bunch of mates. I convinced myself that I had forgotten all about my previous life, and became so totally committed to these guys that the course was almost over before I realized it. We had finished all our examinations. Everybody in my own flight had passed.

That dreadful morning arrived, cold, bleak and miserable.

Was it only two days ago? It seemed like an eternity since I had climbed into the little Warrior for the last time. It surely must have been eons ago that I saw or even thought about Barbara.

No! Not true. I had tried to convince myself that it was true every day for the last eight months, and every day I knew deep down that she was firmly implanted in my subconscious and crept to the surface every time I let my mind wander off my work for the tiniest fraction of time.

Now she was here beside me again. In real life! I finally accepted the fact that she had come to me many times in my dreams during the short nights at the academy. And at the moment of absolute crisis, here she was beside me once more; the last person I expected to see. The only one I wanted to see!

3

Barbara quickly won the hearts of not only the other fellows in my room, but also the transient doctors and nursing staff. On the very first morning that she magically appeared beside me, she immediately took over the more fundamental duties of the wardsmen and nurses. She did everything from changing sheets and bathing my battered body to washing my hair and feeding me, including cooking my food. She absolutely hated the way the nurses treated us, considering them callous and indifferent to our helpless plight.

She spent her entire first day, and most the night, getting the place organized the way she wanted it. She would have even given me my shots if the nurses had allowed it. Instead, she told me in no uncertain terms that I did not need to be relying on those drugs anyway and that I was to stop taking them. I had to learn to live with the pain in my back for the rest of my life, so I might as well start right now.

So I took her at her word and the next time Sister Wang came to give me a shot I told her what she could do with it. Naturally, the good Sister was appropriately distressed. It probably saved me from becoming dependent on the stuff, but it sure made the next few days and nights hell.

Barbara was right, though. In a few days the really severe pain began to wane. I'm sure that I did not notice it so much because of her constant attention.

That day and night went so quickly! Barb finally collapsed around two a.m. the following morning, after running around for me and my room mates, serving our meals, buying flowers to brighten up the room, calling the wardsmen every ten minutes to tell them to take trays away or bring fresh sheets or pillows. They had never worked so hard!

She kissed me good-night and left around two-thirty, promising to be back tomorrow. I did not sleep at all that night. This time it was not the pain that kept me awake, but memories of the day — and the thought of all the wonderful days that were to follow, now that Barb was back.

Her mother came in that morning. I had not seen Nell since the day I left Sydney to head north to the academy. Now here I was, back in Sydney under much less pleasant circumstances, and here was Nellie, my second visitor, preceded only by her daughter. She was her same old cheery self.

"Hi there, boy. How are you? Silly question, I suppose. I knew as soon as we left you alone you would get yourself into all sorts of trouble. I told Barb the news as soon as I heard. I also called your folks and told them. They are on the way down to see you. Has Barb been in yet?"

"Hi Nellie. Good to see you, too," I replied wearily, pecking her on the cheek as she leaned over to give me a hug.

"Thanks for letting my folks know, although knowing my Mum, she knew the moment I crashed that something was wrong. And yes, Barb has been here, all right. She was here when I opened my eyes yesterday morning, and she left only a few hours ago. I hope she is sound asleep by now. She said she was coming back later today."

"She missed you, Rod. She was always talking about you. Of course, I have always told her that you two should never have split up. Maybe you would not be here now if you had stayed together."

"You're probably right, Nellie," I replied. "But at least she is with me again now, when I need her the most. I hope I can do the same for her some day when I have got myself out of this mess."

"Well, we all have faith that you will be walking again soon, so it's up to you to prove it to us — and yourself."

"Yeah. That's what Barb told me in no uncertain terms about five minutes after I woke to find her sitting beside me. It IS up to me. I realize that and I am going to start working on it right away."

"That's the spirit. Never give up hope. There are a lot of people pulling for you."

Nell stayed and chatted for an hour or so. The nursing staff left me alone. I think they were all a bit put out by Barbara's obvious dislike for them. Well, that suited me fine. I did not like them hovering over me with their hypos and bedpans anyway.

As Nell got up to leave, Barb came back into the room, staggering under an armload of supplies.

"Hi Mum," she called, bright as a button, as though she had had a full night's sleep.

"I'm glad you are here. You can give me a hand setting up all this stuff," she added, placing her packages on a nearby table.

She greeted the other three patients with the same enthusiasm as the day before, then came to me and gave me a kiss and a hug, tousled my hair, which she said needed to be washed again, and proceeded to set up her mysterious equipment.

The first thing she extracted from one of the bags was an electric frypan!

She plugged it in, turned on the thermostat control, and pulled already prepared chicken breasts and various peeled and sliced vegetables from another bulging sack. Placing the chicken in the pan, she then poured a pre-mixed home made Marengo sauce over it and began to stir.

It must have taken her hours to prepare all this stuff, so she had gotten little or no sleep when she finally did get home.

"I don't like the food they are serving you guys here," she said, looking around at all of us as she prepared the meal. "I'm going to feed you from now on, and just let them try to stop me," she added, referring to all the hospital staff in general.

Soon the mouth-watering aroma of freshly fried Chicken Marengo was wafting around the halls, and Barb and Nell were both busily serving up huge helpings to Mark, Ken and Brian, when Sister Wang angrily swept in with a pair of beefy interns to back her up.

"You can't cook in here!" she screeched, waving her ample arms frantically. "It is absolutely forbidden to give the patients food like this. It is not good for them! I want you to remove all this . . . this equipment immediately, and take that food away from those patients. I won't have this sort of behavior in my ward!"

Barb strutted up to Sister Wang and stood nose to nose with her.

"Listen SISTER," she emphasized, making it quite obvious she was not referring to her title, "this food is a damn sight better for these guys than any of the junk I have seen you feeding them. What's more, I will give 'em anything I please, any time I want, and you just try to stop me!"

Sister Wang stood there for several moments, her mouth working as if she was trying to speak. No words came forth, however. She had obviously never encountered any problem like this before, and was at a complete loss as to how to handle this mutinous outsider, who had so defiantly encroached upon her personal territory.

Barb stood hands on hips, refusing to budge, staring her down. Sister Wang surrendered first, turned and stomped off trailing her two similarly shocked escorts.

"I will be back," she called over her shoulder. "You won't get away with this. I shall have Doctor Yeoman throw you out of this hospital and you will not ever be allowed back through the front door. You'll see!"

Barbara laughed at the retreating figure and turned back to her self-imposed task.

"Mum, why don't you give Ken and Brian their tucker, while I look after Mark and Rod."

"But what about . . . " Nell began.

"Don't worry about Doctor Yeoman," Barb replied confidently. "I have him eating out of my hand already."

She was not bluffing either.

Sitting down at the table between Mark and myself, she began cutting up a plate full of chicken and vegetables and fed them, spoonful at a time, to Mark whom she had propped up for the occasion. He was obviously delighted by the excitement, and was grinning and laughing and making sounds which were becoming more intelligible every day.

For his part, Mark's attitude had improved tremendously in the past few days and especially since Barb had started talking to him yesterday. Now he was opening his mouth and allowing her to feed him and making earnest attempts to talk and convey his gratitude to her.

As for me, she set a steaming plate on a bed table in front of me and said, "You're on your own, baldy. You are a big boy now. You can feed yourself."

I glowered mockingly at her and then Mark, who rudely poked his tongue at me.

When she had finished feeding Mark, Barb took his hands and began rubbing them, opening and closing his fist, bending his wrist back and forth and then working on his arms.

"It's about time you did a bit of work, too," she told him. "I haven't seen anybody giving you physiotherapy. How do you expect to feed yourself if you are too lazy to move your arms. I am not going to be around forever, you know."

He laughed and let her work on him. It was the first time I had seen him in any mood other than deep depression.

Nell, meanwhile, was bantering with the other two fellows. I had discovered through conversation that both Ken and Brian were paraplegics like myself and were in hospital for recurrent treatment. Both had been injured years before and were confined permanently to wheelchairs, returning to hospital for periodic treatment and examination.

I had finished my excellent meal and Barb was just about to begin a workout on my legs when the dragon-lady returned as promised with the good doctor.

"Aha!" she bellowed. "See, Doctor. This . . . this UNQUALIFIED person is not only cooking in the ward but performing unauthorized and probably damaging therapy on the patients. She must be removed from the premises immediately!"

"Thank you Sister," replied Doctor Yeoman. "I can see what is occurring here. However, I am afraid I see something you have obviously overlooked. Every one of these patients is smiling. Look at Mark. Have you seen him this happy before? Have any of your staff been able to do in six weeks what this young lady has accomplished in one day?"

"Please do not misunderstand me, Sister. I appreciate that you have many other wards and patients to attend to, and you have set standards and procedures to abide by. But let us not stand in the way of someone who can only benefit these chaps and take some of the work-load off your shoulders into the bargain. No. I think Miss Terry — and her mother — may stay and attend to these patients in their own way as long as they so desire."

"However," he added, turning to Barb, "please understand, Miss Terry, that Sister Wang and her staff have certain duties to perform regarding the patients' welfare. I do not want you interfering with those duties or trying to prevent them. Otherwise I will have no choice but to curtail your own very generous activities here. Is that clear?"

Barb gave him that winning, lopsided, smile of hers, threw a mock salute, and came smartly to attention.

"Yes Sir! Perfectly Sir! You will not CATCH me taking liberties ever again, Doctor Yeoman, Sir!"

"Very well, then," the doctor replied, scowling suspiciously at her from beneath bushy brows.

"Furthermore," he added. "Sister Wang is right when she says you must not move Rod's legs like that. There will be time enough for therapy later. He cannot be moved — and I do mean no part of him can be moved for at least six weeks. As I have already explained to you, we have just performed major surgery to implant a steel rod in his spine, replacing that section which was destroyed in the crash. What remains of his own spine must be given time to graft itself onto that steel."

"If he is moved before that begins to happen, the steel implant may well detach itself and we will have to operate again, which means — at the very least — the six weeks will start all over. So please do not move his legs until I give you the word. Promise?"

Barb paled at his words. It obviously had not occurred to her — or to me for that matter — what might have happened with her pulling on my legs.

"I'm very sorry, Doc," she replied meekly.

"I . . . I didn't realize, I mean I won't try any more therapy until you give me the word. I promise."

Doctor Yeoman smiled and nodded, satisfied. He began to walk away, then turned and spoke once more. "One more thing, while we are on the subject. When it IS time for therapy, I have an expert in the field whom I will want you to watch for a while. She will show you what to do. I do not want you doing any more of these pulling and twisting maneuvers until I have you instructed as to how to go about it properly. O.K.?"

"O.K., Doc," she replied humbly.

As if to give us both some encouragement, he then said, "There is, however, absolutely no reason why you should not try yourself to move your toes and legs, Rod. If you mentally keep trying to get some movement out of your lower body, you may eventually succeed in partially overcoming the paralysis. You must not give up hope."

He turned once more and disappeared outside the confines of the small world of my room.

Barb sat down beside my bed, took my hand and held it tightly. "Did I hurt you, mate? I'm awfully sorry. I didn't even think about pulling on your back. I just want you to get well again. But he is right, I guess. It has only been a couple of days and we have to be patient, if you will excuse the pun."

"Don't worry about it, Barb. It never occurred to me either. And it didn't hurt. Well, not much anyway. I will just have to do as the doctor ordered and work on the problem mentally. Not one of my strong points, as you know. Mental stress, that is."

"There is nothing to stop you continuing work on Mark, though, if he will let you. The nurses and that therapist Doctor Yeoman was talking about have been working on him. It can't do him any harm."

"Yes, you're right!" she replied, her grin returning. "He sure needs some encouragement. I'll attend to him some more later. In the meantime, Mum and I will get this mess cleaned up. I hope you enjoyed the lunch. I'll try to bring you all something at least once a day so you get some nourishing food. Just looking at that hospital stuff they dish up makes me sick to my stomach."

"Yeah, it is pretty awful, I must admit," I replied. "And as for that Chicken Marengo, it was just as good, if not better, than when you used to make it at home for us before. It reminded me of the good old days."

"That was the general idea," she grinned. "I want you to think of those days and convince yourself that you are the same person now as you

37

were before the accident. You HAVE to get well. I won't let you live your life in a wheelchair. You ARE going to walk again!"

Before I could reply, she got up and started to fiddle with the used plates and utensils, stacking them and the dirty frypan in the sacks she had brought them in. More than once, I caught her staring at me, then turning away and wiping her eyes. Despite her good cheer, my condition was obviously affecting her deeply. It was going to be a long, hard road for both of us; just like before, and as before, the end result was just as uncertain.

Barb and Nellie finished cleaning up properly, so that Wang and her associates would have nothing to complain about, and then said good-bye to each of the other fellows in turn. Those three thanked them profusely, expressing a fervent desire to see them again tomorrow, or as soon as they could make it back. They had won more than one heart in these bleak surroundings.

Ending up back at my bedside, Nellie bent to kiss me good-bye, and while Barb was still with Mark, whispered softly in my ear.

"Barb still loves you very much, Rod. It's killing her to see you like this. You hurry up and get out of that bed and get back together with her. That's an order! I'll be back to see you as soon as I can."

With that, she toddled off out of the room to wait outside for her wonderful daughter.

Barb left Mark's bedside, promising to return tomorrow to give him a proper workout. Mark, who was becoming quite weary by now with all the excitement, expressed his gratitude as best he could.

It was obvious that he was looking forward to her return as much as I was. She then came to me, bent forward and kissed me tenderly on the lips and rested her head with that shiny black hair lightly on my chest. The aroma of her perfume and her own musky scent filled my head and I began to feel quite dizzy. I knew I had to try my very best to get out of here and back into her arms, no matter what it took, no mater how long it took. I had to walk back to her on my own two legs, just as I had walked away from her a lifetime ago.

I still wonder today how it would have affected the outcome if I knew then what I found out much later, when I finally did leave that dreadful place.

After many long and delicious minutes, she lifted her face towards mine and kissed me once more. She clutched both my hands tightly in hers, stood fully erect again, and spoke so softly I could hardly hear her.

"I love you, Rod. You are going to get out of here, and when you do, I'll be waiting. I am going to take care of you for as long as you want me to. It will be just like before, only better. You wait and see. Get some sleep now, because that's what I'm going to do. I'm bushed. I will be back tonight."

She squeezed my hands again then let go, picked up the remains of her epicurean efforts, and walked quickly out of the room.

The rest of the day dragged on forever. I finally slept a few hours. When I awoke, it was getting dark again. The curtain had been drawn around the bed, so I lay there and tried to concentrate on moving my useless legs.

Nothing!

Not a bloody twitch! It was as if my body had been cut in half, my lower torso and legs as immobile as if they did not exist at all.

After a while I began to think that the messages from my brain were not even getting to the affected area of my body; that it was useless to keep trying to send them down. But perhaps I was not concentrating hard enough. That was it! Visions of Barbara kept creeping back into my head. I must try to block her out and think about nothing but working my legs and toes.

Still nothing!

Close your eyes and try again.

Harder! Harder still!

Hopeless.

I kept it up for what seemed like hours. It was actually probably only a few minutes. I fell asleep again. When I woke this time it was fully dark, the curtain was still drawn closely around the bed, and Barb was once again sitting beside me, her silhouette black against the curtain. I could not believe it. She was a miracle! She sensed, more than saw, in the semi-blackness that I was awake, leaned forward and rested her head on my chest from her sitting position close by the bed, and stroked my hair and whispered to me all night long. Well, it seemed like all night. It was wonderful!

When I woke the next time, Barb was gone, the curtain had been withdrawn, and it was broad daylight again. That night had certainly passed much more quickly and much less painfully than the previous ones.

39

If only she could sit by me like that every night, and take away the pain, the loneliness and the deep depression which was going to be part of me for a very long time. That was too much to ask for, however. Barb had a full-time job, and her nocturnal visits, as well as her daytime absences from work, were going to become evident when she started falling asleep on the job. No. I had to endure this by myself. It was my battle, and nobody could fight it for me. I was completely on my own for this one.

Barb returned that afternoon, and again prepared a delicious lunch for the four of us. She had set a precedent unheard of before in the history of the hospital, and other nursing staff and patients were becoming accustomed to her familiar figure swinging through the halls.

She spoke words of encouragement to many other patients more helpless than I, and came to be known around the wards as a contemporary Florence Nightingale. Her visits became a routine which I and every other patient with whom she had come in contact looked forward to every day.

Mark had improved his own attitude tremendously. He no longer screamed in the middle of the night for somebody to come and end it all for him, nor did he lie in his bed during the day not wanting to try to help himself. Now he insisted on being propped up in bed every day when he thought Barb was due to arrive. He eagerly awaited her manipulations of his useless limbs and really did try to move them for her, although to no avail.

His parents had met Barb on her second visit and considered her presence nothing short of a gift from Heaven. They regaled everybody they met with stories of Mark's amazing improvement since she had begun her ministrations on him.

By the end of my first week there, Barbara Terry was firmly ensconced as a permanent fixture in the Spinal Unit of the Sydney Royal North Shore Hospital.

4

Things were not going so smoothly for me.

My own physical condition had shown absolutely no sign of improvement, despite Barb's continuous encouragement and my efforts to make my lower limbs function.

My parents had called from Brisbane, six hundred miles north of Sydney, the day after I had been admitted to hospital. They were, of course, extremely distressed and concerned. My mother told me that on the day of the accident she had been nervous and restless all day and just knew that something terrible had happened to me. When she received the phone call from Nell Terry that night, she said she did not have to be told the news. She instantly knew what Nell was going to say.

When Mum and Dad first called the hospital, I was still in surgery. It was some time before they finally managed to get someone to tell them the situation. The first flight they could get was the following Saturday, and they arrived right in the middle of my second bout of utter dejection, depression and fear.

They could not have appeared at a more opportune time. I was undergoing regressive depression and displayed the same suicidal tendencies that Mark had been showing when I was admitted.

My first few days of effort at moving my legs or even wiggling my toes or flexing a muscle having produced absolutely no result, and despite Barbara's unflagging support and encouragement, I slipped into a black mood of bitterness at the world in general; what I called the "Why me, Lord?" syndrome.

I quit trying, and nothing could induce me to regain my will to fight. I was once again convinced that I was to spend the rest of my life in a wheelchair. Barb came and went on her self-appointed daily rounds. She was quite disgusted with me at the moment because of my refusal to extract myself from my present mental state. As a result, she was spending more time with Mark than she was with me because, as she put it, at least he now had the guts to try to fight his condition.

This, of course, did nothing to improve my frame of mind.

My Mum and Dad walked in on me in this appalling state of mind. I was lying flat on my back, still the only option open to me, with my hands clasped on my pillow behind my head, not appreciating that this very position was a damn sight more than Mark could ever hope to achieve.

My bed was closest to the doorway and my curtain was drawn aside. My parents appeared in the entrance and I saw them at the same time they saw me. My mother and I broke into tears at the same instant of recognition. For a moment, I forgot my condition and tried to turn over to reach out for them. The surge of pain and lack of movement in my lower body as I tried to roll toward them quickly reminded me of my situation, and I slumped back to the pillow, sobbing uncontrollably.

Mum and Dad came rushing to my bedside, taking chairs on either side of me. They both leaned over and hugged me tightly. I returned their embrace, realizing that I had never in all my years of wandering been so happy to see these two wonderful parents.

I forgot for a moment the terrible feeling of helplessness and futility that had been haunting me, and listened to their words of relief at seeing me still alive.

My Dad sat on my right and my Mum on my left, and they took each of my hands in theirs and held on tight.

Mum spoke first, through a continuing flood of tears.

"Hi mate. It's so good to see you. We have seen Doctor Yeoman on the way up and he has been very honest with us. We have also spoken to Barbara. She tells us you are not coping so well now as you were at first. It's not like you to give up on anything. You must think positively! After all, it has only been a week. You have five more weeks to go before you are even allowed out of bed to start physiotherapy. You must never give up. I, for one, do believe in miracles. I also believe that someone was watching over you in that crash, or you would not be here now."

"Thanks Ma," I replied dejectedly. "I know you are right, and I really have been trying, but it's no good. My legs are useless. No amount of therapy is going to make them work again. My spinal cord is too badly damaged. Doctor Yeoman said so."

At these words, Mum's eyes, which she had been dabbing continuously with a handkerchief, became wet with tears again.

"You don't know that for sure," she replied. "After all, he is only a doctor. He is not God. Anything you have accomplished in your life, you have done because you believed in yourself. You never listened to what anyone said you could or could not do before. Why start now?"

Despite myself, I had to smile at that. She had me there. I could not remember the last time I had heeded advice from her or Dad or anybody else for that matter.

My reply did not convey my amusement at her words.

"Mum, I don't think you quite understand. I am a paraplegic! When I do get out of this bed, it will be into a wheelchair. I know that I am going to have to learn to cope with that, just as millions of others have. But right now the thought of having to be totally dependent on somebody else to look after me is absolutely repugnant.

"I have been a loner for so long. All of a sudden I am crippled, confined to this bed, with no hope of ever walking OR FLYING again. What am I going to do? Where am I going to live? How am I going to take care of myself. Oh God, what am I going to do?" I cried through clenched teeth and flooding tears.

My Mother, still weeping, looked over at my Dad, shaking her head forlornly and biting her lips in anguish at my words of hopelessness.

Dad had not yet spoken. He rarely did unless he had something to say, preferring to leave the chatter to Mum. He sat there holding tightly on to my hand and gazing at me and, I think, crying a little too. I had never seen my father cry, so I could not be sure.

I was about to open my mouth and utter more words of self-pity and misery.

Instead, as though on cue, my Dad began to speak. I will never in my life forget the words he spoke to me on that fateful afternoon.

I did not know it then, but it was to be the turning point for me. When I think about it now, the very idea that those words could change my life seems quite ridiculous. I think the fact that the character to whom he referred, and the achievements of that character — at least as he was portrayed — went deep into my subconscious and remained there as a mental poultice through the long, tedious months ahead.

Today when I relate my father's words of that clear, Spring day so long ago, my listeners scoff and chuckle, but I know deep down that had he spoken any other words in any other way, my life would be vastly different now.

He must have had a powerful feeling that it was up to him. He knew that the only weapon in this battle of mind over matter was words. So far that weapon had failed. He had to give them some practical meaning; some example that would reach me as nothing else had.

He drew a deep breath and began to speak.

"Rodney, what I am going to say may sound corny right now, but I want you to hear me out. No interruptions. You can tell me what you think when I am finished. First of all, who is the one man you have admired all your life?"

"C'mon, Dad," I replied sheepishly, rather embarrassed. "You know the answer to that. What has that got to do with anything?"

"Just listen to me," he went on.

"We both know that you have, for reasons best known to yourself, always been one of John Wayne's greatest fans. I even remember the letter you wrote to him when you were just a boy, asking him for a job as one of his cowboys."

"So what of it?" I asked hotly, feeling the blush rising to my throat.

"I told you, don't interrupt. Just listen to your old man for once in your life."

"You remember that picture he made a long time ago about Navy flyers? He played the part of Admiral Frank Wead, the fellow who pushed the idea of baby aircraft carriers at the Brass in Washington until they finally relented and let him prove his theory. The name of the movie was "Wings of Eagles." Dan Dailey played his Chief Petty Officer. Remember?"

"I remember," I replied, "but I don't see what . . . "

"Well," he went on, as though I had not spoken, "can you recall what happened to him? He had a terrible accident. He fell down the stairs in his home and broke his back, just like you. In about the same place. Only thing was, in those days, they did not have the knowledge and surgery skills they do today. He was put in hospital where the Navy doctors x-rayed him and told him there was absolutely nothing that they could do for him. He was going to be a cripple for life. Paralyzed from the waist down. Just like you. Remember?"

I lay there sullenly and nodded.

"He was in your exact predicament. And he was just as mean and full of self-pity as you are right now. He lay in that hospital bed and sulked and moaned about how life had pulled such a dirty trick on him, not thinking or caring about the thousands of boys dying outside his window in the Pacific War until his Petty Officer showed up with his ridiculous little ukulele. He sat down beside him and told him to pull himself together.

"He pointed out quite bluntly that the only person who could get him back into the fight was himself, so he had better stop whining about how badly life had treated him and start working towards getting himself out of there. Then, if you remember, he picked up that silly little ukulele and composed a one line song on the spot for 'Spig' Wead to memorize and repeat."

"It went like this. 'I'm gonna move that toe, boy, I'm gonna move that toe. I'm gonna move that toe, boy, I'm gonna move that toe.'

"He told him that he had to keep repeating those words over and over and over until he could not get them out of his head. Until his brain was sending those words down to his left big toe every second of every day, even when he was not aware that he was doing it. Day and night. Awake and asleep. Non stop!"

45

"Do you remember that, Rodney?"

"Sure, I remember that. It was one of my favorite films. You know that scene stuck in my mind. I've commented on it enough over the years."

"Well then," he continued, "don't you think it is rather a coincidence that that particular scene did stick in your mind. Why is that, do you think? You know the answer to that, too. Because it took guts and will power and determination and . . . "

Suddenly it dawned on me!

It struck me on the head like a physical blow. I'm not slow! I realized my father was setting me a task I could not refuse; a challenge I could not ignore. He had dug deep into my psyche and found the one thing that would make me fight back. He had thrown down the gauntlet. He had told me obliquely that it was about time I began to live up to the standards set by my hero. And now was the perfect time to begin!

I realized that Dad was speaking again.

"Ah, so you remember those words, do you?" I heard him say through my own turbulent thoughts. "Guts and will power. Frank Wead — or John Wayne — however you prefer to think of him, took those six simple words and planted them firmly in his mind and did not let them leave until he did in fact move that big toe. John Wayne was not accustomed to sending down commands that were not being obeyed; especially by his own body. So they just got stronger and stronger until the mental power overcame the physical refusal to function."

"Eventually, that toe gave up. It said, 'O.K., O.K., gimme a break. There! How do ya like that? Satisfied now?' and began to wiggle. In time, the rest of his leg and thigh muscles followed the example and he ended up being able to walk again. Even if he did have to use a couple of walking sticks. He walked again! That's the main thing. You, Rodney, have got to do the same thing. Starting right now.

"C'mon! I'm gonna move that toe, boy, I'm gonna move that toe. Say it!

"Go on! Say it! I'm gonna move that toe, boy, I'm gonna move that toe!"

By this time, Mark and the other fellows in the room were staring at Dad and me. I was very embarrassed, and getting angry.

"Look Dad," I said, "I get the point. I promise I'll start saying it mentally all the time."

"Not good enough," he replied stubbornly. "I'm not leaving here until I hear you start saying it OUT LOUD, over and over, until you can't stop. Until when you stop saying it out loud, your brain is still saying it in your head. You are going to beat this thing, AND YOU ARE GOING TO START RIGHT NOW!" I surrendered. For the last time in my life, I hope.

My mother, who had remained silent throughout Dad's tirade, now joined in with him, chanting that silly verse from a long-ago movie.

I began to mumble the words. The idea took root. I spoke them more clearly. A feeling of determination that even Barb had not been able to draw out came over me. I started to shout those words. Over and over.

"I'm gonna move that toe, boy, I'm gonna move that toe. I'm gonna move that toe, boy, I'm gonna move that toe."

Mum and Dad were still holding my hands. They began rocking to and fro, swinging my arms as they did so. The three of us were now chanting the words. Soon the mood took hold. The other three guys joined in the spirit of the thing and also started singing.

The six of us were now making so much noise that the nursing staff heard us from their command post halfway down the hall outside. A delegation, led by the indomitable Sister Wang, arrived shortly after and stopped in the doorway, struck speechless by the strange ritual being performed before them.

"Stop this noise," the good Sister bellowed. "Stop it, I say! Immediately! Have you all gone mad? Doctor Yeoman will hear of this! Now stop it! Stop it! Stop it," she wailed.

We stopped it.

Long enough for my Mother, who has always been the outspoken one in the family when it comes to dealing with officious people who are supposed to be serving the community, to put Wang in her place.

She let go of my hand, stood up to her full five feet four inches, and confronted the Sister who towered over her.

"Now you listen to me, you stupid person. This is my son lying here. We are going to do anything we can to help him get over his injuries, including singing, dancing, or howling at the moon if that's what it takes. So why don't you go and tend to the really sick people in this hospital and leave us alone. If we want you or your staff for anything, we will SEND for you. Is THAT plain enough?"

"Well, I never!" the Sister retorted, dumbfounded.

"Well! Ya oughta try it sometime. Aaaah! Aaaah!" Mark chipped in, ending with a gurgling cackle.

Dad pretended to ignore this, glaring at Mark under lowered eyebrows. The rest of us chortled loudly at Wang's expense, once again driving her into a frenzied retreat.

This time there was no return visit from Doctor Yeoman, as had been the case when Barb confronted the battle-axe. We were left entirely alone for the duration of my parents' visit. We continued to sing our lungs out for another ten minutes. Of course, there was no indication that my left big toe — or my right one — or anything else below my waist — had heard any of the command performance. But the objective had been achieved. When we finally stopped saying and singing the lines, I could still hear them going round and round inside my head.

For the rest of my parents' stay, we talked about what we would all do when I got out of here; about how I would go back home to Brisbane with them where I could recuperate in peace and comfort. There was never any mention of wheelchairs or leg braces or crutches. We talked about how I would go back and finish my aviation course and end up flying for QANTAS.

None of it worked out that way, of course.

Mum and Dad remained by my bedside most of that day and retired in the early evening to an apartment on the hospital grounds provided and paid for by the Board. They returned early the following day to find me asleep. My father swears to this day that my lips were moving, saying the magic words!

He is probably right.

That Sunday evening, after another day of encouraging me to believe that I was going to be out of here in no time, they reluctantly left for the airport, where they had to catch the last flight of the day back to Brisbane.

Mum cried, as usual, dabbing her cheeks with a white lace handkerchief as she hugged me and said good-bye. Dad shook my hand, and ruffled my already greasy and unkempt hair. My hairdresser, namely

Barbara, had remained aloof except for a quick visit to be polite to my folks. She knew they would want to be alone with me for the brief time they had here.

Dad said, "Now you be sure to keep repeating those words. Any time you find your head empty of thought — which I know is usually the case anyway," he jibed, "get those words back in there. You are going to make medical history and prove that even your brain's impulses are strong enough to jump the gap in a damaged spinal cord. Look after yourself, mate. We will be thinking of you, and we'll be back down as soon as we can make it."

He turned and strode out pretending to remove some foreign body from his eyes. This time I knew he was crying. I guess there really is a first time for everything.

That was the last time I saw my parents for many weeks. They stayed constantly in touch by telephone, of course, and every time they called, Dad asked how my mental exercises were coming along. He was bound and determined to keep my brain functioning even though he could not be there to personally supervise it.

Barbara's visits were renewed in force and she was very pleased and amazed at the change in my attitude, even though she was not responsible for it. She took up her previous voluntary chores with extra vigor, much to the annoyance and consternation of Sister Wang, who by now thought we were all quite mad.

Mark was overjoyed to see Barb again, as he had slumped into a foul mood at her two day absence.

For my part, I remained on a mental high as a result of Dad's (and the Duke's) influence as well as Barb's re-kindled interest in my welfare.

I found that my father's little pep-talk and session of therapy had indeed worked. The six-word sentence was so firmly implanted in my mind by now that it was in fact becoming a constant source of irritation because I could not turn it on and off when I wanted to.

Even when I was talking with Barb, I was aware of the words nagging away in the back of my head.

"I'm gonna move that toe, boy, I'm gonna move that toe."

Sometimes she became upset because she thought I was not paying attention to her, but it was just that the words were occasionally so forceful, they pressed themselves to the front of my brain, blocking my undivided attention to what was going on around me. At these times, the message was so powerful I felt sure that any second now my toes, if not my legs, would begin thrashing wildly.

But nothing moved.

I think Mark had decided to try the same thing, as I frequently looked across to find him obviously awake, but with his eyes pressed tightly closed, his face scrunched up and his teeth clenched. No doubt he was willing his body from the neck down to produce some sign of life. Barbara was pleased with this progress too, encouraging him and massaging all his limbs whenever she could spare the time.

By the end of the second week, I had more or less come to terms with the dreary hospital routine, punctuated by the joyful hours brought to all of us by Barb. The horrendous pain of the first few days had been replaced by a dull, nagging throb where my lower spine used to be. This, and the chance of bedsores, was alleviated by the wardsmen electrically rotating my bed, with me in it, to varying angles at different time of the day.

At these times, I felt like Paul Hogan's much overdone "shrimp on the barbie."

———————————— ❖ ————————————

5

Weeks passed.

Barbara's visits became less frequent now. Her boss had taken exception to her long lunch hours and inattentiveness to her work. She mostly came at night for a few hours, and usually every weekend, still bearing flowers and food of all kinds.

I did have other visitors, however.

Several times some of my fellow students and instructors from the flying academy called on me to see how I was doing and give me encouragement. These visits depressed me, more than anything else. I'm sure they thought they were doing the right thing, but when they came, they reminded me of where I should be and what I could be doing.

My class had graduated on October 14th. On that day, I had tortured myself by mentally picturing every one of the cadets proudly stepping forward before his family and friends to receive his gold Commercial Pilot's wings from the Academy Director. As the appointed hour of three p.m. grew closer, I became more and more morose, thumping the bed with my fists in frustration that I could not get out of this DAMN bed to go get my wings.

One or two of my colleagues were insensitive enough to come to see me wearing their Academy uniforms with their bright new wings pinned to their chests. This did nothing to improve my frame of mind.

However, there were a few fellows from my class whom I did look forward to seeing. Paul Howard, who had seen my wreck from the air and passed on my radio call for help, had dropped in to see me several times, and so had his mother and father. He and Barb got along well and the three of us joked and kidded around for hours, cheering me up no end.

Paul got into the highly unauthorized habit of smuggling various types of booze, usually beer or wine, but occasionally bourbon or scotch, into the ward, in assorted disguises to thwart the suspicious eyes of Sister Wang and Co.

Two other friends, Shane Lambert and Chris Charles, who are now both airline pilots, also decided the place would be much brighter with a touch of amber cheer.

These sessions usually turned into wild and raucous parties, with the four patients (Ken and Brian had now been replaced by two new temporary patients) and any of their visitors who happened to be present at the time getting outrageously silly, if not positively inebriated.

The whole thing being based on covertly drinking to avoid the wrath of the marauding battle-axe, the persons involved began by passing the liquor around with whispers and subdued giggles, but ended up, completely and hopelessly under the influence, throwing all caution to the winds and shouting and hollering around the room and to hell with the consequences.

Surprisingly enough, Sister Wang, despite many sneak attacks to try to catch us in the act, never did arrive in the room at the precise moment to actually find anyone with a glass or bottle conspicuously in evidence. Of course, the fact that the place reeked like a distillery was not hard enough evidence on which to have us all, patients included, thrown bodily out into the street, which is no doubt what she would have liked to do.

I became disturbed to notice that Barbara's drinking during these sessions was increasing almost by the day. When we had been together before, she had always liked a drink, but now it seemed more evident. When I mentioned it to her, she jumped down my throat.

"Anyone could become an alcoholic having to cope with this every day," she snapped, casting an arm around her head and indicating the surroundings in general.

That was the first time I had seen her really snarl like that. It made me realize that my condition — and Mark's — must take its toll on the people around us who love us. We, the paralyzed ones, were not the only ones who suffered. It must be hell for our families as well.

The little singing voice in my head got louder again.

I shrugged off Barb's vicious remark, and her increased consumption, as being due merely to the stress and fatigue of her continuous visits to the hospital and the worry associated with what was going to become of me.

The real reason did not come to light until much later. By that time it was too late to do anything about it, even if I had wanted to.

Meanwhile, both my mental and physical condition, apart from the fact that I still could not move a muscle from the waist down, were improving by the day. The sessions with my pals had done much to make me feel like I was one of the boys again. This had never meant much to me before the accident. But then, neither had the other ordinary things in life we take so much for granted; like just being able to sit up in bed and throw your feet on to the floor; like standing and stretching and walking and running and bending and a million other things one does without thinking when all one's limbs are functioning.

Well, now I HAD to think about it. In fact, I could think about nothing else. Every second of every day, the part of my feeble brain that was free from the voice of John Wayne's Petty Officer was counting down to the day not long ahead when Doctor Yeoman would come and pronounce me fit enough to be removed from that cursed bed. They would dump me into a wheelchair and take me around to the gym where I would commence physiotherapy, trying to get my now atrophied legs at least partially functional again.

It had been five weeks, four days and ten hours now. Doctor Yeoman had said I could get off this rack in six weeks, and I was looking forward to the day like a long-term prisoner must look forward to being released.

I had heard wondrous tales of other paraplegics who were so swift and nimble in their wheelchairs that they could negotiate their way through the hospital grounds, across the busy highway outside, and into the pub on the other side, where the saloon bar was chock-a-block with wheel-chairs and their occupants, all merrily slurping away at their frothy-topped glasses. Right now, this sounded very much like the Heaven I had come close to seeing when the plane crashed!

The last couple of days dragged on, hour by miserable hour. I became irritable and jumpy, and nothing Barb or Mark could say would pacify my shredded nerves. Every time I saw a wheelchair go past the door, I dragged myself into a sitting position, hoping that it was for me. I simply could not wait. Like all others in my situation, I had never been held prisoner by my own body before, and it was driving me absolutely crazy.

THE day came!

I was awake long before dawn, waiting for Doctor Yeoman to arrive with the good news, a battery of nurses, a sweat suit and a gold-plated wheelchair. Ten o'clock came and went. Every nurse and wardsman who had the effrontery to walk past my door got abused mercilessly.

"Hey you!" I bellowed. "Where's my chair? Today's the day I get out of here. Find Doctor Yeoman for me. He'll put you straight! Now get your act together!"

Twelve o'clock!

They all must have gone to lunch. They will be back soon. Then they'll come to get me.

Two o'clock! Where ARE they, for Christ's sake?

"Nurse! NURSE!! Yes you!" I screamed as a little girl straight out of nursing school poked her head around the doorway.

"Get Wang in here. Tell her I want to see Doctor Yeoman. RIGHT NOW!!"

"WELL??? What are you waiting for?" I bawled, as she stood there, mouth agape, not quite knowing what to do.

I opened my own mouth to shout at her again. She turned tail and disappeared in a flurry of starched white linen.

At ten minutes to four o'clock, Doctor Yeoman, accompanied by a suspiciously smirking Sister Wang, arrived at my bedside with a not too pleasant or reassuring smile on his normally jolly face.

"Good afternoon, Rod," he began cheerily enough. "I really am very sorry I am so late. I know you have been anxiously expecting me, but I got tied up at a neuro-surgeons' conference and I have only just returned."

He flourished his clipboard, pretended to examine it minutely as though it was a record of my criminal activities, which perhaps it was, then spoke again.

"Rod, I am afraid I have some slightly bad news for you."

Without waiting for my suddenly sagging face to get back to more or less normal composure, he continued.

"The bad news is actually based on good news. The fact is that you are so active and so looking forward to getting into serious and heavy therapy when you get out of that bed, I feel you may quite easily overstretch yourself and undo all the good work we have done when we operated on your back. Your spine is still extremely fragile and the bone takes a long time to graft on to that steel implant."

"What are you trying to tell me," I bellowed at him.

"I want you to stay in bed another week," he said succinctly, as if it was just another hour he was talking about.

"Christ," I moaned. "Don't you know I have been looking forward to this day since the minute I came round and found myself in this bed? I am feeling fine. I HAVE to get out of here and start exercising. I've got to GET OUT OF HERE!!"

"I know how you feel, Rod. Believe me, I do know how you feel. That is precisely why I have decided to keep you here another week. I know that the minute you get out of bed you are going to be trying much too hard to move along at a pace which is going to do more harm than good. If you injure yourself again, if you do the slightest damage to that spine, you will be back in bed for at least another six weeks. Maybe longer. Better to give your back another week to strengthen itself for the onslaught now than to end up right back where you started. Don't you agree?"

I grudgingly agreed that he was probably right. I knew damn well that the minute I was up and about, I was going to concentrate non-stop on getting out of the hospital altogether and back into some semblance of normal life.

"I am very glad you see it my way," Doctor Yeoman said. "I shall see you next week. Take it easy until then."

He turned and strode off without further comment. Wang leered evilly at me. It was obvious that she was thoroughly enjoying my disappointment and that she was going to make the most of my extra time in prison.

I slumped down in the bed, folded my arms and glared back at her in silent fury.

She opened her mouth to say something I'm sure would have been rude and vindictive. She did not get the chance, however.

Mark, who had been listening silently to the conversation between Doctor Yeoman and myself, drew a deep breath and released it, using his cheeks and tongue in a most unpleasant sound directed at Sister Wang.

She heeled around to face him, realized that the deliberate and disgusting gesture was entirely for her benefit, turned bright pink, and strutted out of the room, shoulders back, nose high and making threatening rumbles deep in her own throat.

I burst into uncontrollable laughter, and so did Mark and the others.

"Thanks Mark," I said between convulsions. "She deserved that. She was overjoyed that the Doc was bringing me bad news. I guess she really will be so glad to get rid of us, though. I feel sorry for her in a way. Maybe some day we should all do something nice for her. It's not long to Christmas, you know."

That thought prompted the voice in my head to louder effort yet again. I was determined that I was not going to be in this place for Christmas, and that was probably the best gift I could ever give Sister Wang. Not to mention myself!

I pushed my body down on to the pillows again, folded my hands behind the back of my neck, and steeled myself for another week of abject boredom tinged with keen anticipation of the big day's postponed arrival.

Just one more week, then I was going to be free to come and go as I pleased. Oh, I would still have someone hovering over me making sure I did not hurt myself. Hopefully, though, that would be Barbara most of the time, which would be much more pleasant than anyone else I could think of at this moment.

These thoughts lulled me into daydreams of wonderful things to come. Out in the sunshine and fresh air of the hospital grounds strolling, well, not exactly strolling; being strolled around the flower-lined walks, smelling the spring blossoms which would be just awakening into full summer beauty.

The daydreams relaxed me into dozing, and finally I slept deeply. I dreamed that Barb had come to get me and take me home to her place where she was going to look after me and make me well again.

Dreams can be very cruel sometimes.

When I awoke, it was night again. I was alone. The curtain was drawn tightly around my bed. I squinted at my watch. The luminous hands told me it was one a.m. There was no light in the room, except the shaft slanting through the doorway from the corridor outside.

The other three fellows were asleep. I could hear one of them snoring loudly. Laughter drifted to me from somewhere down the hall. Footsteps sounded on the walk beyond the window. I closed my eyes and tried to go back to sleep. Something was bothering me. I could not quite make out what it was. I dozed again.

Another dream. Or was it?

Something was definitely different. What was it I had just dreamed?

Think! Close your eyes. Try to dream it again.

There. That's it!

What was it?

Just that silly damn voice in the back of my head. That's all. It had become so much a part of me now that I did not even realize it was still there. Which, of course, was the object of the exercise.

Over and over again. That voice. "I'm gonna move that toe."

It had kept me awake for days after it was locked in my skull, but ever since then, it was simply there. Just below the conscious level. Now it seemed to be back with renewed vigor.

Damn the voice!

What was it that I had just dreamed, for Pete's sake?

Aha! Got it!

I just dreamed that I moved my big left toe!

God, I wish I would not dream things like that. It's so disappointing to wake and find . . . Wait just a damn minute! I AM awake!

Right now, I AM AWAKE!!

Is it possible?

Nah! Can't be.

I dragged myself up to a sitting position, threw the sheet right off the end of the bed, turned on the bedside lamp, aimed it at my left big toe, and simply stared at it.

The said member drooped lifelessly.

The voice in my head spoke.

I continued to stare at my toe.

Nothing!

I must have been dreaming after all.

The voice spoke again, louder this time.

Still nothing!

Wait!

Did I see a flicker of life in that toe? Just a tiny little flicker of the main tendon that moves the toe?

No. Must be my imagination. Wishful thinking in the dead of night.

There it goes again! I'm not imagining it! That tendon jumped, pulling the toe up just a fraction. Just enough to see — and feel.

"I'm gonna move that toe!"

Again!

It did it again!

It IS responding to the command. It's not just a random nerve twitch.

"I'm gonna move that toe!"

Again. More this time. A positive upward movement of THE toe.

"I'M GONNA MOVE THAT TOE!"

I found myself shouting it out loud.

It moved again, just a flicker.

"I'M GONNA MOVE THAT TOE!!"

"SHUDDUP!!!"

I had woken the snorer. He was not amused.

"I moved my toe," I shouted at him through the curtain.

"I don't care if you moved your bowels," he rudely replied. "I'm trying to sleep."

"I moved my toe, dammit," I repeated.

"O.K., O.K., so you moved your toe. Now go back to sleep!"

Inconsiderate oaf, I thought. What does he know?

"NURSE!" I shouted. "Somebody, come quick."

A moment later, the sound of running footsteps clattered down the hall. The curtain was pulled urgently aside and the face of an unknown nurse peered at me from the end of the bed.

The fact that I did not know this person made me feel rather silly. I could not know whether or not she was familiar with my case and therefore the importance of my discovery.

"I moved my toe," I said rather inadequately.

She stared at me for a moment, then at my feet. I thought she may feel that she was facing a madman, but she quickly set my mind at ease.

"Do it again," she said with a smile, staring at my toes.

"All right, I'll try," I replied.

Once more out loud I cried, "I'm gonna move that toe!"

The left big toe twitched obediently.

"Again!"

"I'm gonna move that toe."

Twitch!

"One more time!" she said enthusiastically.

"I'm gonna move that toe."

Twitch, twitch. It moved twice. Up and down. Up and down.

"Pretty good, huh," I said, with less emotion than I felt.

"Good?" she replied. "It's wonderful! Wait till I tell Sister Wang. She's off duty right now. But she will be absolutely thrilled to hear that you moved your toe. It really is wonderful. Doctor Yeoman will be tickled to death. I am going to call the Sister right now!"

She hurried out of the room, wanting to be the first to break the big news to anyone she could find at that hour of the night.

I was filled with emotion. Tears welled in my eyes. I was alone, so I let them flow down my cheeks in a steady stream.

"YAHOO!!" I cried. "I moved my toe. I really moved my toe."

"SHUDDUP, for Christ's sake. Tell me about it in the morning."

Peasant, I thought.

The remaining hours till dawn went quickly. I could not sleep a wink, of course. I lay awake, hands clasped behind the back of my head, staring at my toe and repeating over and over, silently for the benefit of my ill-mannered room-mate, the magic words.

Every time I did so, the toe in question moved obligingly up and down, up and down. Not much. Just a fraction of an inch. But enough for me to see and feel that it was in fact responding to the command after all these long weeks.

Thanks Dad!! Thanks Duke!! It worked!

With the dawn came Sister Wang. I thought she was going to give me a blast for disturbing my room-mates. Instead, she actually smiled pleasantly at me for the first time. She pulled the curtain all the way back revealing me and my toes to the general public so anyone who wanted to could watch the show.

"O.K.," she began without any discussion. "Let's see it move!"

I looked down at my toe, which was drooping lifelessly, as though it had never considered moving.

I did not want it to let me down. I would look a complete fool if, before a live audience, it failed to obey me.

I drew a deep breath.

"I'm gonna move that toe!"

Nothing. Absolutely zilch!

Wang's eyebrows went skyward in questioning expectation.

I took another breath, stared malevolently at the drooping digit, and shouted. "I'M GOMNA MOVE THAT TOE!!!"

Twitch!

Mark, who had been watching the proceedings with enthralled interest, began to whistle. The other two, including the snorer, clapped effusively. Sister Wang smiled — again. She sniffled. If I did not know better I would have thought she was holding back a tear!

She said nothing. Instead, she turned and rushed from the room.

Mark whistled again.

"Hey Rod, that's great!" he said, genuinely pleased at my small but important achievement.

"Maybe Doc Yeoman will let you off the torture rack early now."

"Not bloody likely," I replied cheerfully, hopeful nevertheless that it may be true.

The morning dragged on.

No further sign of Wang. The wardsmen did their rounds, leaving me to my own ablutions as usual.

At ten a.m. on the dot, Doctor Yeoman, accompanied by a now almost conspiratorial Sister Wang, arrived brandishing his customary clipboard.

"Good morning Rod. Sister Wang tells me you have had some movement in your toe. Let's make sure that it is not just a nerve twitching before we get too excited. Quite often the case in your circumstances."

Cheerful bastard!

"Now let us see what you call movement. Can you induce your toe to move at will?"

"What the devil do you think I have been doing all night?" I asked hotly. "Never mind. I'll show you."

"I'm gonna move that toe!"

Nothing!!

WHAT??

"I'M GONNA MOVE THAT TOE, DAMMIT!!"

Flicker!

That's better! Wake up, you stupid digit.

"Again," said the doctor.

I tried a different command, to relieve the monotony.

"Toe, do your duty."

Twitch!

"H'mmm," said the doctor.

"I think you are right, Rod," he grudgingly admitted. "You really are moving your toe. Amazing! I would not have thought it possible, but it seems you are actually getting a message through that scarred and damaged spinal cord."

He held his left forefinger lightly on the top of my toe.

"Now try it," he said.

This time I said nothing out loud.

Move toe, I said silently.

The weight of the doctor's finger, even though he was barely touching the toe, prevented, it from moving. The tendon, however, rose and fell in compliance with the mental command.

Doctor Yeoman felt the toe try to rise and saw the tendon move.
He smiled broadly.

"Rod, I think you have earned a slightly early reprieve. I shall meet you half-way regarding the extra week in bed. Make it three days from now and you can begin your physiotherapy. How does that sound?"

"You bloody little ripper!" I replied irreverently, totally disregarding his rank and stature in the hospital's pecking order.

"Did you hear that, Mark? The Doc's going to let me up! At last I am going to get out of this bed. YAHOO!!"

"Now just a moment," the doctor replied to my outburst.

"That does not mean you can disregard my comments yesterday concerning your remaining relatively inactive to allow your spine more time to heal. You must take it very easy for the first few weeks out of bed. If I hear of any exploits outside the limits I have imposed, you will be confined to bed again more quickly than you can imagine. Is that perfectly clear?"

"Yes sir!" I replied with a mock salute.

"Absolutely, sir. You won't hear about the slightest disregard of your orders. I promise!"

"I do not want you to promise that I will not HEAR about it. I want you to promise that you will not DISOBEY my orders. Do you so promise?"

He was smarter than I gave him credit for.

"O.K.," I reluctantly agreed. "I promise I will not disregard or disobey your orders till you say otherwise."

"Very well, then. I accept your word as a gentleman. Three days. I shall send a wheelchair for you promptly at ten. First trip will be to the gym and back. No further. Understood?"

"Understood," I lied.

He flourished his clipboard, tucked it under his arm, turned smartly on his heel and left the room. Sister Wang followed, as usual, without a word.

I was beside myself.

Not only was I going to get out if this CURSED bed, but I now had something to look forward to. Something to work with. I had a positive indication that at least part of me was healing. Barbara was going to be thrilled to pieces when she came in and I told her the good news. I could hardly wait for her next visit. She had been stepping up her visits again lately, despite her boss, and had been here at least every other day.

At last we were going to get some action around here.

The rest of the day I spent talking excitedly to Mark — and his parents when they dropped in — about what I was going to do when I got up. In my excitement, I did not notice that he had become glum and moody during my incessant chatter. It did not occur to me that I was making him unhappy and envious by my selfish ramblings. He had been in bed much longer than I, and had little or no chance of ever having any independence again.

As it happened, Barb turned up that very afternoon at about two o'clock. She was absolutely delighted at the fact that I had got some action out of my toe at last. She was also furious at me for upsetting Mark. She could tell instantly what was troubling him. It was not difficult, as I was still raving about what I was going to do when I got out of there.

Barb drew the curtain around my bed and, although in a whisper, told me in no uncertain terms what an inconsiderate clown I was for talking about myself that way.

"Haven't you got any brains at all?" she snapped. "Can't you see that it is killing Mark to hear you talking about getting up? He is more than ten years younger than you, and has no chance of living anything like a normal life again. I know you are excited about getting some movement in your toe. So am I, but can't you see what that does to Mark when he can't move a muscle from the neck down? He is putting on a brave front of being happy for you when it is really tearing his guts inside out."

It was true! Right then I felt about two inches tall. I vowed that I would try to help Barb with her self-imposed task of assisting Mark to regain some of his own self-esteem.

The next three days dragged on more slowly than the previous six weeks. I no longer spoke to Mark about my own plans. Instead, whether Barb was there or not, I concentrated on talking to him about his problems instead of mine. It made a remarkable difference to his attitude, and we soon had him convinced that he too had a chance of regaining some muscle control and movement if he believed it strongly enough.

For my own part, no matter what else I was doing, or who I was talking to, part of my mind was permanently distracted and concentrating on my toes. There was no doubt about the movement in my left big toe now. With every twitch, it seemed to grow stronger. I even thought I detected a flicker or two in the other four left digits from time to time. I could not be sure of this however, so I shrugged it off as imagination for the time being.

Occasionally I concentrated on my right foot for a change, hoping that I could detect some sign of movement there as well. No such luck! It remained as still and lifeless as the day of the accident, and this fact tended to dampen the joy of success with the left toe.

I told myself that I had to learn to get one going again before I could concentrate wholly on the other side. This was sound reasoning, but I was not totally convinced. As long as I never remained quite satisfied with my progress, I found that I never again lapsed into the doldrums of the first few weeks in bed.

———————— ❖ ————————

6

The third day of extra confinement finally came and went.

That last night before my big day arrived, I did not sleep a wink. I lay, uncomfortably rolling from side to side as best I could, without being able to move my lower body. I dozed and dreamed that I was never going to be allowed to get up. I could see Sister Wang with a pair of horns and fangs, laughing scornfully at my plight. That bed became my idea of hell. I HAD to get out!

The minutes and hours ticked slowly by. Dawn finally arrived. I did not volunteer any conversation. When spoken to by Mark or any of the other patients or staff, I replied in monosyllables, looking constantly at my watch.

As ten o'clock approached, I broke out in a cold sweat, fearing a recurrence of what had happened last time when the doctor had shown up late in the afternoon — and then with bad news.

Ten o'clock! Oh please don't let him be late.

I could not stand it if I had to go through that again.

Doctor Yeoman, Sister Wang, Nurse Hoffman and two wardsmen, one carrying pajamas and slippers and the other pushing a wheelchair, arrived in convoy at precisely two minutes and thirty-two seconds past the hour of ten a.m. on the morning of the sixth week and fourth day after my admission to hospital.

I sat up in bed, rubbing my hands with glee and grinning like a Cheshire Cat. I could not think of a happier day in my life so far.

Doctor Yeoman smiled, flourished his ever-present clipboard, and spoke cheerily.

"Good morning Rod. I know how anxious you are to get out of that bed, so we will not waste any more time. Remember one thing, though. When you sit up properly with your feet on the floor for the first time in many weeks, your blood is going to plunge to your feet and you may feel dizzy for a while. Be prepared for it."

"I'm ready for it," I replied with alacrity. "Just get me out of here!"

Sister Wang smiled knowingly. I wondered for a moment what that particular smile meant. I was about to find out!

Nurse Hoffman reached for my sheets and threw them off the end of the bed after drawing the curtain. One of the wardsmen handed me the pajamas and they all watched as I struggled to pull the pants up my useless legs and over my backside. Because I had no muscle control in my legs or lower back, I could not arch my spine to pull the pants up. I had to roll from side to side using my upper torso to drag the lower part, pulling the pants up inch by painful inch as I did so.

My audience looked on, amused and entertained by the performance. They knew damn well that I would not allow them to lift a finger to help me so they did not even bother to try. This was the very first step in the long road to partial independence, and they knew how important it was to me to prove that I could look after myself.

I finally had the pants on — more or less. I sat up again and pulled on the shirt. That was much easier, as I had normal use of my arms.

"O.K. gang, let's get to work," I said, not realizing that it was easier said than done.

Nurse Hoffman and one of the wardsmen reached for my legs to pick them up and place them on the floor.

"NO!" I said emphatically. "I'll do it."

They looked at Doctor Yeoman. He shook his head at them. I reached down with both hands, grabbed my left ankle, picked up my leg and threw it over the side of the bed. It fell to the floor with a terrible thump. The jerk on my spine sent a surge of nausea through me. I fell back on the pillows and let it pass.

I reached for the right leg and repeated the performance. Less nausea this time. Now I had both legs dangling uselessly over the side of the bed with the rest of me lying askew at an awkward angle. I pushed myself up with my arms and sat supported by my palms flat on the sheet behind my back.

For the first few moments I felt fine. Then it hit me. A horrible feeling swept over me. I had never felt anything like it before, even during all the pain of the previous weeks. I began to perspire profusely. An awful, bilious sensation overcame me. Bile filled my throat and I began to dry retch and gag. I just knew I was going to vomit! Black waves of dizziness struck me like physical blows. I fell back on the bed in anguish. I continued to gag. I thought I was going to choke. Red dots exploded before my eyes. I must have passed out for a brief time because I suddenly realized that Doctor Yeoman was speaking to me.

". . . told you what would happen when you sat up, Rod. What you have just experienced is perfectly normal after a long period in the more or less horizontal position. Your heart is not working very hard. It does not have to circulate the blood uphill from your feet as is the case when you are standing. You have had absolutely no exercise for six weeks. Now suddenly you place a simple load on your system by putting your feet on the floor."

"Your blood rushed to your feet, leaving the supply to your brain temporarily short, which causes dizziness and nausea. Then your heart has to double its accustomed work-load to pump the blood back up from your feet and legs and re-supply the brain. The whole process combined to cause what you just felt. A most unpleasant experience, to say the least. I did try to warn you, but I also suspected that you would not heed me, knowing you as I do."

I carefully and tentatively struggled back to a sitting position by placing my hands behind my back and inching my way up little by little. My head began to spin again, but not as badly this time. Finally, I was sitting in more or less erect posture, clutching tightly at the edge of the bed to prevent myself from swaying too much. With no strength or movement in my legs or feet to support my body, I realized for the first time just how difficult it was going to be to perform a simple maneuver like sitting up.

I glowered defiantly at the gathering around me.

"Nothin' to it!" I proclaimed, feeling much less confident as smaller, but nevertheless sickening, waves of nausea pulsed through my body.

"You should have told me how bad it was going to be," I added, scowling accusingly at Doctor Yeoman.

"As I said, there would have been no point. You would not have paid any attention to me. It is quite obvious that you are going to have to learn everything the hard way, as you probably have done all your life, I suspect."

"Balls," I rudely replied, knowing full well that he was absolutely correct. "Well, let's get this show on the road," I added, much less inclined to do so than I had been a few minutes before.

Nurse Hoffman drew back the curtain and I was greeted with a round of raucous applause and cheering from the other occupants of the room. This bolstered my flagging confidence, and I called to the wardsmen to bring up my chair.

They obliged, and rolled the chair alongside the bed. This time, I did not refuse their offer of assistance. I did not want to make a complete fool of myself by falling flat on my face on the floor, my first time out of bed. They each got hold of me under my armpits and lifted me bodily off the bed and into the chair.

It took only a few seconds, but by the time I was firmly seated, I was already beginning to feel the onset of more dizziness. They let me sit there until I declared myself ready to be launched into the routine life of the hospital outside my door.

"O.K. Let's go see what everybody else does for fun around this place. I'm ready for some action!"

I raised my right arm in the fashion of a cavalry trooper, turned to the wardsman who had already taken up the reins of my chair, and called the well-known cry.

"Forward YOOOO!!"

Mark whistled. The other fellows clapped loudly. Doctor Yeoman led off, followed by Sister Wang and Nurse Hoffman in line astern. With one wardsman pushing my chair, and the other bringing up in the rear, we lurched off into the exciting new world of the walking wounded.

Now I was irrepressible. I was so happy to be out and about again. Even if I was confined to a wheelchair! I ignored the nagging pain which had returned to my lower back.

I pretended that the nausea threatening to make me vomit on to the shiny white linoleum floor of the corridor did not exist. I was having too good a time to be bothered by such trivia.

Everybody who passed me in the passageway received a loud, cheery and enthusiastic hail.

"G'day, mate! Lovely day isn't it? We're going to the gym for some exercise. Wanna come?"

Some of them obviously thought I was crazy. Others smiled knowingly and returned my greeting, guessing that I had just been released from maximum security horizontal prison. It was SO good to have at least partial freedom again.

We trundled down the corridor, around a corner, along another corridor, through a pair of big wooden swinging doors held open by Nurse Hoffman, and into the largest gymnasium I had ever seen. All kinds of strange equipment littered the floor and hung on long chains from the high ceiling. I could not decide whether the place looked like a gymnast's heaven or a medieval torture chamber. However, I quickly discovered that the latter description was going to be more accurate in my particular case.

They wheeled me over to a huge canvas-wrapped mat on the floor in the center of the room. Doctor Yeoman spoke to a middle-aged woman who was dressed in a crisply starched white blouse and slacks. I could not quite make out what the doctor was saying to her, as he conveniently had his back to me, but I did hear my name mentioned.

The woman turned to gaze in my direction with raised eyebrows. She caught my eye and smiled. I did not like the looks of that smile. It reminded me of Sister Wang.

Doctor Yeoman turned towards us and spoke again.

"Rod, I would like you to meet Miss Julia Starrett. She is perhaps the finest physiotherapist in the country. She will get the circulation going again in those legs of yours, and hopefully, begin putting some muscle back on them after their long inactivity. The rest, as you already know, is up to you."

"Julia, this is the infamous Rod Lewin. You know his history. He has already had some movement in his left big toe, which in itself is quite incredible under the circumstances. Perhaps you can encourage the rest of him to start doing some work once more."

"We will certainly give it our best shot, won't we Rod," she said, shaking my hand, and smiling again with kindly gray eyes.

I decided instantly that I liked this woman, despite my initial suspicion when she looked at me as the doctor spoke to her. She had compassion in those eyes when I saw them up close. Compassion, kindness and something else I recognized immediately; determination. The same kind of determination that I had to get out of here. I knew she would be working as hard as I was, to help me get some of my old life back again.

Here was my answer to John Wayne's Petty Officer. This woman was going to make damn sure that I did not get a moment's rest until she was convinced that I had done my very best, and was completely exhausted when I went to bed at night. She was going to make me wish that I had never even wanted to get out of that bed!

I shook her hand firmly.

"Hi Julia, I greeted her enthusiastically. "Well, I'm ready when you are. When do we start on the parallel bars?"

She laughed heartily at my optimism. "Very funny. Your first lesson, my boy, is that you literally have to learn to crawl again before you can walk. Let's get you out of that chair and on to the mat. O.K., boys," she said to the wardsmen, "if you will put him on the floor, we can get to work."

They took hold of me under my arms again, lifted me out of the chair, and dumped me unceremoniously on the mat.

"Good luck, Rod," Doctor Yeoman said as he turned to leave. "Remember, don't overdo it. If you start to feel tired, or if your back begins to hurt, tell Julia immediately. She will understand. I will drop in on you again in a few days to see how you are progressing."

He left the room trailed by his ever-present entourage, and I was alone with my new mentor; well, not exactly alone. By now I had realized that the gym was indeed a hive of activity.

Julia Starrett was the boss of this room. There were at least a half dozen other therapists working with other paraplegics and quadriplegics at various instruments and machines around the floor.

I looked on as if I was not a part of this strange scene. For a moment I thought that I was merely a visitor in a land of stricken beings. Then I remembered that I was not a stranger in this land, but one of the local inhabitants. This is where I belonged.

No! Never, I thought. I do not belong here. These are not my people. I AM a stranger here. I am going to prove it.

As if she had been reading my mind, Julia gently pushed me down on to the mat so that I was lying flat on my back. She took hold of my left foot and began working and kneading at the toes, twisting the ankle and raising and lowering the leg, bending the knee at the same time.

"I want you to keep mentally working on that system of yours," she said.

"I have never heard of anything like it before, and I have never known anyone with your spinal damage to have any definite movement like that either. Usually the movement is due to muscle spasm and is quite uncontrollable. What we are going to do is to give your legs some artificial movement. Exercise them as if they were doing it themselves. Make them think that they can in fact move of their own volition."

I listened, fascinated, as she talked and worked on my legs. Bending, squeezing, twisting, bending. Never stopping. Constantly working them for what seemed like hours.

"If you will keep willing them to move, then perhaps that, combined with my therapy which is hopefully rebuilding the muscle that has wasted away, will one day enable you to walk again. Oh, you will have to wear calipers of course, but at least you will be walking."

I looked at her in alarm.

"I'll have to wear what?" I croaked in horror.

"Calipers," she replied. "You know, those steel braces you have seen people wearing. We may even be able to have our equipment specialists make you a pair with bending knee joints so that you can stand and sit

71

more or less normally. It all depends on how much strength we can get back into those legs. You may even become proficient enough on the calipers to end up walking without crutches. But that's all a long . . ."

"Crutches?" I squeaked in disbelief.

"Of course, crutches," she said. "You can't walk on calipers without crutches. You would fall on your face every time you took a step."

My bright new world collapsed around me. It had never occurred to me that if I was ever going to walk again, it would be on practically artificial limbs and crutches. That depressing thought brought me back to reality with a hard jolt.

I looked around the room once more, and decided that I had better get used to the idea that these people in here were, in fact, my own kind now. I was not invading their territory like some stranger from another planet. I was one of them!

Julia continued working my legs, talking all the time about how I was going to be able to learn to become a useful member of society again, despite my handicap. She told me of all the activities that were still open to me even in the immediate future while I was still confined to the wheelchair. I could learn all kinds of fun things like archery, for instance.

"As a matter of fact," she continued, "I just happen to be conducting an archery class this very afternoon. If you feel up to it, you are more than welcome to join in. We have it down in the park in the grounds. It might do you the world of good to get out in the sunshine and fresh air again for a while."

I remembered what Doctor Yeoman had said regarding my immediate return to bed after the session with Julia.

"Thanks Julia, I replied, "but Doc Yeoman told me in no uncertain terms that I have to go straight back to bed when we finish here. I don't want to disobey him on my first day, or he might confine me to that prison cell indefinitely. I did promise him that I would follow his orders. On the other hand, if you, as my therapist, feel it would do me good to get outside, then I can't disregard your advice either. Maybe you can mention it to him."

She flashed me that smile again, this time with a hint of conspiracy in her eyes.

"I think I can convince him that you are up to a little stroll in the garden. Strictly for medicinal purposes, as they say."

"Julia, I think I'm going to like you," I replied. "You are going to be my passport to freedom."

"Now don't go getting any ideas," she responded. "I am not going to let you get away with anything either. If I don't think it is good for you, I will not let you do it. You will not be able to twist me around your little finger and have me cover for you so you can do crazy things like disappearing across the road to the pub for instance. No way, Joe!"

Bloody mindreader!

"Never entered my mind," I lied.

"Just remember, you are not my first patient," she said. "I am awake up to every trick in the book tried by fellows like you. Cross me just once, and I will never do you another favor. On the other hand, if you do as I tell you, I will let you get away with far more than the good doctor ever knows about. Understood?"

"Yes ma'am! It's a deal," I grinned.

"O.K., then. Let's get on with the work. This is only the very first exercise. In a couple of weeks, I will have you sitting, then crawling on your hands and knees, then maybe working the parallel bars, I hope. But your progress is basically up to you. I can't make you work. You have to WANT to do it."

"Don't worry Julia. I'm going to work. I am going to get out of here before Christmas if it kills me."

She was obviously taken aback by that statement, but not wanting to dampen my spirit, said nothing to discourage me.

Julia continued to push and pull at my legs for about an hour. By the end of that time, my back was beginning to throb mercilessly and I could tell that, as usual, nothing in this business was going to be as easy as I had at first imagined. After a while longer, I begged for mercy and Julia stopped for a break herself.

"You sure you are going to want to go down to the park later?" she asked, testing my endurance.

"Sure. Just let me get a bit of rest before I go. What time do you go down?"

"Oh, about three o'clock or so. Don't tell me you want to go back to that bed so soon," she provoked, with a grin to soften the jibe.

"Ha, ha. Very bloody funny. You knew that I would be begging to go back to it after my first time out."

"Of course I knew. Like I said, you are not my first patient. Remember, most people with your type of injury are, or were, active young men. If they had not been, they would not be in here. When you begin to venture forth around the wards, you will discover that most of the people in the spinal unit are in their late teens or early to mid twenties. The usual cause of injury is due to football accidents, falling off motor bikes, etc.; anything that is, by the nature of the sport, inherently dangerous will sometimes cause young men and women to receive spinal injuries."

"Yeah," I replied thoughtfully. "The fella in the bed next to me fits that description exactly. Young Mark Giavelli. Apparently he fell a few feet after a couple of beers at a party and ended up a quad."

"Yes. I know Mark," Julia said. "What a terrible waste. I have not begun to treat him yet. He has been in no shape, physically or psychologically, to try to help him. However, I believe that in the last few weeks his condition has improved greatly, particularly since a certain young lady has been visiting the ward."

"You're right there," I replied, thinking immediately of Barb. She came to look after me, but typical of Barb, who has a soft spot for anything wounded or hurt, she ended up cheering up the entire floor. "I think she has done Mark a lot of good. He should be able to start some kind of treatment soon, I hope."

"I'll have a look at him," she promised. "Maybe I can talk Doc Yeoman into having him brought round here to the gym to begin some basic therapy. It certainly can't do him any harm at this stage."

"As for you, I think that is quite enough for your first day. If we can get you back into that chair, I will take you back to your room myself, and have a talk to Mark while I am there. Also, in future, as well as your workouts in the gym, I will be coming round to give you some minisessions while you are in bed — probably a couple of times a day — just so you won't forget I am here to harass you."

"Sounds great to me," I replied. "The more you harass me, the better chance I have of being home for Christmas."

She did not say so, but I knew she did not think I had a prayer of being out of here until a long, long time after the festive season.

One of the other girls in the gym came across in answer to Julia's call, and between the two of them, and despite my own struggle to help them, they managed to get me back in the wheelchair without too much difficulty. Julia then wheeled me out into the hall and round to my room.

Just as we were turning toward my cell, Barb came striding down the corridor from the direction of the elevators.

"Oho!" she cried. "So this is what you get up to as soon as I stay away for a couple of days. How long has this been going on, anyway?"

We stopped outside the room and I introduced Julia and Barb to each.

"Barb, this is my physiotherapist, Julia Starrett. Julia, meet Barbara."

"Hi Barb. Pleased to meet you," she said, shaking hands. "So you're the Florence Nightingale I have heard so much about lately. Well, I can see why everybody around here has been immensely cheered by your presence."

"Hi Julia," Barb replied, flashing her smile. "Nice to meet you too. Looks like you are doing some good yourself. I've been telling this lazy bum for weeks now that it's about time he got out of bed and started to do some work again. I hope you gave him a real workout."

"I think you could say that. Although, I have promised him he can come down to the archery session in the grounds this afternoon. Perhaps you would like to stay and bring him down?"

"Sounds like a great idea. I don't want to miss his first day out and about."

"Wonderful! I'll see you then."

"See you later, Julia. And thanks."

"Don't mention it," she smiled as she turned away.

Barb took the handles on the back of the chair and wheeled me down the corridor to a sunny spot by the big windows at the end of the hall.

This was the first time I had felt the sun on my face for nearly two months now. It felt so good! I gazed out the window at the peaceful scene seven floors below. Traffic was flowing busily along the Pacific

Highway through the northern suburb of St. Leonards. The skyscrapers of North Sydney and those of downtown, linked across the beautiful harbor by the magnificent Sydney Harbor Bridge, glinted in the midday sun on this wonderful summer day. Down below, a Careflite helicopter sat hunched on the concrete pad waiting patiently for the call that would send its crew off on another mission to bring some seriously injured person under the care of somebody like Doctor John Yeoman.

The hospital grounds were alive with activity, people walking and talking in the bright sunlight. Beautiful flowers of every kind lined the sidewalks, and the Jacaranda trees spilled their millions of pink and purple blossoms onto the ground, making a multi-colored carpet which could be seen and admired more easily from my elevated position.

Barb came round the side of the chair and lightly sat on the left armrest, placing her arm around my shoulders as she did so.

"Beautiful, isn't it?" she remarked, gazing out at the sights and sounds below.

"It sure is," I replied. "I can hardly wait to get out of here. I told Julia that I am going to be out by Christmas. I meant it too! Only thing that worries me is that when I finally do get out of this place, I will have no place to live. I gave up my apartment before I left for the Academy. That was my home before the accident. Now I will have to find some place where I can get around while I am learning to walk again."

"I have already thought about that," Barb said, grinning down at me. "I want you to come home with me. Stay at my place. I have a nice new flat on the beach at Coogee. You can stay with me as long as you want. As long as it takes. The only problem is, it is on the second floor. We may have to do a bit of maneuvering to get you up and down the steps. There is no lift."

As I looked up at her, my arm around her waist, salty tears welled in my eyes. This girl was an answer to a prayer — for the second time. Not only was she sharing her life with me while I was in hospital, she was willing to take me into her own home to look after me when I got out.

At long last, we were going to be together again. This time, I would make very sure that we stayed together. This time, I was going to make it work. Barb was too good to lose twice in one lifetime.

Admiring the view outside the sun-filled window on that wonderful first day out of bed, it was easy to believe that everything was going to be all right. Oh, if only things in real life turned out the way they did in your daydreams!

Barb and I sat in the sun for an hour. She called her boss and told him that she would not be in for the rest of the day. Then, conveniently forgetting Doctor Yeoman's explicit instructions, and hoping Julia would cover for me if he found out, we innocently wheeled our way down the hall to the elevators, waited anxiously expecting to be caught at any moment, and when the lift came, disappeared inside and arrived at the ground floor without being intercepted.

This was a brand new game for me; a completely new adventure. For the first time in months, I was out on my own again; free to come and go as I pleased without the regimen of the hospital staff to bother me, Barb and I wandered through the lovely gardens we had admired from the window on the seventh floor.

The hours passed pleasantly and at three o'clock we made our way down to the park at the bottom of the garden, bumped and bounced across the uneven grass, and arrived just as Julia was getting the archery class under way. There were about a dozen other students, all in wheelchairs and all in various stages of paralysis.

We had a wonderful afternoon, laughing at each other as we all fumbled with the bows and arrows, more than once nearly puncturing a fellow student as our inept, and in some cases paralyzed, fingers struggled to gain some measure of control over the bow and the flight of the arrow.

That was the most enjoyable day I had experienced in a very long time. After a while, my back began to throb from sitting in the chair. I ignored it. All I noticed was the serene beauty of the grounds, the pretty, sweet-smelling flowers, the trees filled with singing birds and the sun gleaming on Barb's jet-black hair.

Maybe life was not going to be so bad after all.

7

Now that I was more or less free to come and go as I pleased, life took on a whole new interest. It also became a lot more work. But, at least I had a challenge every day to get up and prove that I could do better than I had done yesterday.

The routine began at about ten a.m. every morning, when Barb, or if she was not available, one of the nurses or wardsmen, came to my room with the wheelchair to escort me round to the gym for my session with Julia. I could see no reason why I could not wheel myself around, so I had been doing just that, despite objections that I might run amok and injure some innocent bystander.

For the first week, Julia did nothing more than what she did on that first day. She simply pushed and pulled and twisted at my legs, all the time telling me to keep working mentally on my toes. Since the initial movement of the big left toe, there had been no further improvement. That toe was obviously becoming stronger, and the movement was definitely more pronounced, but there appeared to be no action from any of the other digits.

We spent anywhere from one to three hours in the gym, depending on how tired and sore and irritable I got. I was mighty bored with this routine now, and craved some different kind of exercise. I was impatient to start showing some signs of improvement so that I could begin learning to walk again, calipers or not!

On the third day of the second week out of bed, Julia surprised me by beginning a new series of exercises. First, she had me roll over on my stomach. Then, with my palms flat on the mat, she made me raise my upper torso up as if I was doing push-ups. At the same time, she hauled my backside into the air until I was precariously balanced on all fours. There was no way I could stay there under my own power, so she held me in that position until I fairly trembled with fatigue and pain.

The minute she let go her support of my back, I flopped over on my side, crashing on to the mat. This was extremely discouraging, as it served to painfully point out that I could not even crawl yet, let alone learn to walk again; I did not realize, of course, that in order to crawl I had to have some strength and control in the thigh muscles, which at the moment were as useless as the rest of my leg and foot muscles.

I wheeled myself back to the room that morning in an evil temper at my lack of progress, not thinking at all about the fact that I was already miles ahead of where I was a week ago, by virtue of my mobility alone. I was never going to be satisfied, and that was the only way to be if I ever intended to get out of this DAMN prison!

That afternoon, sitting in my now favorite position in the sun at the end of the corridor, and contemplating my uselessness to the world in general, I received a sudden burst of unexpected encouragement. I was squirming in the wheelchair, trying to adjust my position to relieve the pain in my back. I happened to glance at my feet and . . . could it be?

Surely not!

Yes!! There they go again. The other four left toes were moving in sympathy with the big one.

When I was moving my body in the chair, I was unconsciously instructing my toes to adjust to a better position on the footrest — and by God, they were responding!

I spun round in the chair, grabbed the huge rear wheels, and took off with a squeal of rubber on the polished floor, totally disregarding the safety of all the pedestrian traffic in my path.

Julia was still in the gym with another patient. I charged over to her, barely stopping in time at the edge of the mat, and almost hurling myself on to it as a result.

"Julia! Julia!" I yelled, rudely interrupting her conversation with her patient. "My toes! My toes! They're moving! Look! They're moving!"

Both Julia and her patient stared at me for a moment as if I had gone quite mad. Then she got up from the mat, came over to me, and lifted my foot gently off the chair rest.

"Show me," she said calmly.

I looked sternly at my left foot and mentally willed the toes to perform. Slowly the big toe raised and lowered itself, and then the other four followed in unison. I could not get them to move individually, but there was no doubt that they were all moving up and down on command.

Julia looked up at me with a new light in her eyes. "Why, that's absolutely marvelous," she cried. "When did you notice that they were responding?"

"Just now, out in the hall," I replied effusively. "I was sitting in the sun down there at the end of the corridor, squirming around in the chair trying to get more comfortable, when I noticed that they were moving. Do you think there is a chance that my spinal cord might be starting to heal?"

"Well, I don't want to get your hopes up this early in your recovery, but this does appear to be some indication that the damage is partially repairing itself."

I smiled down at her, feeling much better than I had when I left her after my therapy.

"I surely hope so, Julia. I can't wait to get into some real exercise, so I can learn to walk again. I don't care even if I do have to wear calipers for a few weeks, just so long as I am walking."

"Whoa there," she said, raising her hands, palms towards me.

"I don't know where you got this idea that you would only be wearing calipers for a few weeks. But if and when your legs ever get strong enough to wear them, it will probably be permanently. I'm sorry Rod, but you will have to get used to the fact that your legs will never again be able to support you by themselves. The chances of recovering full movement and strength in your muscles are very slim, and you will most likely suffer from what is commonly called 'dropfoot.' That is to say, the muscles which control the ability to hold your feet up so that you don't trip over them, will not be able to support them without the help of calipers. No, Rod. You MUST face the fact that you are going to be limited in your activities from now on, despite these encouraging signs of movement in your toes."

"NO!" I almost shouted at her. "No. I won't accept that. I AM going to walk again, dammit, and I'll do it under my own power if it kills me. I am tired of everybody telling me what I can't do. Julia, I want to be fitted out for calipers next week whether I am strong enough or not! Obviously the whole purpose of the damn things is to help you walk when your own legs can't carry you, so the sooner I get into 'em, and start walking on 'em, the sooner my own muscles will be forced into action."

I wheeled that chair around and took off in another squeal of rubber, fuming at the abject pessimism of everyone around here.

It was driving me crazy. Ever since my first day in this nuthouse, people were telling me what I could not do any more. Well, the hell with all of them! I was going to walk out of this institution for the permanently brainwashed, and I was going to do it before Christmas!

I charged back to my room in disgust, once again disregarding the safety of the pedestrian traffic. By now, most of the regular nursing staff knew me — and knew me well enough to stay out of my way.

On the way back to my room, I ran into another paraplegic, Don Richardson, who had been in a wheelchair since he was twelve years old, as a result of an automobile accident. He was in the spinal unit on a routine visit for examination and therapy.

We stopped to pass the time of day, and he informed me that he was going across the road to have a few beers at the "Wheelchair Watering Hole," as the pub was affectionately known.

"Would you like to come? It's about time you had a change of scenery, isn't it?" he asked temptingly.

"Would I!" I responded eagerly. "I'd jump at the change to get out of this madhouse for a bit. Let's go!

Without further ado, we wheeled around and headed for the elevators at the end of the corridor.

Just like on the first occasion when I left the building with Barb, I felt guilty and thought that at any moment, somebody would spot me, realize that I was not allowed out, and have me arrested and thrown into solitary confinement. So far, to my knowledge, Doctor Yeoman had not discovered my truant activities.

The elevator arrived and we rolled inside, innocently chatting amidst a throng of nurses coming back from their lunch break. Lucky people! Just take off whenever they feel like it. They walk, they run, they jump, they play wonderful games.

Talk about pessimism! I am getting as bad as the staff in this place. Of course games are not out of my reach. What is this caper I am embarking on now, if not a game? I may not be running or jumping yet, but I sure am going out on the town to have a few beers with the boys, just like in the old days. And pretty soon, I WILL be doing everything anyone else can do — including flying aeroplanes!

We rolled out of the building, down the walk which wound through the gardens and out the main gate. By this time, I was becoming reasonably proficient and comfortable with handling the chair in most situations. However, this was the first time I had been outside the hospital grounds. It was rather unsettling to be in the outside world again, with people bustling by, traffic whipping up and down the highway, dogs barking and chasing cats around the block. God, it was wonderful to be out again, even if it was a bit nerve-racking at first.

We waited on the edge of the sidewalk at the pedestrian crossing conveniently located right in front of the hospital gates on our side, and the pub on the other side. I noticed with some alarm that there was no break in the curb for a wheelchair to enter the street. However, before I could think about it, the light changed to "WALK" and we took off, wheeling ourselves across the road in defiance of the temporarily stopped traffic. Getting off the curb was no trouble at all, and I rolled across the road licking my lips and imagining the bitter taste of the cold, frothy, amber nectar as it passed down my throat for the first time in months.

Don had taken off like the expert he was as soon as the light changed. He was waiting on the other side before I was halfway across. As I approached the opposite curb, the problem of getting back up over the edge and on to the sidewalk loomed ahead. I had watched as Don easily shifted his ample weight aft, deftly tilting his chair rearward so that the small front wheels left the ground and were raised high enough to plant them firmly on the concrete of the sidewalk. In this tilted attitude, he rolled forward until the large rear wheels were touching the curb, and then heaved himself up and over the edge with a firm push.

Nothing to it!

As I approached the curb, I slowed the rolling chair with a light grip on the rear wheels. When the front wheels were almost touching the edge, I threw my body backwards as Don had done, raising the front wheels off the ground. Everything looked fine. The front wheels were balanced at just the right height to pass over the curb. I gripped the rear wheels tightly, rolling them forward as I did so.

Suddenly, as if it had a mind of its own, the chair began to tilt further back. I don't quite recall what happened after that, but the next thing I remembered was lying flat on my back, still in the chair, my legs completely out of control as usual, and hanging askew around the armrests, the front wheels turning uselessly in mid-air.

The combined mess of me and the chair was poking dangerously into the street. Traffic was backing up as drivers braked hard and swerved to skid around me. Horns were honking furiously, and onlookers were gathering on the sidewalk, wondering what to do about the bizarre scene before them.

I was like a turtle turned on its back, and was totally helpless. Don quickly took charge of the situation, and called to two of the closest bystanders to lend a hand to get my chair upright.

An approaching police car stopped at the pedestrian crossing with lights flashing. The officer stepped out and began to return some measure of control to the traffic flow which was by now, with the drivers slowing down and turning to gawk at the strange sight, almost total chaos.

I was not hurt, but I was still lying helplessly on my back when the two volunteers recruited by Don came to my aid. They soon had me upright and safely removed to the sidewalk.

Don wheeled over to me, his face ashen.

"It's all my fault," he said, wringing his hands in despair. "Are you

O.K., Rod? We had better get you straight back to the hospital and let Doc Yeoman have a look at you. This is awful! It's all my fault," he repeated.

"Don't worry about it, Don," I replied. "I'm fine. Really. It was my own stupid fault for trying to imitate you. It did not occur to me that you have been doing stunts like that for years. I was just getting way ahead of myself, as usual. Besides, if you think I am crossing that bloody road again, to face the wrath of Doc Yeoman before I have had a beer, you're crazy! I do not want to die sober. Let's get inside out of this crowd."

The police officer came over and asked if I was O.K., and whether or not I needed an ambulance. I told him I was fine and thanked him for keeping the traffic from mercilessly running me down.

The crowd began to disperse, now that the excitement was over. I thanked my two rescuers, who were still hovering in the wings in case I needed further assistance. Don and I then spun our chairs around and wheeled in through the open doors of the pub. Some of the patrons of the bar had obviously been onlookers outside, who had returned to their posts once the show had finished. They cheered as we entered the premises, and made way for us as we approached the bar.

The place was literally choc-a-bloc with wheelchairs. I had never seen so many people in various stages of handicap in one place at one time. Men and women both, they were all cheerily quaffing beer, laughing and joking, and generally having a ball. I wondered if Sister Wang knew about this place. Probably not, or she would have had it condemned as a menace to public safety!

We each ordered a beer from a nonchalant barman who did not even bat an eye at our condition or our presence. He was obviously quite accustomed to people like us in his establishment. We wedged the frosty glasses between our legs, and as we backed away from the bar, I was thinking that those useless limbs did come in handy for something.

Soon we were conversing freely with a group of other inmates from the spinal unit, and I was realizing that these people were really pretty remarkable to be able to learn to cope with a life-style which up until now had been totally foreign to me.

Time passed, the meager contents of my wallet diminished at an alarming rate which was directly proportional to the increasing pain in my bladder, and soon I had to ask Don for guidance to the bathroom.

As I maneuvered through the crowd in response to his directions, the importance of what I was doing suddenly hit me. I was going to the bathroom! I had been holding the recently consumed and processed beer in my bladder. Up until now, I had been led to believe that my spinal injuries, in addition to causing the paralysis, had caused total loss of control over my bodily functions. When I awoke for the first time after my operation, one of the things I had noticed through the blinding pain was a catheter protruding obscenely out of my lower stomach wall, leading to a plastic bag hanging over the side of the bed. This awkward contraption (although a vast improvement on the older, more painful and embarrassing method) had been with me ever since, and any liquid I had subsequently taken in had been automatically vented overboard.

I now discreetly looked over the side of the chair at the ever-present bag, and was amazed to discover that it was empty. By God, I was holding the wonderful stuff inside me! My bladder muscles were working again! This was fantastic! I found the bathroom, shoved open the door, rolled into the wheelchair-sized cubicle, and with more ease than I had imagined, transferred myself out of the chair and on to the pedestal.

Now this might sound like a small thing, but the relief and satisfaction I felt at the outcome of this minor victory was possibly even greater than the first movement of my big toe. I was free of yet another encumbrance.

I rolled out of there and back into the bar, relieved in more than one way. I found Don amidst the crowd, and pushed through to him.

"Don, Don, guess what?" I shouted above the din. "I just went to the bathroom!"

"Congratulations," he responded, with a remarkable lack of enthusiasm.

"No, no, you don't understand," I replied excitedly. "The bag's empty. My bladder is holding water again. Isn't that great?"

"My God!" he responded with rolling eyes. "That fall must have done you some good after all. Think I'll try the same trick. It would be wonderful to be able to take a voluntary piss again. Oh well, fortunes of war, and all that."

"Don, I think I'll mosey on back to the funny farm now. I don't want to be charged with being drunk in charge of a wheelchair. If Doc Yeoman finds out what I have been up to today, he will clap me in irons — and I don't mean calipers. As for the old battle-axe, she will summarily execute me if SHE finds out, God help me!"

The crowd around us laughed in unison at that last remark. Obviously Sister Wang was well-known to the majority of people here.

Don was understandably reluctant to leave just yet, but would no doubt have escorted me had I asked him. I thanked him for inviting me, and for the good time I had, despite my embarrassing re-entry to the vehicular world.

"Thanks gang," I shouted to the bar in general as the group parted to let me through.

"Nice to meet you all. I had a great time today. This is the first time I have been to a pub, or anywhere else, for months. I wonder if I could impose on one of you two-legged types to get me across the road in one piece. I am not taking another chance on getting mown down by those lunatics out there."

One of the group standing at the bar separated himself from the crowd and came over to escort me across the highway. The rest of them laughed again at the reminder of my near-disaster, waved good-bye, and returned to serious drinking. This time, I gratefully allowed my escort to raise my chair to the safety of the sidewalk outside the hospital gates. I thanked him, and he waved as he headed back across the road to his mates in the pub.

I wheeled around and trundled into the relative safety of the hospital grounds, pushed myself up the incline to the main entrance and in through the lobby to the elevators. I was feeling pretty smug, and just a little bit light-headed as I entered the elevator and rode it up to the seventh floor. The doors slid open quietly and I wheeled out — straight into the waiting arms of a reception committee led by Doctor Yeoman and Mata Hari!

"Oh my God," I muttered through trembling lips.

"Not even He can help you now," purred the good sister from behind a dark and evil smile.

She personally took a firm grip on the handles of my chair and with an ungentle lurch, shoved me off in the direction of my room.

I was done for!

Dear Lord, what were they going to do to me? They were obviously aware of my little outing, and if they knew about my visit to the pub, they also knew about my disrupting influence on the mid-afternoon flow of rush hour traffic along the main artery through North Sydney.

Doctor Yeoman had not yet spoken. He was no doubt deeply disappointed in me for breaking my promise to him. But surely that only applied to the first day or two out of bed. I had only breached the promise once, on that first day out in the gardens with Barb.

Please, Doc. Please don't revoke my new-found freedom, I mentally begged.

We arrived in my now rarely visited room, and I was unceremoniously dumped out of the chair and into the bed by a couple of waiting wardsmen. I lay there quietly, expecting at any second to receive a blistering tirade from Doc Yeoman. He just stood there looking down at me with a strange, dull, gleam in his eyes. He said nothing as he clutched his clipboard tightly to his ample chest with both arms folded, suffocating his stethoscope as he did so. Sister Wang obviously could not stand the silence either. She stood there fidgeting for a few moments more, then decided to bring down the wrath of God on me herself.

"What in blue blazes do you think you were doing out there, Lewin? In one afternoon, you have single-handedly done more to damage the good reputation of this establishment than all the rest of the patients in the spinal unit put together, past and present. We have had calls not only from the local Police, wanting to know why we cannot control the activities of the mobile patients under our care, but also from concerned citizens, afraid that we are letting lunatics loose on the general unsuspecting public. I told the doctor that he was making a grave mistake to let you wander around without an escort, preferably armed. My worst fears have been realized. I knew if you . . . "

"Thank you Sister," interjected the doctor, "that will be quite enough."

"But Doctor Yeoman, this . . . this PERSON has flagrantly disregarded not only your own direct orders, but also every rule and regulation laid down by the hospital for the safety of the patients. You simply MUST take the sternest disciplinary measures against him, or the rest of the patients will think they have the right to do what they please!"

Doctor Yeoman turned his steady blue gaze from me to Sister Wang.

"You are absolutely correct, Sister. We certainly do need to take some severe action here. Please leave me alone with him. I do not want anybody else to be present to hear what I am about to do to him. Please draw the curtains and leave the room. All of you. It is a pity we cannot remove the other patients to save their embarrassment, but perhaps they will learn something from the example I am about to make of Mr. Lewin."

Sister Wang smiled evilly at me again. The doctor was probably going to have me thrown out of the hospital to fend for myself in some nursing home. At last, she was going to be rid of me and my disturbing influence on her sterile little world. She turned sharply on her heel, drew the curtain around the bed, and followed by her minions, left the room with one ear cocked, hoping to hear the beginning of the terrible retribution she was expecting.

Doctor Yeoman stood there silently until the retreating footsteps were well out of earshot. He still had not spoken one word to me since I had been recaptured. I could tolerate Sister Wang's manic outbursts. I was accustomed to that; but this silent treatment was driving me crazy! I lay there awkwardly, staring up at him in utter dejection, not knowing what to say to appease him. As I gazed at his face, I noticed a change in his stern expression. His frown eased, then the corners of his mouth and the creases around his eyes began a peculiar twitching.

Suddenly, his whole visage cracked into a huge grin, and the next moment, a noise which sounded suspiciously like a chuckle began deep in his throat and erupted in an uncontrollable, hysterical, snorting belly laugh which made his entire body fairly tremble and shake like a giant jelly.

I could not believe my own eyes and ears. I had expected him to roast me alive, not only for my blatant disobedience, but also for my thoughtless stupidity in risking further damage to my spine with the wheelchair stunt. Instead, here was Doctor John Yeoman, one of the truly great men in the field of neurosurgery, a highly regarded and respected professional in every sense of the word, guffawing uncontrollably with tears of laughter streaming down his cheeks! My mouth dropped open in utter astonishment at this amazing turn of events. I could not for the life of me fathom this remarkable change from apparently deep anger to obviously genuine humor.

Finally, his hysterics died down to an occasional chuckle. He cleared his throat with a loud "Harrumph," wiped the jovial expression from his face, and replaced it with one of stern severity, peeked through the curtain to make sure Sister Wang had not doubled back to hear what was going on, and spoke for the first time.

"Rod, you will be the death of me. You and I both know that Sister Wang is absolutely correct in what she said to you. However, I simply cannot find it in my heart to punish you. You have, from the day you arrived here, shown an incredible determination to set things right in your own world. Unfortunately, this has had some undesirable repercussions on the neat, orderly life of this hospital and its staff. I cannot condone what you did today. You took a foolish risk — several, in fact — but you survived — again."

"I think it best, for both you and the hospital, that you leave here as soon as possible, so with that in mind, combined with your own obvious determination to achieve the same objective," he raised his hand to silence my attempted interruption, "I am having you fitted for calipers. Today. Right now, in fact. The sooner, the better. It will take about a week for them to be constructed. In the meantime, I want every ounce of your energy to be expended on exercise in the gymnasium with Miss Starrett. You are strictly confined to the hospital grounds. Any further breaches will result in my placing your calipers on permanent hold, you will be further restricted to your room again, and I will allow Sister Wang to have total control over your movements. You will both have to learn to live with each for a long, long time. Do I make myself perfectly clear?"

This was incredible! Instead of being punished, I was being patted on the back AND given my ticket to freedom in one breath.

"Very clear, Doc," I replied, barely able to contain the relief and excitement I felt at this latest remarkable development. "This time, I really do promise. You won't hear a peep out of me. I'll work hard, and I won't do anything to antagonize Sister Wang. No more visits to the pub. I will spend all my time in the gym getting my legs ready for the irons. I swear it!"

I held out my hand and Doctor Yeoman extended his own and shook it firmly.

"I will send you an escort — unarmed, despite Sister Wang's advice — just to show you the way," he smiled. "You can go down to the basement and have the technicians measure your legs. I will tell Sister Wang, so she will not have you shot on sight. Remember, from now on, you are on your best behavior."

He turned, drew the curtain aside, and left without another word. I pulled the curtain all the way back, to reveal Mark's face grinning at from the adjacent bed.

"Good on yer, mate," he said with deep feeling. "I wish I could go with you ."

"You will, Mark," I replied with renewed enthusiasm. "Some day real soon, you will. I just know it!"

———————— ❖ ————————

8

The caliper specialists were waiting to receive me, and they soon had my legs measured and fitted for the irons. I was not prepared for the detail and precision to which these people worked, and had, of course, given absolutely no thought to the technical aspects of fitting a person with virtually artificial limbs. They had to be able to bend at the knees so that I could sit down easily. They had to be braced and hinged at the ankle to allow me to walk flat-footed, so my drooping, lifeless feet would not trip me up. They had to be padded with felt at thigh, calf and ankle, otherwise my skin would chafe and be rubbed raw. At the same time, they had to firmly grip those parts, so no slippage occurred when I raised my leg to take a step.

By the time the technicians had finished with me, I was convinced that I would be walking again in no time; perhaps a little stiffly, but without the aid of the crutches which Julia was adamant I had to learn to live with.

As usual, I was blinded by ignorance and exuberance.

It was well and truly dark by the time the experts let me go. I went back to my room for supper, and sat in my chair regaling Mark and the others with exaggerated tales of my day's adventures. That night, I slept more soundly than I had for a long time. I dreamed that Barb had come to take me home for Christmas, but when I woke in the cold, gray light of dawn, there was no Barb and I was stiff and sore from yesterday's activity.

My chair was beside the bed so I leaned forward, hauled my legs up and over the side, and, grabbing hold of the arm rest, heaved myself into the chair. I wheeled around to the bathroom, cleaned myself up, found with deep satisfaction that I was still holding and passing water — a minor detail I had forgotten to mention to Doctor Yeoman in the excitement — then trundled off to the gym in search of Julia.

She was not there. In fact, nobody was there. It was much too early. Oh well. I might as well do something constructive while I am here, I thought. I threw myself out of the chair and on to the canvas and sat with my hands flat on the mat behind me, supporting me upright with my legs stretched straight out in front of me. While sitting there watching my left toes wiggle, I tried in vain to lift my leg.

"I'm gonna lift that leg!" I said to myself, trying the same old formula.

Nothing, of course. I had not really expected anything to happen, but I was still disappointed that my leg did not rise as instructed. There had been no movement in anything but my left toes so far. So again!

"I'm gonna lift that leg!" I commanded mentally.

Still nothing.

Wait! What was that?

Again.

"I'm gonna lift that leg!"

No. The leg did not move. But that thigh muscle — or what was left of it — on the front of the leg above the knee, the one that lifts the leg, did that twitch?

"I'M GONNA LIFT THAT BLOODY LEG!!"

It DID move! That muscle twitched! Again and again I commanded the leg to move. Again and again the muscle responded with a twitch.

I had to tell somebody about this wonderful new turn of events. The gym was still deserted, so I rolled over, dragged myself to the edge of the mat, grabbed hold of the armrests on the chair, and hauled myself up into it from the ground. I found that as I turned my upper torso to drop into the chair, my useless lower half just naturally followed, although with some considerable pain in my back. However, the maneuver proved to be less difficult than I had at first imagined, and I had now gained one more small victory on the road to independence.

In a matter of seconds I was off, wheeling away in search of somebody to whom I could tell the good news. I searched around all the corridors, poking my head into rooms and offices, and asking every doctor, nurse and patient I came across if they had seen Doctor Yeoman or Julia Starrett. No luck! I guessed that it was still too early for anybody to have arrived. Even Sister Wang was conspicuous by her absence.

I rolled back to the gym to wait. Throwing myself on to the mat once more, I took up my previous position, and continued to work on willing that thigh muscle to move. By the time I had been at it for an hour or so, I was absolutely exhausted and my wrists ached from supporting my body in that awkward position for so long. But not without results! I had watched that muscle increase its movement from an almost invisible twitching to a positive and clearly evident contraction with every mental command.

As I sat there alone on the floor of that huge room, I reflected on the fact that it had been a rather eventful twenty-four hours, one way or another.

What with my toes beginning to wiggle yesterday morning, followed by my attempted suicide by throwing myself into a stream of traffic, discovering that I could control my bladder, almost getting castrated by Sister Wang, being fitted for calipers, and now this morning moving my left thigh muscle, I could smugly afford to call it a fairly full day.

I gazed around the empty room. My eyes came to rest on a large picture calendar on the opposite wall. The date stared back at me. Today was the 20th of November. Two months yesterday since the crash. Ye gods! Yesterday was the 19th! Brilliant observation, Lewin! All those things had happened to me, including being nearly killed again, on the exact same day two months after my accident. Now today, I had discovered the first sign of movement in my left leg. There was still no sign of any kind of action on the right side, but I was becoming more and more hopeful that this would soon follow. I really might be out of here before Christmas!

This reminded me that I had not seen or heard from Barb for several days. I could hardly wait to tell her all the news. Maybe I would be going home with her sooner than either of us had hoped. I was sure that she would be pleased to hear that.

Just then, the big double doors of the gym were thrown open, and Julia and three of her assistants marched in, wheeling a similar number of patients before them. Julia came straight over to me, obviously surprised that I was here so early.

"Hi Rod. What's up? I thought you would be over at the pub by now," she jibed.

Apparently the news of my errant behavior had spread like wildfire all around the hospital.

"Ha! Ha! Very funny," I replied, feeling a hot blush which began at the base of my throat and worked all the way up to my forehead until I could tell that my entire face must be a deep red.

"Sorry. Just kidding," she said, smiling to reassure me that she did not mean it.

"That's O.K.," I replied. "I guess I deserve that anyway. I must have been crazy to pull a stunt like that yesterday. Hey, guess what? I have been sitting here since daybreak. I got bored, so I started flexing my left thigh muscle just for something to do."

"Well, that's nice," she replied. "It's about time you . . . you what?"

"I have been flexing my left thigh muscle," I repeated calmly.

"Dear God! Let me see!"

This time I was confident that I did not have to speak the command aloud. I simply stared at my left leg just above the knee and mentally instructed it to move.

The muscle in question obeyed instantly and positively. So much so this time that the lower leg itself actually twitched.

"Dear God," Julia repeated unnecessarily.

"That's what I said, more or less, when I discovered it. It started with just a twitch this morning. I have been sitting here ever since, working on it. It has been getting stronger by the hour. Isn't that fantastic?"

"It certainly is! It's marvelous. Doctor Yeoman has also informed me that you have been fitted for your calipers. I told him I think it is much too soon, of course, but he says it is best for the general safety and welfare of the hospital that you get well enough to leave as soon as possible. I don't quite understand what he means by that, but I have no doubt you know what he is talking about?"

"Yeah, I kinda know what he's getting at," I replied sheepishly.

When I did not elaborate, she let it pass and, stepping onto the mat, got down to the business at hand.

"Right," she said. "Seeing you are doing so well, we shall continue trying to get you to balance on your hands and knees. This is the most important exercise you can accomplish before you get your calipers. By learning to crawl again, you are working the same muscles you will need to use when you are walking. So. Roll over onto your stomach and I will haul you up on all fours. O.K.?"

I did as she requested and soon she had me upright on my hands and knees, wavering in an unsteady crouch. I could feel my left thigh muscle quivering with effort and fatigue. My right leg was still useless and wanted to give way under me, so I favored the left side and soon found that I could balance there practically under my own power with only one of Julia's hands on my rump to steady me.

This quickly became tedious and I yearned for some variety. Without any word from Julia, I shifted my weight from the left to the right side in an attempt to raise my left leg and move it forward — and promptly fell flat on my face as my right leg gave way under me.

Julia gasped in horror.

"Are you all right," she cried, gripping my hips and rolling me on my side to see if I was hurt.

"Yeah, I'm fine. Just getting way ahead of myself as usual."

"O.K.," she said with a sigh of relief. "Let's try it one more time."

I rolled over and again she hauled me up. Once more, I could feel my left thigh muscle trembling with the effort. This time I stayed put and did not try anything else. Eventually my left leg, which I was still favoring because of the partial movement in it, became weak with fatigue and I had to let it fall out from under me, though not as heavily as when I had tried to crawl. We took a break until my leg stopped quivering, then repeated the exercise.

The best part of the morning was spent doing the same thing over and over again. By the time lunch came around, Julia was ready to call it a day. Not me!

I had a quick bite to eat from the meals-on-wheels cart which the volunteer staff brought round, then continued with the torture. I was determined that I was going to at least take one crawling step by the end of the day, now that I had some control over my left leg.

Julia stepped out for a few minutes, leaving me balanced on all fours. I took the opportunity to again attempt to move my left leg forward. Once more, I slowly transferred my weight to my right side and, tottering on the brink of collapse, managed to drag my left leg a fraction of an inch forward before I did in fact topple over again.

When Julia returned, I told her between panting breaths that I had indeed managed to take my first crawling half step before I fell. She hauled me up and we repeated the performance for her benefit. Lean, lift, drag, fall. As I did this, she became more and more excited, clapping her hands and laughing with joy.

"That's wonderful, Rod. It's simply wonderful. And guess what? You cannot see it, but when you drag your leg like that, the tendons behind your left knee are beginning to stand out. That means your calf muscles in back of your leg are also trying to work. This is absolutely tremendous!"

I felt tears beginning to well in my eyes; and it was not just from pain and exhaustion, either.

Her words and feeling made me more determined to finish this day with a positive accomplishment. I kept up the routine.

Lean, lift, drag, fall. Lean, lift, drag, fall.

After each collapse to the mat, Julia would help me up, as no matter how hard I tried, I could not get all the way up on to all fours by myself. I could get my front up, but because of the lack of movement in my legs, I simply could not get on to my knees.

Damned frustrating!

Oh well.

Lean, lift, drag, fall. Lean, lift, drag, fall. Over and over again.

After what seemed like about five years of this, I finally made it to the end of the mat, a total distance of ten feet. I collapsed for the last time and lay sprawled, panting for breath, with my arms and legs stretched straight out before and behind me. I had not realized it, but I had gained a curious audience of patients and therapists who had halted their various activities to watch my painful, snail-like progress across the mat. When I finally reached the end of it, they all clapped and cheered, then turned back to their own projects.

The mid-afternoon sun was casting hazy, slanting, rays of dust-filled light through the giant windows of the gym. It was enough. I had exceeded my own objective for the day. My back ached so badly, I thought I had damaged it again. My knees were bruised and swollen, and the skin on them was rubbed raw. My hands and wrists and arms throbbed and trembled with the effort of supporting my body for so long. My left thigh muscle quivered unceasingly. I still had no feeling in either leg, but I was sure that if I had, both of them would hurt abominably.

Julia brought the wheelchair round to where I lay, practically unconscious. I was unable to move another inch. The chair towered above me as I strained my neck to look up at it. No way. There was no way I was going to be able to haul myself up and into that thing now. So I tried anyway, as a finishing touch. I struggled to lift one arm and then the other and place my palms flat on the mat one more time. My wrists screamed at me. I pushed up until my arms were straight.

Julia leaned over to assist me.

"NO!" I bellowed rudely. "Sorry, Julia," I said more calmly. "I didn't mean to yell. I'm just very tired. Let me have a go at it. If I can't manage, you can pull me up. O.K.?"

Frowning, she stood aside to watch.

I reached up and grabbed the right armrest with my left hand, then took hold of the left rest with my right hand. I inhaled deeply, took my weight on my arms, dragged myself up — and promptly turned the chair upside down on top of me.

Fortunately, Julia was prepared for such a catastrophe, and stepped up to intercept the downward flight of the chair. Had she not done so, the heavy metal footrest would probably have severely dented my thick skull, which had followed my face to the mat with a sickly splat when I instinctively let go of the handles to cushion my return to the horizontal.

"Have you had enough now?" she asked gently, as she returned the chair to its normal upright position.

I could but nod my head as I gingerly felt my jaw to see if it was still intact.

She took hold of me under the arms and in one fluid movement, lifted me, turned me over, and hauled me up into the chair, much as I had done earlier, when I was still fresh and strong.

"O.K., let's get you back to your room. You have had more than enough for one day. If Doctor Yeoman finds out what we have been doing here today, he will have both our hides. That obviously doesn't worry you. But I have to work here, and I would like to keep my job."

With that, she took hold of the handles and personally wheeled me off in the direction of my room. She was taking no further chances with me. When she deposited me safely in my room, her responsibility would end there.

I do not remember the ride back, or even being put to bed when I got there. I must have instantly fallen asleep and remained that way for hours. When I awoke, it was pitch black. I looked at the luminous hands of my watch. It was nearly eleven p.m. I had been asleep for more than seven hours, and did not even remember hitting the bed. Just goes to show what a good day's workout does for you, I thought, as I promptly fell asleep again.

Something woke me for the second time that night. It was several hours later. Nothing stirred. Not even any talking or laughing from the night staff outside. What was it that had woken me? The pain in my back? Could be. It was killing me. Though nothing like the first few days in hospital. My left thigh muscle? It too was aching, and twitching uncontrollably now. What the hell was nagging at me? Everything else seemed to be as it should be, yet . . . ? Something definitely was different. I could not identify the anomaly for the life of me. I was lying on my back, as usual, the easiest and most comfortable position for me. It still hurt to roll over, twisting my body and dragging my useless legs behind.

Something was not right! I reached over and switched on the bedside light. I looked at my legs and discovered the reason for the discomfort. My legs were close together, my right ankle atop my left, my feet crossed as in an old habit I had, when lying awake at night, unable to sleep.

Without consciously thinking about it, I dragged my right foot off the left, whereupon it flopped back to the mattress and . . .

I DID WHAT????

I stared in stupefaction at my right foot, as if I had never seen it before. Yep. It was mine, all right. Now run that by me again! My right foot had been resting on top of my left.

How in God's name did it get there? But what was even more incredible, did I or did I not just witness that same foot — and leg — move under its own power and remove itself from that position when subconsciously instructed to do so, JUST LIKE A NORMAL, UNPARALYZED, LIMB?

Weak, yes. Uncontrolled, certainly. BUT MY RIGHT LEG HAD MOVED OF ITS OWN VOLITION!!! This was . . . miraculous! Could it be possible?

My right toes, foot and leg had up until now shown not the slightest desire or intention to ever move again. Indeed, I had been so busy concentrating on the left side, before and since the first movement of the big left toe, that I had — I thought — been totally neglecting the right side altogether.

Was it possible that I had been so preoccupied with trying to see some kind of continual improvement in the left side that I had not even been aware of movement in the right? Yet, there was no doubt that it had moved. Well, let's try it again.

"I'm gonna move that leg!"

Nothing.

"I'M GONNA MOVE THAT LEG!"

Still nothing!

I gritted my teeth and tried again, concentrating as hard as I could on trying to move my right leg. Beads of sweat broke out on my brow. I could almost feel the command as it surged down my spine and into my leg. I just knew it was getting through. It must be that my muscles were so weak and atrophied from lack of use, nothing wanted to function.

"I'M . . . GONNA . . . MOVE . . . THAT . . . LEG!!"

Slowly, with such tiny movements as to be almost invisible, my right leg moved closer to the left. It was obviously not going to lift up again, but it WAS moving. By the time I had finally succeeded in bringing my right heel up to my left, I was perspiring freely and the veins in the sides of my neck stood out, as I grunted and groaned and gripped the sides of the bed with both hands so tightly that I was beginning to tear the sheet.

"Are you all right, Rod?"

Mark's voice penetrated my concentration and startled me into letting go of the sides of the bed, causing me to flop back on to the pillows, exhausted and frustrated and panting like a wounded animal.

"Rod! Are you O.K.?" came his worried voice again through the drawn curtain.

"Yeah, I'm fine," I finally wheezed. "Just doing my morning calisthenics."

"Your what?"

"Never mind. Go back to sleep. I'm sorry I woke you. I was just trying to move my right leg."

"And . . . ?"

"Oh, I finally got my heels together. God knows how!"

Silence.

Then, "You mean you really did move your leg?"

"I think so."

Silence again.

Then a strange noise began drifting through the curtain. I reached over, pulled it aside, and aimed my flashlight over towards Mark. Tears were rolling down his cheeks, glistening in the beam of light. He sniffled, unable to blow his own nose or wipe his eyes.

"Oh God, Mark! Are YOU all right?"

I grabbed my legs, tossed them over the side of the bed, heaved myself into the wheelchair, and taking a box of tissues with me, rolled the few feet over to his bed and wiped his face for him. By this time, I was bawling uncontrollably myself and the two of us unashamedly continued to cry in the still of the night for a long time. Finally, the mood of depression and loneliness passed, and we were down to an occasional sob and sniffle.

"I . . . I'm sorry, Rod. I just couldn't help it. I'm so happy for you each time you have a small victory over your body . . . yet, at the same time, I am envious and frustrated that I can't do the same. If only I could get out of this DAMN bed for just a little while, I know I would feel better."

"I know you would too, Mark. You have to believe that you are going to beat this thing. That is the only way I have been getting anywhere. I realize it's a lot more difficult for you to do, but you HAVE to keep telling yourself you are going to get out of that bed and go home to live with your folks again. I think Barb's absence recently has also had a bad effect on both of us. But when you come right down to it, nobody can help us but ourselves."

"This is a strictly personal battle, and one we will probably have to fight for the rest of our lives. So don't let it get you down. Get mad instead! Fight it! The will to fight is the only thing that is going to get you out of here."

"Thanks, mate. You're right, of course. Sometimes though, in the middle of the night, I wake up with an itch somewhere and I can't even scratch it and it drives me crazy. I wish I could at least move my arms like you can. But, you are right. Each of us has his own problems to face. Mine are just different from yours, that's all."

"That's the spirit! And when you get an itch, pretend you are an astronaut."

"What?"

"Yeah, pretend you're an astronaut. You think those guys can scratch an itch when they're lying around in a spacesuit?"

"You're right!"

"I'm always right! Now go back to sleep and keep telling yourself over and over again that you are going to move something. Pick a finger — your brain won't have to send the message so far — and concentrate on it and don't ever let it get out of your mind. Some day you WILL get it to move, then you can start on something else. Oh . . . and if you really need anything scratched, I'll be happy to help you out; within reason, that is."

I grinned to let him know I was not patronizing him, tousled his hair, wheeled back to my own bed, heaved myself into it, and immediately fell into a deep and contented sleep.

The next morning I woke, wondering if it had all been a dream.

However, when I looked down at my right foot, without any apparent effort or command, the ankle twitched, moving the foot of its own free will. I tried wiggling the toes. Amazingly enough, the big toe moved up and down a fraction of an inch, just as the left one had done at first. I was so excited, I just about threw myself off the bed and on to the floor as I heaved my legs overboard so I could get into the chair.

It was after nine a.m. and the gym was a hive of activity when I got there. Julia was again busy with another patient when I rudely rolled to a squealing stop at the edge of the mat, hurled myself on to it, and announced myself ready to begin crawling exercises.

"Well, what's eating you now?" Julia asked, slightly miffed at my intrusion. "I thought after yesterday you would be happy to rest awhile. I guess I should have known better. Anyway, just hold your horses for a moment and I will get to you shortly. I'm nearly through with Mrs. Donnelly here."

"I'm sorry, Julia," I replied, suitably chastened. "It's just that I am so excited. I got my right foot and toes going last night, you see!"

She had been massaging Mrs. Donnelly's legs. Her head jerked up and she stared at me in blank disbelief. She really was the most wonderful tonic for me, as she regarded every little piece of news I gave her with renewed wonder and awe. A broad smile cracked her face. She continued working on her present task without making any comment, but I knew she was pleased. I sat there patiently until she was finished, casually and nonchalantly twitching my right foot a tiny fraction of an inch from side to side. That was all I could do, but it did not go unnoticed.

When she finally got round to me, she was plainly tickled pink.

"I don't know how you are doing it, Rod. In all my years of working with paras and quads, I have never seen such rapid recovery. I still say, however, that you had better not get your hopes up too high. The fact remains that you have had massive spinal damage, and it is very likely that the tiny movements you do have will never be any more than that. The scar tissue in your spinal cord may very well prevent any more improvement. Anyway, enough of that. Let's get on with the exercise, and see what you can do."

BLOODY PESSIMIST!!

The rest of the day went much like yesterday. Except that by the end of it, I was able to crouch on all fours without support and without falling over. By late afternoon, I was taking my first unsteady crawling steps on my knees, slowly and painfully dragging first the left one, then amazingly enough, the right one. I still lost my balance and toppled with every other step, particularly when I tried to drag the right leg, but now I was finding that with tremendous effort and much agony I could raise myself back to my knees after falling.

It was coming along!

In the last few days I had received more encouragement and shown more improvement than in all the previous frustrating and agonizing weeks.

Oh Dear God, please let me walk again!

———————— ❖ ————————

9

The week dragged on.

Every day before nine a.m., I was in the gym waiting for Julia, doing my crawling exercises. By the fifth day, I was confidently getting around the mat without falling over. Both legs were still terribly weak, and even though there appeared to be limited movement in all my leg and foot muscles now, they did not seem to be getting any stronger, just as Julia had predicted. I was still confident, however, that I could start them working when I got my calipers.

THE day finally arrived. Julia wheeled me down to the basement one week to the day after my fitting. Doctor Yeoman and Sister Wang were waiting with the two technicians, Sam and Bob, when we arrived. They were no doubt as anxious as I was to see that they fitted correctly.

The room was littered with all kinds of mechanical contrivances, artificial limbs, wheelchairs and walking aids, and I was as amazed by it all as I had been on my first visit here. Standing up against the workbench was a gleaming new pair of stainless steel calipers, leather at the thighs, knees and ankles and padded on the inside with soft felt.

One of the technicians walked up to me and promptly hauled off my pajama pants while I sat in the wheelchair.

"O.K., Rod," he said without further ado, "let's see how good we are. These should fit you like a glove, but if they are the slightest bit tight — or loose for that matter — they will have to be adjusted. We can't have them chafing you. Your skin is very sensitive to abrasion at the moment, and any raw skin will take a long time to heal."

They took the left one first. One raised my foot off the rest while the other took the caliper and slid the large top end over my left foot and ankle and up my leg. The big thigh strap, already partially buckled, was re-fastened until it fit snugly around my upper leg just below my groin. The same was done just below the knee, and again at the ankle. Then they took one of my socks and shoes, put them on and slipped the heel over the metal cross brace which supported my foot.

They pulled a wire behind the knee which unlocked the joint, allowing it to bend so that I could sit normally instead of having my legs thrust straight out in front of me.

The whole procedure was repeated with the right side, then each of the technicians took hold of one of my hands and pulled me out of the chair. As soon as I was upright, the knee joints immediately locked back into position with a healthy snap, and I was standing for the first time in nearly three months.

They steadied me as I felt a minor repetition of the horrible sensation I had when I first sat up in bed. I wobbled, trembling as the familiar dizziness and nausea swept over me. Then it was gone, leaving me feeling reasonably confident that I was able to stand on my own two feet again without any assistance. The braces gripped my legs comfortably, although the left one felt slightly too long and dug painfully into my crotch.

The experts hovered around me like a couple of mother hens, adjusting the straps, tightening screws here and there, checking the support to make sure that my feet were properly braced so as not to droop. Finally, they seemed satisfied, and asked me if I was.

"I think so. They feel good, except for the left one, which is cutting into my groin a bit," I replied with a satisfied grin.

"O.K., we'll soon have that fixed. Let's whip it off again Sam, and adjust the length while we have him here to try it. No sense in having him wait any longer than he has to for the things."

"Here, here," agreed Sister Wang, who had remained abnormally silent during the entire proceedings.

I let it pass. This was too exciting a moment to be dampened by anything the dragon-lady could say to me.

While the guys were adjusting the length of the left iron, Doctor Yeoman took the opportunity to brief me on a whole new set of rules regarding my behavior when I became 'upwardly mobile' again.

"Now then, Rod," he began, and waited until he had my undivided attention before he went on, "I want you to listen very carefully to what I have to say. It is particularly important that you do exactly as I tell you this time, or you may not be so lucky as the last time you disobeyed me."

"First of all, before you do any walking at all, I want you to spend as long as Miss Starrett deems necessary, in the gym practicing on the parallel bars. It is going to take quite some time for you — and your legs — to become accustomed to walking with the calipers. Remember that your legs have no feeling, the muscles are weak and unused to any exercise. Remember, too, that you will be walking stiff-legged, and you will have no spring in your ankles or toes or hamstring muscles for a normal stride. You will be walking somewhat like a robot, and the only muscles that are providing you with the ability to lift your legs are those in your thighs, which have miraculously begun to function, together with a hip swing which Julia will show you."

"I absolutely forbid, repeat forbid, you to attempt to leave the environs of the seventh floor until you have my permission. Any breach of this order will result in the immediate confiscation of your calipers for an indefinite period. Is THAT perfectly understood?"

I opened my mouth to make a tongue-in-cheek reply, thought better of it, and snapped my jaws closed again.

"Well?" the doctor said, staring at me without a trace of humor.

"Yes sir," I replied in my most placating voice. "Perfectly understood sir. I told you after the last time that you would not have any more trouble with me. I promise."

"Very well, then. I accept your word as a gentlemen."

Sister Wang made a disagreeable noise in her throat.

Doctor Yeoman glared at her and went on. "One more thing. Now that you have some of your leg muscles functioning again, I want you to begin some hydrotherapy to see if you can strengthen them. Julia will take you down to the indoor pool this afternoon for your first session. If you feel comfortable with it, you can do it every day. It will increase the rate at which your operative muscles regain their ability to cope with the weight of the calipers. You will find that a few minutes on the parallel bars will be all your legs can handle at a time. The pool exercises should assist tremendously with that problem."

"Now I have my rounds to attend to, so if you have no questions, I will see you later. Good luck, Rod. Come along, Sister."

He strode off towards the basement elevator, closely followed by his shadow, the indomitable Sister Wang.

I relaxed and waited for the two technicians to finish my left iron alterations. Sam turned to me from the bench and looked over a pair of rimless half spectacles at me.

"He's right, you know. You won't be able to get across the road to the pub quick enough in these things. The light will change before you are half way across, then you know what will happen. You had better take it steady for a while, m'boy. It's not as easy as it may sound."

I just smiled at him. I was already a million miles away, planning what I was going to do when I did get out, and trying to work out the best way of getting up and down the steps to Barbara's apartment.

It took them about five minutes to adjust the length of the left iron. When they had finished, Bob, the senior technician, brought it back to my chair. Sam once again held my leg up. This time, they left all the straps undone to demonstrate how I was to put the thing on myself. It was quite simple, really. With the straps open, I merely had to lift my leg with one hand and lay the caliper under it with the other, then lower the leg into the steel frame and buckle the straps together.

Sam told me the only thing I had to remember was to put my sock and shoe on first in order to set the shoe in the support at the bottom of the brace. That, however, brought up another problem. The normally fundamental task of putting on one's shoe was hampered by the fact that I did not have enough control over my ankles and toes. When I tried to push my foot into the shoe, the foot itself would wobble about making it difficult to get the shoe even part way on. The second, most annoying thing, was that when I finally managed, with much pulling and tugging and holding my ankle steady, to get the damn shoe over my heel, I could not get it all the way on. This turned out to be caused by the fact that the toes, not being strong enough to resist the pressure of the shoe being pulled on, simply turned under. Because I had no feeling in them, I did not even know what had happened until I pulled the shoe off again and found them all curled up inside the sock.

Obviously this was not going to be as easy as it first appeared. One of these years, I was going to realize this, and make allowances accordingly.

We overcame this obstacle by opening up the shoe laces as wide as possible so that the tongue was completely exposed. Then, holding the foot steady with one hand, and pulling back on the top of the sock at the same time, so as to raise the toes, I found that I could just barely get the shoe all the way on without curling them under.

WHEW! What a job!

I was not going to need to be in any hurry to get mobile when I was putting these things on. There had better not be a fire in the building where I was sleeping, that's all! Not unless I intended to sleep in my shoes and braces.

Naturally, I had insisted, after they first showed me how to get into the calipers, on trying to get the things on myself. About half an hour later, I was more or less ready to try getting out of the chair.

Next came the crutches. A pair of aluminum crutches — the kind with a single stem, a round upper arm support and a single lower handgrip — was leaning by the workbench. Sam brought them over and handed them to me with a wink and a smile.

"Now's your big chance, me bucko," he said. "Let's see you walk."

"O.K., I will!" I beamed.

"Now you be careful, Rod," said Julia. "It is not as easy as it looks. Just take it slowly, please."

"No worries, Julia. Piece of cake."

I took the proffered crutches, got a good grip on the handles, took the weight on my hands and arms, and heaved myself out of the chair and on to my feet, where I would have hurtled forward on to my face if Sam had not been there to grab my shoulders and arrest the fall.

I stood there trembling for a few moments, wondering what damage I would have done if Sam had not been there.

"Thanks, Sam," I told him sincerely.

I attempted to take a step forward with my left foot. Nothing happened. I was stuck firmly, rigid as a totem pole. This was ridiculous!

"Well, c'mon then," Sam encouraged. "Let's see some action! We haven't got all bloody day, you know."

Bob stood leaning against the bench rolling a hand-made cigarette, a knowing smile on his thin lips.

Julia came forward to show me what I was doing wrong. "Now listen to me Rod. Remember the crawling exercises in the gym. We were not doing that because we had nothing better to do. You are just fortunate that your thigh muscles began to work again when they did, otherwise this would be much more difficult — if not impossible."

"What I want you to do is pretend you are crawling again. You are going to work exactly the same muscle in exactly the same way. Only now you are standing on your full leg instead of your knees. The principle is still precisely the same. If you are going to lead with your left foot, you should first place your left crutch slightly forward of it, then take your weight on your right crutch and roll your body forward, lifting your leg with your left thigh muscle, exactly as you have been doing when walking on your knees. Got it?"

"I . . . I think so," I stammered, now totally unsure of myself and very self-conscious.

Doing as she instructed, I placed my left crutch forward, leaned to the right, rolled my left hip forward — actually it was my entire left side raising it as I did so by lowering my right shoulder, and dragged my left leg through. At the end of that one step, I was panting as if I had run a marathon. I stood there gasping and trembling with the effort.

I had done it! I had taken my first step since becoming paralyzed! Oh, I was still almost a total paraplegic, all right. I had virtually no feeling in my legs, I had only my thigh muscles weakly working, my ankles wobbling and my toes wriggling, but it was a start. I was walking, dammit! Julia, Bob and Sam clapped in unison.

109

"Let's see it again," Sam shouted with delight.

Bob continued leaning and smoking, a blue aura of hand-rolled tobacco smoke encircling his head. Julia was feverishly biting her nails.

"All right, here we go," I said with much more confidence than I felt.

I performed the reverse of what I had just done, although with even greater difficulty. My right thigh was still considerably weaker than the left, and screamed at me that it could not possibly carry the leg through with that heavy steel on it.

SHUDDUP AND GET TO WORK!

Pole, lean, roll, drag.

Simple!

Pole, lean, roll, drag. Pole, lean, roll, drag. Pole, lean, . . .

Nothing to it! Or so I thought. After about the sixth or seventh painful step, my thighs throbbed and trembled, my groin felt as if it was on fire and my arms ached with fatigue. I gazed at my watch. It had taken me nearly twenty-five minutes to stagger a half-dozen steps.

I was all in! I mean, I was completely and utterly exhausted. The wheelchair was going to feel awfully good after this effort; which brought another minor problem to mind. The chair was behind me. How the devil was I going to turn around?

"Julia!"

"Yes, I'm here. I bet I know what you are going to ask me. How do you turn around, right?"

"O.K., O.K., so I'm stupid. I've walked myself into a corner and now I can't get out of it. You are not going to tell me I have to walk backwards, I hope!"

"Of course not, silly. Actually, it is quite simple, really."

"Naturally!"

"Very well. First you take the crutch on the side of the direction in which you wish to turn. Then, you swivel your upper body toward that crutch. Your braced leg will follow the direction in which you swivel. Then, you move the crutch further back behind you and swivel again. That's it. Lean on the crutch you are not turning on, place the other one slightly behind you, and swivel towards it. Go on. Give it a go. You're doing great. Much better than I had hoped for, actually. I thought you would be tired out after the first step."

I could not tell her that was precisely the case, of course.

"O.K., here we go again."

I did as instructed, and got partially turned around, only to find that the leg opposite the turn was getting tangled up behind me. As I could not lift it, I had to drag it from behind, then around the turning leg. Finally, after a six point turn, I was facing back toward the wheelchair. It might as well have been a hundred miles away. There was no way I was going to reach it. NO WAY! So I started towards it anyway.

Here we go again. Pole, lean, roll, drag. I was already totally exhausted when I began the long journey back. I stumbled and nearly fell several times, but by putting one of the crutches out in front of me, I saved myself without assistance.

Twenty minutes later, after many stops to regain my breath and rest my arms and groin, which was by now badly chafed and hurting abominably, I arrived at the chair. Now I had to turn around again. I had the knack of it now though, and a few seconds later I was slumped in the chair, legs straight out in front of me, as I had forgotten to release the knee locks before I sat down. I was simply too beat to worry about such a public courtesy as bending my knees while seated.

"Well, how do they feel?" asked the ever jovial Sam.

"Bloody awful, seeing you asked," I replied acidly.

"I think you have ruined my manhood — what was left of it! And that's not all! I think they are rubbing against my ankles. If I could feel them, I think they would be killing me!"

"All right, we'll take a look at them. Let's have 'em off!"

They both moved in and quickly had the braces off my legs. What a relief! They had begun to weigh a ton. It felt so good to have them off. It was typical! I could not wait to get the things on, and then I could not wait to get them off again.

I looked down at my legs and was horrified to see that my ankles on both sides had been rubbed raw. Similarly, my groin on both sides of my jocks was a glaring red mess. I had attempted too much too soon, as usual.

Julia took one look at the injuries and her face turned ashen.

"All right, that's it. You are going straight back to bed. There will be no hydrotherapy — or any other kind — for the rest of the day. I am going to have some explaining to do if Doctor Yeoman or Sister Wang see that lot. Fortunately, I have some excellent salve which works wonders on burns like that, but you won't be doing any more on the calipers until that skin has had a chance to dry up."

With that, she wheeled me to the elevator, waving good-bye to the two technicians.

"See you later, guys," I said cheerily. "Thanks a lot. See if you can't readjust and put a bit more padding on those things before I come down again tomorrow."

They laughed, thinking I was joking. Julia was not at all amused. She knew I was never more serious, despite her orders to the contrary. Fortunately for both of us, we did not run into Doctor Yeoman on the way back upstairs. Julia dumped me in bed and went away in search of her miracle salve, which I sincerely hoped would work as well as she promised. Because I was going to be on those calipers again tomorrow if it killed me.

I was going to be in the gym on the parallel bars instead of the crutches. That way, I could take most of my weight on my hands and arms, lifting myself bodily off the ground if necessary, to ease the pain which I knew would come after a very few minutes of wearing the braces. Once again, I should have heeded the doctor's advice, and once again, I was now paying the price for not doing so.

Lost in my own thoughts, I suddenly became conscious of the fact that Mark was speaking to me.

"Well? How did it go? Aren't you talking to me now?"

"Huh? Oh! I'm sorry, Mark. I didn't hear you. I was thinking about something else. Yeah, it went fine. Much harder than I thought it would be. I have the burns and chafe marks to prove it."

"It will get easier. At least you're walking!" he said huffily.

"Yeah, I guess so. How are you? You doing what I told you?"

"I sure am. And you know what? I feel better. I mean, I really do feel as though, some day, something in me will move again. I can't explain it, I just feel it."

"That's the spirit, mate! You believe it yourself, and it will happen. I know. You heard the Doc say I would never walk again, didn't you?"

Julia returned just then with the ointment and some large, white, plastic-coated bandages. She quickly and efficiently rubbed the burn cream into the affected areas, eliciting some cat calls from Mark when she rubbed it around my groin.

"Hey, now I know why you wanted those braces so badly," he jibed, grinning from ear to ear.

"You people are impossible!" Julia scoffed, embarrassed at his remark. "I guess I will see you tomorrow then," she said to me, heaving a frustrated sigh.

Bloody mind reader!

At eight a.m. the next morning, I was waiting in the basement for Bob and Sam to turn up. For once, I had realized the value of taking some advice, and had rested for the remainder of the day yesterday. The chafed areas felt good enough to again attempt a workout with the calipers.

The two technicians finally arrived at about eight forty, made some joking remarks about my lust for punishment, unlocked their cabinets, and brought out my braces. We went through the fitting procedure again, and I found to my surprise and pleasure that they had considerably shortened both calipers so that they now reached only to my mid-thigh, instead of all the way up to my groin.

This made an immediate improvement to the feel, as well as decreasing the weight. When I asked them about this, they told me that they normally made them as close to the groin as possible because most people in my situation had little or no control over their muscles and needed the full length calipers to provide total support for their body. They had seen in my case, however, that I had considerable control over my thigh muscles now, which eliminated the need for full-length irons. This pleased me immensely. It was a good, positive beginning to the day, and I looked forward to getting upstairs and on to the parallel bars.

I left the calipers on, as the extra felt padding the guys had installed made a big difference, and even my raw ankles did not hurt too much. I stayed in the chair, bent the knees on the braces, and hauled my steel-shrouded legs on to the foot rests.

"Thanks fellas. I really appreciate your time and effort with these things. You will never know how much they mean to me."

"Oh, I think we do," Bob said in his slow outback drawl. "Good luck, my boy. And be careful."

"Don't worry, I will," I lied.

They grinned knowingly. They had obviously seen too many like me pass through their portals.

---- ❖ ----

10

Early the next morning, I was already on the parallel bars in the gym.

As usual at this time of the morning, the place was deserted, which gave me an excellent opportunity to get in a bit of practice before Julia or any of her staff and patients arrived.

I rolled the chair up to the end of the bars, reached up and grabbed the ends of them, and hauled myself up, leaving the crutches leaning against the side of the chair. I took a deep breath and started on down the length of the bars, using the same method as I had been taught yesterday. It was much easier today, partly because of the stability of the bars and partly because the calipers themselves were much more comfortable than they had been.

My thigh muscles seemed to be stronger, despite Julia's pessimistic views that they had gone about as far as they could go. It was still a slow process, however, and I had not even got to the end of the bars the first time when the room began filling with people, some of whom came walking or wheeling over to watch my progress. Pretty soon I had the hang of it though, and I was stumping up and down the length of the bars quite confidently by about the third lap.

Julia strolled in at about nine-thirty, accompanied by Doctor Yeoman.

The two of them immediately spotted me and hurried over to watch my performance. I stumped down one more length of the bars, lurching and rolling like a drunken sailor. For some reason on that particular lap, as I staggered along, I thought of Douglas Bader, the famous British fighter ace, who had lost both his legs in a plane crash in the early 1930s. His life story had been made famous by the well-known Australian author and novelist, Paul Brickhill, in 'Reach for the Sky.' After the crash, the doctors had given Bader a pair of tin legs, but they told him he would never walk again without the aid of crutches. He proved everybody wrong, threw away his crutches and walking sticks and forever stumped and lurched around unaided. Not only did he fly Hurricanes and Spitfires again, until he was shot down and taken prisoner in Germany, but he also played golf and tennis — and very proficiently, at that. If Douglas Bader could do it with no legs, surely I could do it with legs, even if they were partly crippled, had no feeling, and were bound in stainless steel supports.

I vowed to myself right at that moment that I too would walk unaided. Oh, I may well be stuck with the calipers, but they would be hidden under my trousers most of the time, just like Bader's tin legs. There was no doubt that my lurching gait would attract attention, but not as much as if I had to get around on crutches — or for that matter in a wheelchair.

My reverie was broken by Doctor Yeoman clearing his throat, his customary preamble to a lecture.

"Good morning, Rod; and a good morning it indeed appears to be for you. It seems you do not like us very much in here. You are apparently determined to leave us as soon as possible. I must say, I would not have believed it if I had not witnessed it with my own eyes. Modestly speaking, I know that my surgical procedures are the best in the business, but if someone had told me that you would be walking around in here today, barely two months after becoming a paraplegic, I would have said it was impossible. In fact, I DID say it was impossible; to several people, including yourself."

The old boy has got his wind up today, I thought. What a speech! And it was all good, for a change. Something else must be coming. I opened my mouth to thank him for the compliment, but before I could speak, he continued his monologue.

"Now then, Rod, let's get you out from behind those bars, where incidentally, Sister Wang declares you permanently belong, and see what you can really do. How do the calipers feel? Are they comfortable? They usually rub and chafe a bit for the first few days. If that happens, you must immediately get off them and stay off until the chafing heals."

I glanced suspiciously at Julia, who was conveniently covering her face with her hands. I imagined it must have been as scarlet as her throat, which was where it seemed the blush began. Fortunately, the doctor was looking directly at me, and did not appear to notice.

"I . . . uh, no, they're just fine, honest. They feel great. Perfect fit. Those guys in the basement really know their stuff!"

"Amazing! Usually, it takes several fittings to get them just right," he replied with a strange smile.

I did not know whether he was taking a rise out of me, or whether he really did know what had happened and was just stringing me along. I decided to play out the charade, whether he knew or not.

"Nope. They really are a perfect fit. I wouldn't change a thing."

"Very well, then. If you think you can manage it, I want to see what you can do without the support of the parallel bars. I would not normally ask this of you at this early stage, but you have proved that you are not normal — at least, when it comes to recovery."

"I'm glad you clarified that, Doc," I replied, relieved that he did not ask me to drop my pajama pants to let him examine the fit of the calipers.

I leaned forward from the end of the bars nearest the wheelchair, took up my crutches, positioned them under my arms, and stepped out on to the open floor. By this time, I had an audience of fifteen or twenty people in the gym, all watching, and some no doubt waiting for me to make a spectacle of myself by firmly striking the floor with my head.

The mat on which I was doing my exercises was about fifteen feet away from where I stood. I was aiming for that, hoping I would reach it before I fell. I put my left crutch forward and, as I had learned yesterday and practised this morning, leaned to the right, rolled to the left, and lifted and dragged my left foot forward. It was not nearly as difficult with the calipers lighter and lower on my legs. I found I could devote my concentration to the movement in my legs instead of the pain in my groin.

A couple of times the leg I was trying to bring forward got tangled up behind the other one, bringing me to the edge of a fall, but I somehow managed to save it, and went thumping out across the floor, the rubber end of the crutch sounding in dull unison to the clank-thud of the shoe brace and heel as they struck the polished boards.

I huffed and puffed and panted and grunted my way across the room and finally reached the safety of the mat, onto which I tossed the crutches and gratefully fell, gasping for air.

The crowd clapped and cheered. Some of them came over to congratulate me and wish me well. Julia rushed up to examine me and make sure I was O.K. before Doctor Yeoman decided to do the same. The doctor walked up and beamed down at me over his clipboard.

"That, Rod, was excellent! You have adapted to the calipers much better and much more quickly than I would have expected. Keep up the good work."

"Julia tells me you did not make it to the pool yesterday. See that you have a session today. I am sure you will find that it works wonders on your legs. Less weight, you see. Your limbs are lighter in the water, so it is easier to exercise them. We have had some success even with limbs which are much worse than yours. Give it a try, and let me know how you get on."

A thought suddenly struck me.

"Hey Doc, what about Mark? You know, in the bed next to me? Wouldn't that hydrotherapy do him some good? It might improve his morale, if nothing else. I know he is really trying to fight his condition and get some movement back."

"Yes, we have been meaning to get him into it for some time. Unfortunately, as you know, his condition is considerably worse than your own. He has also suffered from very bad bedsores, despite constant attention to try to prevent that particularly nasty distress. However, he is doing better and has nearly recovered from that problem, so we should be able to get him down quite soon. Would you like to look after him in the pool?"

"Yes. I think I can help him. I have watched his outlook on life go from suicidal to positively chirpy. Maybe we can work together."

"Wonderful! I shall arrange to have him attend at the same time as you. It may do you both the world of good. I will look in on you again in a few days. Don't overdo it now. And don't forget. No excursions beyond this floor, except to go to the pool."

"Don't worry. I'm too tired after this to go anywhere but back to bed," I lied.

He nodded, turned and marched out in search of other prey.

"Whew, that was close," Julia sighed. "I thought for sure he was going to want to inspect your legs and the calipers. Do you think he suspected anything?"

"I don't know. He either knows everything, and is playing cagey or he is dumber than he looks. If I had to guess, I'd say the former. I'd say Doctor John Yeoman knows everything that goes on in his domain practically before it happens. He has seen enough of people like me to be awake up to every trick in the book."

"I suppose so," she reluctantly agreed. "Anyway, let's get on with some work which is a little less strenuous on both of us."

Soon we were into the crawling again. This was now a snap after walking with the calipers. I still lost my balance on my weak legs from time to time. I still had no movement or control over all of my lower muscles, and my ankles flopped around uselessly. But I was crawling.

We moved on to the weight machines. These were similar to those found in any normal gym, with a few adaptations for control by the therapist instead of the user.

Julia quickly had me on my back facing a foot exerciser designed to increase strength in the ankles and hamstrings.

The work on these gadgets proved to be the most frustrating and difficult task I was ever to encounter during my stay. It was one thing to be able to move my toes and ankles. It was quite another to be able to convert that movement into practical and useful energy. No matter how hard I tried, I simply could not bring any pressure to bear on the bar under my toes. I had some slight success when it came to pushing the bar with my entire leg. By lifting my leg with my hand and placing it on the bar, I found I then had enough strength in that thigh muscle to raise the bar a fraction of an inch. That, however, was not doing my ankle or toes any good whatsoever.

Oh well, it would come. I had learned by now that nothing was quick or easy in this business, except for walking with the calipers, which I thought should have been the most difficult.

By the end of the morning, I was tired and cranky and ready to get into the pool for a change of pace. Maybe I could get some satisfaction out of my useless appendages when I immersed them in water.

Julia offered to buy me lunch in the hospital cafeteria, which made a pleasant change from the stuff they served in the wards. I was glad she offered to buy, as I was not at all sure of my financial situation at the moment. The Department of Social Security had been sending me a regular sickness benefits check, but nobody had told me how much I owed for all this, and I was not asking. Whatever it was, I sure did not have it!

After a pleasant hour watching hospital visitors and staff come and go, we made our way along an endless passageway on the ground floor which finally led to a huge indoor swimming pool of Olympic proportions. There were several therapists and patients working out in the water, and I sat and watched for a while, a little nervous about being dumped into a pool after such a long absence from any body of water bigger than a bathtub.

We went round to the shallow end, where Julia took a life-vest from a supply hanging on the wall nearby, slipped it over my head and tied it in place.

"Just in case," was her encouraging remark.

"Oh great!" I replied in mock alarm.

"O.K., here's what we are going to do," she said. "First of all I assume you have your swim trunks on?"

"Of course not," I laughingly replied. "I thought we'd go in together starkers."

As she began to blush, I set her mind at ease.

"Just kidding. Of course I do. I put 'em on this morning, in anticipation of this wondrous event."

"Thank God for that," she replied with a sigh of relief. "Knowing you, I wouldn't put it past you to jump in starkers."

"Not me! I'm the shy, bashful type," I said, lowering my head to stare at my knees.

"Very funny! Now listen, this is serious. If you don't pay attention, you could slip and badly hurt yourself. Then you would be back in bed indefinitely. I am sure NOBODY wants that! Now, I am going to lift you out of the chair and lower you to the floor. I don't want you trying to do it yourself. This is solid concrete, not the soft mat you are used to throwing yourself on. Then, I want you to take hold of your legs and support them, while I place your butt on the side of the pool. You can then lower your legs into the water, and you will be sitting on the edge ready to jump in. Got that?"

"Sure! Nothin' to it."

I had removed the calipers prior to beginning the weight machine exercises, so I let her lift me as planned, and soon I was perched on the edge of the pool with my legs dangling over the side in the water.

"All right. The water is four feet deep here. I am going to get in and lift you off the side and into the water," Julia continued.

"There is a bar running around the side of the pool for you to hang on to. Grab it as soon as you're in, and we will take it from there."

A moment later, she had me in the water. I was surprised at her strength and ability to lift me with such ease until I remembered that I was only about two thirds of my normal weight due to the atrophy and muscle loss in my legs.

I was instantly amazed at the difference the water made to my ability to stand. Gripping the bar on the side, I maneuvered myself down the length of the pool until I was standing in water up to my shoulders. I found I could actually use my thigh muscles to lift my legs almost knee high with relative ease. I stood with my feet flat on the bottom of the pool and tried to raise myself on to my toes. Strictly no go! My ankles and hamstring muscles were showing no sign of life at all yet, but I was sure that if I kept this up with the same method I had done in bed to move my toes, they would eventually come good.

I took an instant liking to the pool and the possibilities it presented for independent activity. Here was a place I could come at any time, day or night, and providing I could master the slight problem of getting in and out of the water, I could work out with possibly the same results I could achieve on the machines in the gym, without the encumbrance of assistance or supervision.

Julia and I stayed in the pool for about an hour, and she showed me how to exercise what muscles I had immediately available and how to try moving those which still refused to operate.

At the end of the session, when it came time to get out, I swam back to the shallow end using my arms only, reached up and placed my palms flat on the concrete deck surrounding the pool, and heaved myself out using the strength in my arms. At the same time, I spun my upper torso around and came to rest in a sitting position on the side of the pool, my legs dangling in the water, just as I had been before entering the pool.

Like I said, nothing to it!

From there it was easy to drag myself back to my chair and haul myself up into it, as I had already been doing. The only part that might present some difficulty was getting out of the chair and on to the floor. So I had another go at this before we left to go back upstairs.

First, I placed my palms flat on the seat of the chair under my backside. Then, I took the weight on my arms, lifted and lowered myself down on to the footrest. The only problem with this was that my legs, still basically useless as I could not yet raise them an inch from a sitting position, got in the way. So I had to first place them on the floor as far out in front of the footrest as they would stretch. Then when my rear end was on the rest, I repeated the procedure, and I was on the floor. Dragging myself over to the side of the pool was the easy part. I had surmounted another hurdle on the road to independence and freedom.

As we wheeled along the corridors to take the elevator back up to the seventh floor, I excitedly spoke with Julia about the possibilities presented by the pool, and how I was going to enjoy going down there every day. She laughingly agreed that it was definitely the way for me to use my time more productively when not in the gym, not suspecting for a moment just how much time I intended to spend in that pool from now on.

The days passed more quickly now, as I spent each morning in the gym, practicing on my calipers both on and off the parallel bars, as well as exercising as much as my limbs would allow with the machines. In the afternoon, I would go down to the pool and try to get more movement from my legs, both in and out of the water. I even found that by sitting on the side of the pool with my legs dangling, I could do something there which worked some muscles.

When I first started with the pool, I was acutely aware of the fact that when sitting on the side, I could not even draw my heels back to touch the inside wall, even though the minimal weight of my legs was further reduced by the effect of the water. After a couple of days, I found that I could pull my legs back perhaps an inch toward the side. After a week, I was able to draw my legs back all the way so that my heels were contacting the side wall of the pool. This was a tremendous boost to my morale, as it showed that there were now positive signs of movement in all my leg muscles.

My ankles were becoming controllable, instead of uselessly flopping around. All my toes were now moving, although there was no strength in the movement, and the slightest external pressure applied to them rendered them immobile. Strangely enough, although it had been my left toes and leg that first moved, my right side now appeared to be rapidly gaining strength in all muscles, while the left was not making such good progress.

Meanwhile, true to his word, Doctor Yeoman pronounced Mark fit for hydrotherapy, and the two of us looked forward to exercising in the pool together. Mark had been allowed for some time now to be wheeled into the gym for physiotherapy, although it had had little effect. He had also been permitted to be taken down into the gardens by his parents and brother, to give him a change of scenery. The pool had a wonderful effect on his personal outlook and his general condition.

On his sixteenth day in the pool, Mark moved his right hand and arm! It was a weak and jerky and uncontrolled movement, to be sure; but it WAS movement! This truly was a miracle!

Mark had broken his neck, and it was believed that his spinal cord had been severed at the top of the spine. Mark had moved his arm, which proved two things; an incredible will power on his behalf, and the fact that his spinal cord was either not severed, or was partially repairing itself. As the latter was — and still is — widely believed by the experts to be impossible, it was apparent that Mark had a chance, after all this time, of regaining some use of his limbs. This was truly fantastic, and he now received constant and affectionate attention from nurses and therapists alike.

Together we were daily amazed and delighted at each other's triumphs over a condition which seemed at first to be utterly hopeless and impossible to reverse.

However, we had both been severely depressed by the sudden and inexplicable disappearance of Barbara. I had tried on several occasions to call her at work and at home. She never answered the phone at her apartment, and the couple of times I had managed to contact her at work, she said she could not talk and she would come back to see us as soon as possible. When I called Nell to try to find out what the problem was, she too was vague and unable to give me a reasonable explanation. This was becoming a serious threat to my morale. I had truly believed that when I got out of here I could take up life with Barb where we had left off before.

In fact, I did not realize just how much I had been counting on her being there to look after me when I was released from hospital. Now that there appeared to be a chance that she may not be there, I became perplexed, unsure of what was waiting for me in the outside world where, at least for some months and possibly years, I must face the fact that I was not going to be totally independent. I needed someone. I needed Barbara, dammit! Where WAS she?

It was getting on towards Christmas, and I was beginning to think that I may have to spend that wonderful season inside these barren walls after all.

Mark had been told that he could go home with his parents at least for Christmas, and possibly longer, now that the necessary renovations to their house to accommodate his wheelchair had been completed.

I had been making great progress since receiving my calipers. My thigh muscles were now strong enough to carry me comfortably on the braces, and I was confident of getting around without falling over. My right leg was still improving in leaps and bounds, and I now had almost all the muscles and tendons from toes to thigh at least partially functioning. My left leg remained stubbornly inactive, despite the initial burst of encouraging energy after my big toe moved.

On the 11th day of December, two weeks to the day before Christmas, at 8.30 a.m., just as I was about to leave my room for the gym, Doctor Yeoman and Sister Wang appeared in the doorway on an unexpected visit. The good sister was smiling — almost grinning — uncontrollably, causing me to wonder what unpleasantness I was about to have inflicted upon me.

"Good morning, Rod," said the doctor brightly, viciously clutching his clipboard.

"Good morning to you, sir. I think," I replied with deep apprehension.

"Ah yes, my boy, it really is a wonderful morning, isn't it Sister?" he went on, gazing with raised eyebrows at Sister Wang, who was still grinning.

My apprehension grew.

"We have some exciting news for you, Rod. At nine a.m. on the 19th of December, one week from tomorrow, providing you do nothing to hinder it, you are to be released from the spinal unit and placed on outpatient status. You have shown such incredible improvement over the past few weeks, and your ability on the calipers is such that I feel there is little to be gained from keeping you here any longer, taking up bed space which could be put to use by someone in much more need of care and attention than you now require. What do you think of that?"

I could not believe my ears! From the moment I heard the words 're- leased' and 'outpatient,' my mind had flooded with beautiful thoughts of once living in the normal world out there. Emotion welled inside me.

I was going home!

In my wild exuberance, it never occurred to me that I did not have a home to go to, unless I trekked up to Brisbane and moved in with my folks again, which would be a very real and not unpleasant alternative. The only thing I could think of was that I was getting out of this place, and I was going to be able to live my own life again.

I realized that Doctor Yeoman was speaking.

"Well? Did you hear me Rod? I am going to release you."

He knew I had heard, all right. He also knew I was so full of emotion that I could not speak for fear of my voice breaking up. I finally got enough control of myself to reply.

"Yes, I heard you, Doc. I . . . I'm sorry. I thought I'd never hear you say those words. It's almost too good to be true. I have been telling myself for months that I was going to get out of here before Christmas, but I was beginning to doubt it. Thank you — both of you — for all you have done for me. You, Doc, for giving me another crack at life, and you Sister for keeping me on the straight and narrow. I know we have not exactly been the best of friends, but I also know that you were only doing your job. I really am sorry if I made life a little difficult for you at times."

Sister Wang sniffled, dabbed at her eyes, then turned and ran from the room. It was only the second time I had seen her display any form of emotion other than anger and officiousness.

"Well!" exclaimed Doctor Yeoman. "I have never seen her react like that before. I do believe the old girl will be sorry to see you go after all. Anyway, just wanted to let you know the good news. The same old rule applies. No taking your life in your hands by leaving the hospital until you are out of my care and jurisdiction. Otherwise, you WILL be here for Christmas."

"Don't worry, Doc. I'll be a perfect angel. Trust me. I am going to need to spend every waking second exercising and practicing on my calipers so I don't trip and get run over by a truck the minute I walk out the gates. That would kind of undo all the good work you have done, wouldn't it?"

"It's happened before," he replied dejectedly. "But I am sure you are going to be fine. After seeing how far you have come, when I honestly believed that you would never walk again, I would not be surprised to see you flying a jumbo jet in a couple of years. Well, I must be off on my rounds. Take care of yourself. I will see you in a couple of days."

I was so elated I could hardly contain myself. I grabbed my legs, which although now much stronger, were still unable to raise and lower themselves with any control, and threw them over the side of the bed. I took my calipers which were leaning against the bedside table and strapped them on with practiced ease, then picked up my crutches and stumped over to Mark, who was still asleep, to tell him the good news.

"Hey Mark, wake up! Wake up! Guess what? I'm getting out of here."

Mark dopily opened his eyes, recognized me and what I was saying, and his face broke into a wide and infectious grin.

"That's great, mate. Maybe you can come to my place for a while over Christmas; if you want to, that is. I think I'm getting out at the end of the week too. Maybe for good. I can't wait I've been in here forEVER!"

"I'd love to visit you and your folks at Christmas. Thanks for asking. Now I'm going out in search of people to whom I can convey the good news. I hope Julia is around. She will be tickled to death! See you later, Mark."

"See you down at the pool?" he replied hopefully with a slight and jerky movement of his right arm which translated into a wave.

I turned and stumped and rolled my way out of the room and down the corridor towards the gym. I rounded the corner and literally bumped into Barbara who was heading towards my room. She just about knocked me off my feet and as I fought to regain my precarious balance, she began a hurried apology, not realizing who I was.

"I'm terribly sorry," she said, "Clumsy of me. I should have been watching . . . "

"Hi Barb," I said, grinning at the fact that she did not recognize me in a vertical position. She had not seen me since I had been walking.

"Rod! What are you . . . ? Why, this is terrific! How long have you been on your feet? Why didn't you tell me?"

"I tried to. Several times," I replied rather huffily.

"I know. I really am very sorry, Rod. I've had a few things to sort out in my own life. Unfortunately our renewed relationship has affected me in more ways than you could know. Let's go somewhere where we can be alone. I don't want to talk in front of Mark, O.K.?"

My heart leapt into my throat and began to race, and I felt as if there was a block of ice sitting in the pit of my stomach.

"Sure," I replied as calmly as possible. "Let's go out into the garden, where we went on my first day out of bed. It's a nice day outside, isn't it?"

"It's beautiful," she replied, taking hold of my right arm just above the elbow ring of the crutch.

Neither of us spoke again as we slowly made our way along the corridor, down the elevator, through the main lobby and out into the sun-drenched gardens where the heat and humidity of a Sydney midsummer day struck me like a physical blow after being cocooned in the artificial atmosphere of the hospital for so long.

We sat on a bench under a large ironbark gum tree. The harsh sunlight filtered through the limbs and branches to become a soft and dappled glow. The pungent, but not unpleasant, aroma of eucalyptus leaves rustling in the gentle breeze filled the air. I sat silently, waiting for the bad news which I felt sure was about to counter the good tidings I had received from Doctor Yeoman just a short time before.

When Barb finally spoke, she confirmed my worst fears.

"Rod, please try to understand what I am going to tell you. This isn't exactly easy for me, although I know the last couple of months have not been a picnic for you either. That's what has made the whole thing more and more complicated as time went by. Look Rod, the plain fact of the matter is that I am engaged. I have been for six months, but when I heard about your accident, I had to come and see you. The minute I did, my heart went out to you and since that first day I began falling in love with you all over again, and that is what has made it more and more difficult for me to come to see you."

"But what about . . ." I began to protest.

"Please let me finish Rod. At first it was easy to visit you. You were wounded and lost and hurt, and you know what I'm like when it comes to looking after wounded things — animals or people. Then it started to get complicated, because I knew I really was falling in love with you again. I also realized that you were going to recover. I knew that, given half a chance, you would get out of here. I wanted you to come home with me. I really thought I could look after you, not telling you the truth. But I also knew that sooner or later, because of our own past, you would suspect something, especially when you recovered enough to want to . . . to . . . "

"Make love?" I finished the sentence for her, unable to completely hide the sneer which had begun to curl my lip.

"Yes," she replied, tears filling her eyes. "I do love you Rod, but I love my fiance too. I don't know what to do. I've been drinking myself to death, practically becoming an alcoholic. Between visiting you and recovering from hangovers, I have hardly been at work at all the last couple of months; until recently, when I was given an ultimatum. That's one of the reasons I have not been to see you lately."

"Who is he?" I asked, my own eyes clouding with tears which I was desperately trying to hold back.

"He is my boss at work," she replied, finally letting go and beginning to sob uncontrollably, covering her face with her hands.

I sat in stunned silence.

The light dawned! So that was why she had been able to get so much time off work! So that was why she never wanted to talk to me when I called her there, and why she never answered the phone at her apartment. She probably only went there to change clothes occasionally, if at all.

Despite my shock and anger, I could not help placing my arm around her and gently drawing her head down on to my shoulder. She did not resist. Her body shuddered with the heavy and sincere sobs which I knew she must have held back for so long.

I could not believe this was happening. Here I was, about to be released from hospital, counting each second till the day came when I could begin life all over again with this very girl whose soft ebony hair now flowed over my shoulder. Only she was telling me it had all been a dream; a beautiful, romantic, wonderful, impossible dream. I could not believe it. I WOULD not believe it! I simply wouldn't damn well HAVE it!

"Why on earth didn't you TELL me, Barb?" I found myself asking her through clenched teeth, the bitter truth of her recent odd behavior finally sinking in as my mind flashed back to some of the bizarre and uncharacteristic things she had said and done the last few times I had seen her.

"I couldn't!" she cried. "I just couldn't! I tried and tried. But I could not bring myself to do it. I didn't have the guts to hurt you any more than you had been hurt already."

"Oh God," I sobbed. "Not again! I am not going to lose you again, am I? I have been through all THIS and I am still going to lose you AGAIN?"

"Don't, Rod! Please don't! Just give me a little more time to work it out. You have not lost me again, or I would not have even come back. The easiest thing for me to have done would be to have just not come back. But I knew that would have hurt you more than the truth. Now that you know, give me a chance to work it out my own way. Don't push me. Don't pressure me. Just leave me be till I sort it out. O.K.,?"

"Are you living with him?" I asked, angrily, wiping the tears from my eyes.

"NO! Well . . . not exactly. Sort of, I guess. I still have my own apartment."

"For show, for your family's sake, I suppose?" I sneered.

"No. I need my independence. Sometimes I have to get away. I . . . I'm not really sure that I want to marry him. Specially now!"

She suddenly shivered, pulled herself away from me and stood up.

"I have to go, Rod. This is not getting us anywhere, and I really do have to get back to work. He has been patient with me, but he has told me it has gone far enough and he can get me fired if he wants to. He would, too, out of spite, if he thought for a moment that there was anything between us."

"You mean, he doesn't KNOW?" I asked incredulously.

"I told him you were just a very good friend. Fortunately, he also knows and tolerates the fact that I am a sucker for anything that hurts. Except myself."

A multitude of feelings swept over me.

Anger, that she had been deceiving me; hurt, that she had found and loved somebody else; fear, that I was losing her again; pride, that she had risked her job and her happiness for our renewed love.

When I thought about it, she sure would have gotten the rough end of the stick. She would have been sacrificing a safe, secure marriage to a normal person for the sake of taking on a has-been; a semi-cripple with no hope of any decent future prospects. A nobody. And only half a nobody at that!

Oh STOP feeling so BLOODY sorry for yourself! You have faced up to and overcome worse things than this in the last few weeks, I told myself.

She must have read my mind, because she gently took my cheeks between the palms of her hands, leaned over me until the sweet smell of her perfume filled all my senses, and kissed me lightly on the lips.

"Don't you go feeling sorry for yourself, mate. Or for me. We'll work this thing out. I know we will. Now that it is out in the open, we will find a solution. Don't worry. Remember, whatever happens, I love you. I love you, Rod."

My eyes became misty again. I opened my mouth to whisper the same to her. She put a forefinger softly to my lips to stop me. Two giant tears rolled down her cheeks. She pulled away from me, turned and ran down the flowered walk towards the hospital gates, her short black mini-skirt riding high to reveal those slender, shapely legs I remembered so well.

I sat there stunned, my mind completely blank, my dreams and hopes and plans shattered. Suddenly the world outside those gates seemed cold and hostile. A terrible feeling of foreboding swept over me and I shuddered as a cold chill ran up my steel spine, despite the heat of the afternoon.

I do not know how long I sat there. I was beginning to attract the stares of passers-by. The calipers were starting to hurt my legs where the pads were rubbing the still tender skin.

I took my crutches and straightened up. The resounding clicks of my artificial knees as they locked into place gave me some strange measure of comfort. They were the only tangible things I could feel in the dream-turned-nightmare world in which I was walking.

❖

11

I don't remember returning to my room, removing my calipers, or getting into bed. I pulled the curtain closely around it, ignoring Mark as he tried to speak to me. I do remember screaming at the nurse who came in response to Mark's worried call.

"GET OUT!!" I yelled. "Leave me alone!"

The rest of that day and night, I stayed in bed and sulked morosely, spurning all offers of kindness and sympathy. I dragged through the next day, forcing myself to go through the motions of exercise and therapy. I did not know why. Where was I going now anyway?

Late that next day, I finally broke down and told Mark what was troubling me. He too had been missing Barb, and he had a right to know why she had not returned. He turned out to be a tower of strength, and showed tremendous compassion and understanding for one so young and plagued with his own problems, which were, after all, so much greater than mine.

By the time he had finished talking to me, I felt thoroughly ashamed of myself for my selfish and childish behavior. The mental crisis passed, as had the physical one before it.

Barb called me several times over the next few days, but each time, she still had not made the big decision, and seemed to be prolonging it as long as possible.

It began to appear as if I was definitely going to be on my own when I got out, so I started making plans accordingly.

The week passed.

The night of December 18th was a wonderful experience. At about six p.m. that evening, the time we normally had dinner served, Doctor Yeoman, Sister Wang and Julia Starrett, leading a contingent of Spinal Unit staff, arrived unexpectedly in my room.

Doctor Yeoman carried his clipboard, naturally. Sister Wang followed closely behind bearing a huge chocolate cake with a million multi-colored candles. Julia brought up the rear with — I could not believe my eyes — a silver salver on which were no fewer than a dozen bottles of champagne. The nurse immediately behind her carried another tray with real champagne glasses! None of your plastic or paper cups for this lot!

Mark and the two recent arrivals opposite were obviously conspirators in the event, and loudly applauded as the convoy arrived with much pomp and ceremony at my bedside.

The wardsmen in the rear guard brought enough chairs into the room to seat everybody. They were scattered around all four beds.

Sister Wang placed the gigantic cake on the bedside table between Mark and me. The three of them sat where they could face both of us, and the rest of the staff spread themselves around the room.

Julia placed the champagne on a folding table brought into the room for the purpose. Her assistant put the glasses down beside the bottles and began to pop corks.

As the bottles were opened, Julia began filling glasses which were then carried round the room by her nurse-waitress, who offered a glass to me first, followed by the Doctor, then Sister Wang, Julia (who also held Mark's glass for him) and the remainder of the patients and staff.

When all hands held a glass, Doctor Yeoman stood once more, and brandishing his clipboard in one hand and his champagne glass in the other, began a speech which brought tears of joy and pride to my eyes.

"Ladies and gentlemen," he began. "On this, the eve of departure from our humble home of one of our more colorful characters, we gather here to celebrate his quite incredible achievements since his admittance to our unit. You are all aware, no doubt, of the history of Rod's aeroplane accident, his amazing escape from a horrible death by fire, his subsequent admission here, and his miraculous recovery. That his recovery is indeed miraculous should serve as a shining example to all our patients of what one can achieve, despite all known fact and evidence to the contrary, if one is determined, by sheer will power, to prove the purveyors of such fact and evidence to be incorrect."

He turned to me and raised his glass.

"Rod, your stay here has affected us all in some way or other, some good, some . . . well, not so good," he said, turning and smiling at Sister Wang, and waiting for the resulting laughter, including hers, to die down.

"One thing I know for sure," he went on, "if you had taken my word about your injuries, if you had lain back and not tried to do something about them, you would probably be permanently in a wheelchair, as I indeed predicted, instead of walking again as you are now. I continue to be astounded by your day-to-day improvement, and I really do believe you will not be satisfied until you are flying again. Here's to you Rod. We all wish you the very best in your new life outside these walls which I know you have considered more of a prison than a hospital. Good luck, and good health in the future!"

Every person in the room raised his glass and loudly cheered, "HERE, HERE!"

They all took a sip of their champagne and somebody — Mark, I think shouted, "SPEECH, SPEECH!"

The room became politely silent again.

I had been overcome with emotion during the Doctor's oration, and took some time to compose myself. Everyone looked expectantly at me as they waited for me to respond.

"I . . . I don't know what to say — for once!" I began. A ripple of laughter again spread through the room.

"This is all so unexpected. I mean, I know some of you will be glad to see the back of me, but this is a little obvious, isn't it?"

I waited again for the mirth to subside.

"Anyway, it has been a long, frustrating road for me, and I know I have made it difficult for all of you a lot of the time with my stubborn-ness, not to mention my total lack of consideration in sometimes refusing to allow the normal running of the hospital to get in the way of my own recovery. For that, I humbly apologize. You all did your best to look after me under very trying conditions, and I want to thank each and every one of you for helping me literally get back on my feet. But enough of this idle chit-chat! I don't know about you lot, but I for one don't want all this lovely champagne to get warm and go to waste after all the trouble you went to stealing it. So let's get into some serious drinking."

Amid further laughter, they all responded to that suggestion, and the party began in earnest.

Somebody yelled at me to blow out the candles on the cake so they could get something to eat. I obliged with the help of Doctor Yeoman, and Sister Wang cut the cake and passed out portions to the revelers.

Some time later, a huge platter of mixed canapes and other mouth-watering snacks arrived instead of our usual hum-drum hospital food, and soon everyone was eating and drinking merrily.

The very loud sound of voices and laughter wafted out into the corri-dor, bringing more staffers and patients in wheelchairs homing in on the din. Soon the room was choc-a-bloc with people, all talking and joking and generally having a great time.

I do not know about anyone else, but I had a ball. Before I knew it, my head was positively reeling. I could hear myself talking shorthand, and hoped that everyone else sounded as silly as I did. I have no idea what time the party ended. When I eventually passed out, the room was still full of people, noise and more people.

It was just after midnight when I woke with a terrible ringing in my ears. Mark's bedside light was still on, and as I painfully turned my head towards him, he spoke in a garbled voice indicating his own libationary condition.

"Wel . . . welcome back, you . . . bloody piker! You passed out and left me to deal with all those people. They kept pouring that stuff down my throat and I couldn't even raise my hands to stop 'em. Arr! Arr!"

"Wha . . . Didja ge' the number of th' truck?" I intelligently replied, tenderly touching my forehead with trembling hands, surprised to find that it was still intact.

"Lord, what a party," I said more coherently as my blurred vision began to clear. Hard to believe the Doc and Wang were responsible.

"Yeah, it . . . sure . . . was," Mark stammered. "I thought they'd never leave."

"What time did they go?" I inquired, between throbs in my head.

"Oh, I dunno. The last one left about an hour ago, I suppose."

"Grief! That late? I wonder if Doc Yeoman felt like I did when he left. I remember even the battle-axe was positively charming. . . . "

A loud snore interrupted my sentence. I again turned toward Mark to find him out like a light. His nose was pointed straight at the ceiling, his mouth agape, allowing the disgusting sound to escape with a vengeance.

I turned on my side, which was much easier these days, thanks to the partial movement in my thighs. With my back to Mark and a pillow wedged tightly against my exposed ear, I finally fell asleep again, blissfully aware that this was my last night in the Royal North Shore Hospital.

Despite my champagne-numbed brain, I was wide awake at seven the following morning. I was like a cat on hot bricks and could not wait for my escort party to arrive with my worldly goods and chattels. Too nervous and impatient to even take the time to put on my calipers, I threw myself into the wheelchair still parked by my bed, wheeled myself round to the bathroom where I quickly showered and shaved, then hurtled back to the room and waited in the chair with growing impatience as the appointed hour drew closer.

Mark and I chatted more soberly about the events of the previous night, but he grew tired of me looking at my watch every five seconds, and after a while, he just lay there in a silent vigil with me.

I was becoming increasingly alarmed by the fact that I had absolutely nowhere to go when I walked out of the hospital gates. I kept hoping of course, that at any moment Barbara would appear with the good news that she had dumped her fiance in my favor and that she was taking me home to her place to live happily ever after.

However, there were also my parents to consider. They had only seen me once since their very first visit. On that occasion, they were both flabbergasted by the improvement in my physical and mental condition.

They were unable to meet me today, but they naturally wanted me to fly home to Brisbane to rest and recuperate with them.

I was very tempted to do just that, but I knew I would only be running away from and postponing the problem with Barb, not to mention delaying my own prospects for the future, with or without her.

No! I had to stay in Sydney, find myself an apartment, and learn to cope with my disability on my own, while at the same time continuing a physiotherapy program to try to get myself fit enough to somehow pass an aviation medical examination again.

The minutes ticked by as these thoughts tumbled through my mind. My palms became sweaty with anticipation. I stared at my watch for the thousandth time. The morning sunlight streamed through the window, bringing with it the warmth of another summer day in Sydney. I did not know it yet, but the warmth I was enjoying now was going to pose a very great problem for me in the near future.

Nine o'clock was drawing painfully near. No sign of Doctor Yeoman! I remembered with sickening clarity the morning I was to be allowed to get out of bed for the first time. Surely he would not do THAT again!

Footsteps in the hall! I turned to face the doorway, my palms slipping on the wheels of the chair. A figure stopped in the hall, bathed in the rays of the bright light. It was not Barb. It was, however, her mother Nellie, whom I had not seen now for over a month.

She came over to me, pecked me on the cheek like the second mother she had come to be, and sat heavily on the bed.

"Hi man. It's good to see you looking so well on your big day. I guess you're wondering why I'm here. If you are thinking what I think you are, I am afraid I'm going to disappoint you."

"Hi Nellie. It's good to see you, too. What . . . what do you mean? Is she coming?"

Nell shook her graying head as she sadly lowered her eyes to her knees.

"Rod, you know I always wanted you to be my son-in-law. I think of you as a second son anyway, and Col regards you as a brother, I know."

She continued as my heart sank into deep despair, even though I had tried to steel myself for this moment.

"Barb wanted me to tell you that she still hasn't decided what to do about Chris. That's his name, if she didn't tell you. She and I have been fighting over this for some time, but you know what she's like. Pig-headed, just like her father. Try to tell her you don't want her to do something, and she will do it all the more. Anyway, the thing is that without her, you have no place to stay. So . . . it's simple. You will stay with me. For as long as you like, rent-free. If you want to find a place of your own, I'll understand that perfectly, but until you do, my home is your home."

I could not help it this time. Tears of sorrow, regret and self-pity, that Barb had spurned me again; and at the same time, tears of relief and joy and gratitude, that this woman, who owed me nothing, would take me into her home, knowing I would be a handful, disabled as I was, yet still wanting to give me a roof over my head for as long as I wanted or needed. I sniffled and wiped my eyes on my sleeve, rolled the chair over to Nellie, put my arms around her huge shoulders, and cheek to cheek, hugged her with all my might.

"Oh Nellie," I cried, "You will never know how good it sounds to hear that. I had no idea where I was going to stay, or even how I was going to find a place. But I will pay you room and board, and I will have no argument about that. And, I'll try to get into an apartment as quickly as possible."

"Like I said, Rod, you can stay as long as you like. The main thing is for you to concentrate on getting well enough to fly again, which is what you really want to do. I'll be happy for the company."

Just at that moment, Doctor Yeoman and Sister Wang walked in. The Sister carried my suitcase with all my clothes, which had been brought down from the Academy by one of my flying buddies shortly after the accident.

"Well, Rod, I guess this is it," said the doctor, shaking my hand. "I believe last night was a fitting end to a saga I am sure we here on the seventh floor will never forget, eh Sister?"

"Yes, Doctor, you are SO right about that. We will never forget what's-his-name," she jibed, grinning pleasantly to show me she was just kidding and all was forgiven, now that I was leaving.

"Thanks again, Doc, and you too Sister, for all you have done for me. And thanks for the party last night. That was a great surprise."

"It was our pleasure. Now don't forget, Rod. Your battle is not yet over; not by a long shot. You still have a lot of hard work and pain and frustration ahead of you before you can be considered safe on the streets. That means coming back here every day for outpatient therapy. No slacking off. If you do, all the work you — and I — have done has been for nothing and you might as well give up on any idea of a normal life. Do you understand?"

"Ever the optimist," I replied sarcastically. "Don't worry, Doc. I do NOT want to ever take up residence in this building again. I don't intend to give up until I am walking. And I do mean walking, without crutches, canes, or even calipers."

"I think that even you are being a little unrealistic there, my boy. You will never have enough strength or control or feeling in your legs to be able to walk completely unaided . . . but then again, I seem to recall saying the same thing to you once before — about walking at all. Yes. If anyone can do it, I believe you can. I shall expect to hear from you regularly regarding your progress."

"Don't worry. You will."

He smiled and nodded as we shook hands again. Then, still gripping his clipboard, which I was by now firmly convinced was grafted to his chest, he turned and swiftly marched out of the room on the rest of his rounds.

"Good luck, Rod," said Sister Wang. "And the same to the rest of the unsuspecting country, now that you are loose in it again."

She smiled, briefly took my hand, turned and rushed from the room, raising her hand to her face as she went. Maybe I had sadly misjudged the Hard-Hearted Sister from Hunter's Hill!

I sighed, deftly pulled on my irons, limped over to Mark, tousled his hair and took his hand.

"See ya later, digger," I said with feeling. "Take it easy. Keep working on that arm. It's come a long way. I'll drop by to see you whenever I'm in for therapy, and I'll see you next week for Christmas anyway. O.K.?"

"O.K., mate. Sounds great! Good luck, and you take it easy yourself. They tell me it's a jungle out there!" he ended with a grin.

"I'll manage," I replied with more confidence than I felt.

"See you later guys," I said, waving to the two transients opposite.

I picked up my crutches, looked around the familiar surroundings for the last time, and stumped out followed by Nell, who was wheeling my suitcase and other belongings in the chair.

As we approached the elevator, I was deeply moved to find two lines of people, staffers and patients alike, standing there waiting for me. I slowly limped through the gauntlet, shaking hands and saying good-bye to all of them, finally coming to Julia, who was standing holding the elevator doors open.

"Bye Rod. Don't be a stranger now. I expect to see you every day anyway, so this is not really good-bye. Be good and be careful."

I kissed her on the cheek and hugged her tightly.

"Thanks Julia, for everything. Don't worry, I'll be back. I won't let you down. I'll see you tomorrow."

As the elevator doors silently closed, Nell looked at me quizzically and said, "Seems like you made a lot of friends over the last few months."

"I sure did. Probably more than I will ever realize. They are wonderful, brave people in there. All of them!"

We rode down to the ground floor, walked through the main reception area, stepped out into the bright, hot sun of a new day, and threw my gear into the cab which was waiting outside the main entrance. Nell got in the back first, while I struggled for a bit to unlock the knees on my calipers. I had to reach down and behind me with one hand, while bracing myself on the door of the cab with the other so that I would not immediately collapse and make a spectacle of myself in the first five minutes of my release.

Finally I got them both unlocked and, taking my weight on the arm holding the door frame, I hand-lifted one leg into the cab, dropped my backside on to the seat, then lifted the other leg inside. Piece of cake! Nell gave the cabby her address, and he sped away down the hospital drive and out the gates into the rush hour traffic of a busy Sydney work day.

I was free again at last!

12

"Oh well. Life wasn't meant to be easy."

That brilliant statement was made famous by a former Australian Prime Minister in answer to a question posed to him about some particularly difficult economic times the country as a whole had been suffering. It was ridiculous by virtue of fact that he uttered it while sitting and sipping on the front porch of his opulent homestead, gazing out upon the thousands of lush acres of his wealthy family sheep property.

Well, he was right in one way. Life certainly was not meant to be easy for most of us. It was not meant to be easy for all those afflicted people I had recently left in the hospital. It was not meant to be easy for me either, having to learn to cope with the everyday problems of normal life again; like how to get from A to B with no transport; like how to earn money to pay for public transport while spending it commuting to the hospital by cab until I was strong enough to earn some kind of income.

And life certainly was not meant to be easy for Nellie, who had to suffer, as a very poor pensioner and widow, the privation and indignity of living in a dilapidated, almost century old house, the only tolerable advantage of which was the magnificent view it presented of Sydney Harbor.

It was under these difficult circumstances that I found myself attempting to put the long-severed threads of my life back together. The whole situation was made considerably worse by the fact that memories of Barbara filled every room. Pictures, discarded clothes, school trophies, bits and pieces of twenty years of a girl growing up littered the house.

For the first few days out of hospital, I found myself increasingly morose and irritable, which was quite the contrary to what I should have been feeling. I attributed these moods to the constant thoughts of my second failed relationship with Barb, accentuated by the house filled with memories of her. However, I gradually came to realize that the simple fact of being out in the world again, yet unable to do all the things I had previously taken for granted, was what was getting me down. Of course, the fact that Barb often came home to visit her mother and me no doubt played a part in my bouts of depression.

After a few days of this brooding, I began to face life with fresh enthusiasm, treating each difficulty I encountered as a new challenge, just as I had done in the hospital. Initially, I had been returning to the hospital by cab for my therapy treatment, as this was the easiest method for me to get around. This was an expensive mode of transport, and I quickly calculated that spending about fifteen dollars a day on cab fares, plus what I insisted on giving Nell for food and board, was going to deplete the last of my meager savings in very short order.

Although I was glad to be out of hospital for Christmas, as I had promised myself, the day itself turned out to be an anticlimax. I was unable to make it to Mark's place as arranged, because his parents lived in a far western suburb of Sydney and there was simply no way for me to get there from Nell's house, as she neither drove nor owned a car. So I called him instead, and we had a long chat about our respective new lives in the outside world.

Nell's son, Colin, and his wife Christine, picked us up and had the two of us to their apartment for Christmas dinner. I called my parents, and we had a long talk about my progress and my plans for the future. Naturally, they wanted to know how soon I could come home to Brisbane, but I had to disappoint them by telling them that it was quite impossible at the moment. Apart from the therapy I had to do every day with Julia, I had to learn to survive here first, before I went back to friends and relatives. It was a matter of pride.

I took Christmas and the following day off from visiting the hospital. Since I had been staying with Nell, I had developed the habit of not putting my calipers on until I was ready to leave the house for my daily therapy. Instead, I got around on crutches alone, using my now stronger thigh muscles to partially support me between faltering steps.

The second day after Christmas, I determined to set myself a new challenge. I was going to attempt to travel to the hospital by means of the city council bus service — a harrowing experience even for normal commuters! This meant that instead of merely having to walk to the front gate to climb into a cab, I would have to stagger two blocks to the nearest bus stop, wait under the staring eyes of curious onlookers, struggle up the two high steps of the bus, do the same in reverse when alighting, and then hobble up the quarter mile sloped path inside the hospital grounds. And then do it all over again a couple of hours later when I had finished my therapy!

When the time came to leave the house, my stomach was knotted so tightly with tension that I thought I was going to be sick. I said good-bye to Nell and left her standing on her doorstep, protesting loudly and vehemently about my stupid and stubborn desire to be re-admitted to hospital as a result of being mashed by a recklessly driven vehicle (and not necessarily the council bus I was attempting to board).

I stumped out the gate and across the street, round the corner past the bank and the post office, and found myself on the sidewalk of busy Victoria Road, the main artery through the north-east suburbs of Sydney.

The rush and roar of traffic petrified me. I swallowed several times with fear and apprehension, wondering what madness had inspired my previous ill-fated attempt to confront this vehicular bedlam when I crossed the road to the pub in the wheelchair. Lord, what a man would do for a drink! No wonder they say it'll kill you in the end.

I swayed and rolled my tottering way up the slight incline to the bus stop, about fifty yards from the corner I had just rounded. By the time I got there, I was breathing heavily, soaked in sweat, and the places on my legs where the caliper padding rubbed, were once again raw and burning.

There were about a dozen people at the bus stop, and every one of them turned to stare at me, wondering no doubt what my affliction was and why I was out on the street unaided. At least, that's what I thought, being very self-conscious of my obvious handicap. However, they quickly lost interest when I came to a halt and stood there waiting for the bus like the rest of them. The really embarrassing moment was yet to come!

A few minutes later, the right bus came along, and the would-be passengers stepped graciously aside to let me on first. I had, of course, given absolutely no consideration to precisely how I was going to perform this tricky maneuver. As the bus doors swished open, I attempted to hurriedly step up, so as not to keep the other people waiting too long. I lifted my left leg with my left hand, forgetting in the rush to unlock the knee joint. Having got my left heel on the bottom step, I was now forced to stand at an unnatural angle, leaning backwards with the leg fully outstretched at about forty-five degrees from my body. Not wanting to appear too clumsy, or to make anyone aware that this was indeed my first attempt to venture forth into the world again, I tried to climb into the bus from that awkward position. It required an enormous thrust by my arms on the crutches. I almost made it through the center of gravity, teetered for a moment on the brink of a fine balance, then fell; straight back into the waiting crowd impatiently milling around at the bottom of the steps!

Fortunately, there was a large man immediately behind me who was reasonably alert. As I tumbled helplessly backwards, he caught me in his outstretched arms and took the brunt of my collapsing weight, thereby preventing me from contacting the pavement, flat on my back, with what would have been a terrible impact. He lifted me into an erect position once more, and I turned to thank him, feeling the crimson flood of embarrassment rising from my throat to my forehead.

"Are you O.K., son?" he inquired with genuine concern. "You oughta be more careful! You could get hurt that way!"

You don't know the half of it, I thought.

"Yes. I'm fine, thanks to you. Let me try it again," I replied, by now acutely aware of the renewed stares and mumbles from the rest of the crowd, who were by now becoming increasingly impatient in their desire to board the bus themselves, before the driver decided to take off without any of us.

"Do you need a hand?" the same man asked apprehensively.

"No thanks. This is my first time. I've got to learn to do it myself," I muttered.

"You've got to learn . . . " he said, his mouth agape as the implication of what I was saying dawned on him.

I ignored him and once more attempted the boarding procedure.

This time, I tried something different. I realized that it would be time-consuming, if not impossible, for me to unlock both knees at once without collapsing in an untidy heap. This would require leaning precariously on alternate crutches as I raised each leg by hand to the step, then pushed myself upright, re-locked the knees, then went through the whole damn thing for the next step. So I repeated the last maneuver with a slight variation.

I left the knees locked as before so my legs could support my weight. This time, however, I leaned my left crutch against the side of the bus, once again hand-lifted my left leg up on to the step, took hold of the left handrail of the doorway, placed my weight on my right leg, leaned my right crutch against the bus, took hold of the right handrail, and pulled myself up and forward at the same time. My left leg was already on the step and my right leg just naturally followed my body up, and there I was, safely on the step. The entire procedure took about fifteen seconds. All that remained was for me to perform the same trick on the next step, then have somebody pass my crutches up to me.

So bloody simple!

The crowd applauded the circus act, glad to be able to board the bus themselves at last. The man behind me, watching the performance with amazement, had the foresight to take my crutches and hand them up to me. I thanked him, turned and rolled my way down the aisle, trying to ignore the curious stares of the passengers already seated. I came to an empty aisle seat, collapsed into it with my legs outstretched, unlocked the knee joints, and pulled both legs into the safety of the space between my seat and the one in front, taking my crutches between my thighs as I did so. Nothing to it!

My heart was pounding, my arms were trembling and my legs were aching, but I sat there, smugly pleased with myself, despite the somewhat resentful looks of a few of the people boarding behind me. So I had delayed them for a couple of minutes. So what? I had put on a good show for them, hadn't I?

The lady next to me ignored me, so I rode in silence, gazing out on the bustling scene of a typical Sydney summer day, immensely relieved and pleased to be a part of it all once more.

My stomach tightened again as the bus approached the hospital stop, and I struggled past the standing passengers well in advance to let the driver know that I wanted to get off there. He opened the doors for me and watched fearfully, remembering the previous episode. He need not have worried.

Getting off, it transpired, was a whole lot easier than getting on. I simply placed both crutches on the step below me, raised my body up by stretching both arms up vertically on the crutches, and lowered both legs simultaneously to the step, repeating the exercise to get to the ground.

Within seconds, I found myself standing on the sidewalk outside the hospital gates, immediately opposite THE pub. The great temptation crossed my mind. Should I or shouldn't I? I took a faltering step forward to the curb, then thought better of it. No point in tempting fate twice for the sake of a cold frothy-top. It WAS tempting, though!

I turned around and stumped through the gates, staggered up the hill and into the lobby of the hospital, where the canned air immediately chilled my freely perspiring body.

Two hours later, after my therapy with Julia had ended for the day, it was time for the return journey. It was literally downhill all the way, and was not nearly as difficult as the first trauma. Using the experience I had painfully gained on my previous ride, I boarded the bus without further incident, sat down and rode home without raising so much as an eyebrow from my fellow passengers.

One more obstacle overcome on the long, long journey.

Nellie was almost beside herself with worry by the time I got home. She sat me down with a cup of her strong coffee, and listened with wild amusement as I told her of my harrowing adventure.

146

Steel Spine, Iron Will

New Year's Eve passed quietly and uneventfully at home. Nell and I celebrated with a bottle of inexpensive champagne as we stood on her back doorstep, gazing out across the harbor at the gaudily lighted Sydney Harbor Bridge and the magnificent Opera House fireworks display.

I awoke on the following morning, the first day of the new year, with a burning desire, stronger than any before, to dispose of my handicap completely, once and for all, and get on with my life — and my flying career. I had been riding the bus to hospital for a week now, and felt confident and comfortable in that particular aspect of mixing with the public. But it was not enough, of course.

As my legs seemed to be getting stronger, and more feeling was coming back to them, I began to practice stumping up and down the hallway of Nell's house with only one crutch, much to her horror and chagrin. This exercise caused a great deal of damage to the already peeling wall paint, and scratched and dented furniture as I banged my way along, rocking and rolling from one side with the crutch to the other with my unsupported leg and caliper, swinging my free arm as I desperately strove for balance.

Soon, I was confident that I had mastered the peculiarities of this semi-assisted method of walking sufficiently well to brave the unprotected streets. Accordingly, on the first day of the second week in January, I limped heavily out on to the street, where I boarded the bus bound for downtown Sydney. I had not been downtown since before the accident, and I figured this was as good a time as any to see the sights of the city again.

I would go by bus to the famous Circular Quay, wander around the ferry and hydrofoil wharves for a while, then board another bus for the short ride to the beautiful Botanical Gardens which would be alive with spectacular summer flower gardens, huge shady trees hundreds of years old, manicured walks and lawns, and surrounded by the blue waters of the harbor lapping gently at the convict quarried stone retaining walls of the grounds. Everything went as planned, almost.

I found it in fact easier to board the bus with only one crutch to worry about. Getting off presented no particular problem either, as I simply substituted one of the handrails for the missing crutch when lowering myself to the ground.

For an hour or more, I roamed happily around the souvenir stands and take-away food shops on the waterfront, bought some greasy fried fish of doubtful origin — and fries, of course — and stood leaning against the black iron railing surrounding the quay, delightedly smelling the pungent aroma of the salty air and watching the sea-gulls as they wheeled and screeched overhead, ever searching for a scrap of discarded food.

Suddenly, the urge came upon me to buy a ferry ticket and go for a cruise on the harbor, something I had not done for years. I went up to one of the booths and bought a round trip ticket to Manly, one of the North Shore seaside suburbs which was accessible from the Harbor without having to go outside Sydney Heads and into the open ocean. The ferry was just about to pull away as I stumped through the turnstiles and down the ramp to the gangway. I levered myself up the plank, holding grimly on to the rail with my free hand as I struggled to alternately raise my hips and plant my stiff steel legs on the slope ahead.

Everything went well until I got to the top of the plank. The vessel was rolling quite smartly in a swell induced by the passing of a hydrofoil behind, and at the exact moment I stepped off the plank and let go of the rail, the deck rose up to meet my momentarily unbalanced body.

My stiff legs had no seamanship qualities whatsoever, being unable to bend voluntarily at the knee for balance. On only one crutch, I had absolutely no control over lateral movement, and I was inexorably hurtled forward and sideways, only to be bounced sharply off the side bulkhead of the upper passenger cabin, and thrown back to the edge of the deck which was protected only by a four inch wide wooden railing. This thin white rail was suddenly the only tangible support to prevent my plunging headlong over the edge and into the murky waters below, to be either crushed between the side of the ferry and the pylons of the wharf if I floated, or drowned as I was pulled to the bottom by the weight of my own calipers if I didn't!

Neither choice greatly appealed to my shocked and outraged senses, and as I was thrown to the deck, sliding on my stomach and face towards certain death, I reached up desperately with both hands, one for the rail and one for a stanchion which had now conveniently placed itself directly in front of my rapidly approaching face. Closing my eyes, I put my head down, electing to receive a generous allowance of splinters in my nose and cheeks, rather than a steel stanchion between my eyes. Reaching up with both hands — the solitary crutch had long since gone its separate way — I miraculously felt the solidness of wood in one hand and steel in the other as I came to an abrupt and painful halt at the very brink of the deck. Carefully opening my eyes, I found my nose to be about one inch from a securing cleat I had not previously noticed in my long slide. I lay there panting with shock and relief as I gazed in stunned stupefaction over the side of the ferry immediately before my bruised and bleeding face.

A deck hand, who had witnessed my plight from the bridge above, raced down a ladder to the deck where I lay and assisted me to my feet, which along with the rest of me, were trembling uncontrollably.

"Are . . . are you all right mister?" he inquired, staring with bulging eyes at my battered and bleeding face.

"I . . . ah . . . think so," I replied stupidly, not knowing whether I was all right, or whether I was indeed bleeding to death, as appeared to be the case from the profuse amount of blood which was dripping to the rolling deck between my stiff and unsteady legs.

I gripped the rail with one hand and his shoulder with the other while searching desperately around the deck for my missing crutch. My eyes finally came to rest upon it, balanced precariously on the edge of the deck with only one of the rail support stanchions barely preventing it from taking the plunge I had so recently avoided at much cost to the only part of me which had been up to now reasonably intact; my face.

"Would . . . would you mind retrieving my crutch over there please?" I asked hesitantly, pointing towards the edge of the deck where it was about to disappear overboard.

He looked at me as if he expected me to jump over the side the minute his back was turned.

"You be O.K. if I let go of you?"

"I'll . . . be fine. I'll just hang on to the rail here till you come back. Honest, it will be O.K. But I have to have that crutch. I can't walk without it. Steel legs, you see," I said, raising my pants leg to show him what caused the problem with my balance.

"Oh," was his intelligent reply, as he trotted off to get my crutch.

I soon had it firmly planted under my right arm again, and using the sailor for balance against the roll of the ferry, I made it to a seat safely inside the upper cabin, where I sat down without further incident. There was no way I was going to attempt to get down the steps to the lower deck. The sailor disappeared and just as quickly reappeared with a bowl of hot water and some hand towels and bandages. Amid the stares of the ever-present curious onlookers, which I was by now learning to ignore as part of my re-introduction to the world, he deftly and gently wiped away the blood, removed the worst of the splinters with a pair of tweezers, and covered the not-too-many seeping gouges with band-aid strips.

By the time he had finished, the ferry was well out into the harbor and we were just coming abeam the famous Opera House, its creamy-white tile sails reflecting the rays of the mid-morning sun as it climbed over downtown Sydney on its long journey west to the Great Outback. I sat there leaning on my crutch, doing some reflecting of my own. I was rapidly becoming a public nuisance. I would simply have to control these mad impulses to try to do things that normal, perambulatory people took for granted. It was going to take time; that's all there was to it.

Gazing out over the brilliant, white-capped blue of the harbor, with its myriad of vessels of every size and description from tiny sailboats billowing multi-colored sheets of canvas and nylon, to giant ocean liners and container ships, to every kind of warship in the Australian Navy inventory docked at Garden Island, I felt a deep satisfaction and contentment seep down into my inner being. The bayside suburbs drifted lazily past on both sides of the ferry, reminding me of many happy times spent strolling through the ritzy, wealthy, tree-lined streets and parks of Double Bay, Point Piper and the old flying boat base of Rose Bay.

This really was a beautiful city!

I had often wondered which of the two cities I preferred; Sydney or San Francisco. Each one had its own special charm and appeal to the wandering spirit. But as I sat there with the hot summer sun beating down on me, its fierce energy offset by the gentle ocean breeze sweeping up the Harbor from the Heads, bringing with it the tangy aroma of salt ozone, I knew that Sydney was and always would be my favorite town in all the world.

We chugged past old Fort Denison, or "Pinchgut," as the convicts who built it used to call it because of the starvation they endured if sentenced to live there. It was conveniently located right in the middle of the harbor, just like Alcatraz, so that the only means of escape was to dive into the dark waters and become shark-bait.

I squinted through the glare at the thousands of old red-tile roofed pre-World War One houses nestled alongside the more modern, swimming pool and tennis court adorned villas and estates with their finely mown lawns rolling down to the water's edge.

Yes indeed! Sydney was a good place to have grown to manhood and to have found true love, even if that love was not meant to blossom into the rare and wonderful life-long relationship I so desperately sought.

13

Before I realized where the time had gone, the ferry had crossed the Harbor to the North Shore and docked at Manly Pier. Rather than run the risk of repeating my previous attempt at breaking the world underwater endurance record, I remained on board, watching the bustling activity on the shore with a rapidly growing desire to become a part of it. Parents were taking their children to the Aquarium just beyond the pier to show them the multitude of sealife displayed there, including one of the world's greatest collection of sharks. People everywhere were scantily clad in brief shorts or briefer swimming costumes or bikinis, heading to or from the very popular Manly Beach, aptly though not deliberately named for the thousands of well built bodies of both sexes loafing or frolicking in the sand, soaking up the famous Australian sunshine, or playing in the huge surf that pounded the beach.

The ferry was secured firmly to the pier so I did take a chance on stumping to the rail, planning every step first and making sure I had something to hang on to with my free hand before I took the next step. Breathing deeply of the salty air, I gazed with longing over the colorful dock area, very glad to be once more a part of the mainstream of life and not imprisoned in the backwater of pain and frustration from which I had so recently escaped.

Too soon, the ferry skipper sounded the horn, warning would-be passengers of the vessel's imminent departure. I staggered back to my seat as quickly as I could so as not to be caught on my feet when we began moving. As I stepped ungracefully over the low coaming of the doorway, I collided heavily with the same deck hand who had earlier administered my first aid treatment.

"Jesus, mister, don't you ever give up?" he profanely inquired, inspecting with critical eye his handiwork literally plastered all over my face.

"Sorry," I mumbled. "Hey, thanks for your help before; and in answer to your question, no. I don't ever give up. That's why I'm here."

He stared uncomprehendingly after my retreating figure as I stumped back to my seat and fell heavily into it. The sailor wandered away on his duties, shaking his head at the weirdos that he had to tolerate on this job. He reflected that if he didn't love the work so much, he would leave all the loonies to somebody else and go find an ordinary job as a landlubber somewhere!

The return journey, as always, seemed so much quicker and easier than the outbound one. Before I was quite aware of it, I was once again standing safely on the pier at Circular Quay, having found, as with the bus experience, that it was much less effort to go down things with my stiff, steel legs than to go up.

I limped slowly up the sloping ramp and through the turnstiles to the street, stopping frequently to regain my breath which was coming in short, ragged pants as a result of the extra effort required to maintain balance on one crutch.

There was a bus stop right outside the entrance to the ferry pier, and I was soon aboard for the short ride round the dock area to the botanical gardens. I managed to arrive safely inside the grounds without incident, where for the rest of the day, I divided my time between walking up and down the flowered paths, bending as low as I could to smell the incredible variety of blooms, and sitting on park benches watching the hundreds of other people stroll by enjoying the blue and green summer day.

Once I even managed to negotiate my way over the uneven grass to the sandstone retaining wall quarried and constructed by convicts just a hundred and fifty years ago. I turned back-to-the-wall and with my palms flat on the top of it, boosted myself up to come to rest sitting on the edge. Unlocking my steel knees, I sat swinging my strengthening legs to and fro as I squinted out across the sweeping lawns to the turreted colonial sandstone buildings of Government House and the Music Conservatory.

Another hour passed. I lowered myself to the ground and slowly made my way back to the park entrance, where I reluctantly hopped a bus for the return trip to Nell's place. It had been a good day! I was now convinced that I was going to make it in the world, even if I was going to have to get uglier, if that was possible, in the process.

I made it back to Nellie's house without further incident, where I slumped into one of her battered arm-chairs in the front lounge and gratefully accepted an icy orange juice from her.

By now we were both pretty well convinced that Barb had made up her mind not to re-establish our relationship, despite indications by her to the contrary whenever she found time to visit us. Those visits were becoming fewer and fewer, however, and I knew deep down in my bones that I had probably found her again, only to lose her once more — forever, this time.

The days and weeks passed slowly now, as I became more and more impatient for progress in my self-imposed quest for a return to normal life. I began to skip therapy at the hospital on a frequency directly proportional to my desire to venture instead into the outside world. Julia began to severely chastise me for my increasing tardiness in both attendance and concentration on my exercises when I did attend.

Since the day of my downtown foray on one crutch, I had virtually thrown away the other one, and had not used it in public again, although I still practiced with it at home, without the calipers on my legs, trying — so far in vain — to walk unaided by the support of the irons.

At the end of January, on one of my trips to the hospital, I received a surprise visit from Doctor Yeoman while I was in the gym working out with Julia. This was the first time I had seen or spoken to him since my release.

"Well, well, well," he beamed in his usual cheery way, "if it isn't our own prodigal son, returning to regale us with tales of his wild adventures in the world beyond these cheerless walls. How are you, my boy? Let me take a look at you!"

"Hi Doc," I replied, genuinely delighted to see him again. "I'm doing just fine. How are you? And how is the battle . . . I mean, Sister Wang?"

"Oh, I am well enough. I have not had a patient like you recently, to challenge my exceptional talents. Sister Wang is still her same, shall we say, effusive and ebullient old self. I believe she actually misses the daily verbal tournaments with you and your friends, you know."

I had to chuckle at that. I kind of missed them myself.

I noticed that he still had his clipboard firmly clutched to his chest by both arms, as though he was afraid it might escape, but he suddenly released it and lowered his arms and came toward me, a sure sign that I was in for an examination.

"They tell me you have been doing exceptionally well, and that you are walking with the assistance of only one crutch now. Let's have a look at you and see if we can't streamline you a little more."

I did not like the sound of that, but I sat quietly on the old familiar canvas mat, already stripped to shorts and T-shirt for my work-out, and let him pull and jab and twist and poke at my legs, which were by now considerably larger and stronger — at least in the upper thighs and buttocks, where the muscles were returning rapidly now.

"H'mmm. Yes. Very Good! Very good indeed!" were the abstract sounds issuing from the Doctor's throat in various tones of enthusiasm, as he spoke to himself while prodding at me.

"What does all that mean, exactly?" I asked him with mounting anticipation and not a little uneasiness.

"H'mmm?" he muttered again. "Oh, nothing. Just thinking aloud. Stand up for me, would you?" he said suddenly, gazing at me over the top of his gold half-moon spectacles as he knelt beside me.

I reached for the calipers lying beside me, intending to strap them on.

"No, no," he said, waving his hands. "Leave the calipers. Just the crutches! I want to see just how strong your thighs really are."

I frowned at him, wondering how he had guessed that I had been doing just this very thing at home.

155

Rolling on to my stomach, I pushed myself up on to all fours, still amazed at the ease of this maneuver which I thought I would never be able to accomplish when I first attempted it months ago, balanced myself on one arm and two knees as I reached for the crutches nearby, pushed myself erect on my knees and placed the crutches in position, but out at a forward angle of about thirty degrees. Then, digging the rubber tips of the crutches deeply into the mat, I leaned my body as far forward as I could, at the same time heaving myself up by my arms with my hands firmly gripping the handles of the crutches. My lower legs and feet were still dragging, but as my body came erect over the crutches, the lower legs just had to follow, and in seconds, I was standing precariously on the mat, having lifted my upper legs high enough in the process to allow my still drooping feet to clear the mat and enable them to be placed firmly on it.

I stood there, panting with the effort, but relieved and proud that I had been able to perform this tricky task for the Doctor without any of my customary misadventures.

"Amazing!" remarked that worthy gentleman, as he stood there once more in his usual pose, head cocked on one side as if examining a specimen in a jar. "Can you walk like that?" he casually inquired.

"A little," I replied. "It's difficult because I still can't lift my feet and I keep tripping over them. I have to lift each leg far enough to allow my feet to be placed so they will not turn under at the ankle with every step."

"H'mmm," he said again, tapping his teeth with a ballpoint pen he had removed from his coat pocket.

"Put your calipers on and come with me. Julia, I think it is time we updated his equipment. Let's go visit our friends in the basement."

I did not have a clue what he was talking about, but Julia obviously did, and was plainly delighted.

"Yes! What a good idea. I really didn't think he was quite ready for it, but he is already starting to shirk his therapy, opting for his own brand. You never know when or if we are going to see him again, so perhaps it's best."

I didn't know what she was talking about either. They apparently had this coded language that was totally unfamiliar to ordinary people. I collapsed to the mat again, where I quickly and expertly strapped on the calipers, then got to my feet once more.

Minutes later, we were in the basement where the technicians built the equipment, and I was talking to my old friends for the first time since I had left the hospital.

They had me sit in the same old hard-backed chair I remembered from last time. Discarding my old calipers, they rummaged through a pile of bits and pieces on the cluttered bench and came up with a pair which showed obvious signs of much use. They were quite different from mine, however. They were only half the size and had no knees! Sam quickly tried them on me for size. They came up to about two inches below my own knees and had only one strap around the upper calf muscle. At the ankle, they were the same, with a support for my shoe which was hinged at the ankle to allow a more or less normal step to be artificially induced as my foot was placed on the ground, as I had not the strength or movement in my own feet or ankles to accomplish this simple task.

Soon they were both in place. They felt enormously comfortable and light-weight compared to the old ones. I felt as if a great burden had been lifted from my body, and my spirits soared. Real progress at last!

Doctor Yeoman and Julia had stood by silently, watching and enjoying my delight at this new freedom. When the 'new' irons were in place, I immediately grabbed my crutches and attempted to rise to try them out. Doctor Yeoman stepped quickly forward and pushed me lightly back into the chair.

"Not so fast," he said gently. "As with everything else, there are a few rules you have to learn to follow first. If you don't, you will pay dearly in later life. Now listen to me! I don't know what you have been doing at home, but if you have been trying to walk without your calipers, there is a good chance you have already done irreparable damage to your knee-joints. You see, your knees are very delicately held together by fine muscles and ligaments. When you stand, even though you are not consciously aware of it, you always have your knees slightly bent. In your case, your old calipers have been doing that job for you, as your weight has been entirely supported at the knees by the straps of your artificial ones."

"Now then," he went on, as I sat there swallowing in silent dismay at my own stupidity, "if you stand with no strength to support your legs naturally with bent knee, the unfortunate alternative is to stand with your legs perfectly straight up and down and your knees locked. This is not a natural position, and if you walk like that — that is, with locked knee joints, you will very quickly damage those delicate ligaments and you will very probably begin to suffer excruciating pain in those joints. Eventually, you will have to undergo knee surgery to repair the damage you have done. The solution in your case is simple. Do not, I repeat, do not, walk with stiff legs to counter your lack of strength in your calf and thigh muscles. Always use your crutches to support your weight and keep your knees bent slightly at all costs. Do I make myself clear, Rod?"

I swallowed again as his words sank in. I had, of course, been doing precisely what I was not supposed to be doing. Naturally!

"Ah . . . yes . . . I think so," I replied, looking very embarrassed and guilty. It would be all too obvious to both of them that I had been transgressing, as usual.

"Very well, then, Doctor Yeoman continued. Bearing in mind what I have just told you, see how you get on, unencumbered by the full-length calipers. Remember, support your upper weight on your crutches — not your knees!"

I stood up slowly, paying careful attention to what he had said. I felt myself stiffening at the knees, and instantly relaxed to let my crutches take the weight.

Taking a deep breath, I stepped out. I placed my left leg forward, followed by my left crutch, then my right leg and right crutch. Nothing to it!

I had the hang of it in no time, and was soon thumping around the room more easily and quickly than I had ever been able to do before.

"This is great!" I shouted, unable to hide my enthusiasm.

Talk about 'mastering the possibilities'! My head literally began swimming with ideas for my new-found freedom. No more having to unlock steel knees every time I wanted sit down, no more struggling with the weight of my legs as I tried to lift them by hand. I now found I could lift my leg almost half-way to knee height without the aid of my hand. I could step into and on to just about every kind of public transport — including ferryboats — without risk of falling flat on my face.

I was free! I might even be able to drive a car myself. I would have to seriously investigate THAT possibility! I clumped around the room, stopped before each of these wonderfully devoted people, and pumped their hands with gratitude and relief.

Once more I wondered what would have become of me had I not been fortunate enough to have been brought under their expert and never-ending care. I owed my life, but even more important to me — my mobility — to them. A debt I could never repay. I would repay them, however. I would repay them by continuing with my recovery until it was complete. I knew now what I was going to do.

I was going to fly again!!

I was really going to fly again. But not only fly. I was going after the ultimate; I was not going to be satisfied until I was flying for an airline! That would satisfy them — and prove to all other people in my position that it could be done, that there was hope for anyone who wanted to 'give it a go, mate'!

Saying good-bye for the second time to my friends, the backroom boys, I quickly got into my street clothes, which Julia had been thoughtful enough to bring with her from the gym. Oh, it was so easy to pull my pants on over these baby calipers. I simply sat in the chair with my own bent knees and pulled them on, almost like a person with normal movement.

The three of us rode up in the elevator to the lobby, where I once more shook Julia's and Doc Yeoman's hands, thanked them for the hundredth time, turned and thumped out the front doors into the wonderful, glorious, ninety degree heat of the day.

Except for the crutches, I was walking almost like I remembered, so long ago now. A lifetime ago! As I boarded the bus with practiced ease, more swiftly than I had ever been able to do before, I was already thinking of ways to dispose of the crutches! By the time I had arrived at Nell's place, I had the answer.

Without so much as a greeting, and ignoring her frantic questions about what I was doing, I stumped straight down the long, central hallway of the old house, out the back door and down the half dozen steps, barely noticing the magnificent harbor view as I went.

There was an old galvanized iron shed in the back yard, filled with a lifetime of junk that Nell and Bob had acquired over the last forty years or so. I remembered having seen, at some time while I was rummaging around down there trying to get the lawn mower started, a very old pair of matched ebony walking canes with round, carved handles. I wanted them!

After several minutes of desperate hunting, I finally laid my hands on one of them, then the other, buried under a pile of debris. Taking them up one at a time, I admired the smooth, hard, black wood, scratched, scarred and scraped by endless years of neglect and disuse. They were like a rare and wondrous treasure to me! I instantly discarded my crutches, left them lying where I had dropped them in the shed, took up the twin canes, and attempted the experiment.

Although a little unsteady at first, lacking the familiar support of the crutches at the elbows and upper arms, I quickly got the hang of walking with the sticks as I staggered around the shed and back yard. I was completely oblivious to Nellie, who was standing at the top of the back steps staring, mouth agape, at my latest departure from the sane and normal world to which she was accustomed.

Finally, I came to a breathless halt and squinted up at her with the light of new triumph shining in my eyes.

"Well Nellie, what do you think?"

"I think you're out of your mind, that's what I think! Where did you find those old things anyway?"

"In the shed, hidden under all that other old junk of yours. Is it O.K. if I borrow them for a few weeks? Just until I can walk without them?"

"Have you been drinking again? What makes you think you can walk with them at all, let alone for only a few weeks? What happened at the hospital anyway?"

I leaned heavily on the right stick, bent over and raised my left trouser leg with my free hand.

"I got short braces," I replied with great pride. "They think I have enough strength in my legs now to go to half length irons. Isn't that

160

great? So I am going to get rid of those bloody crutches as well. Is it O.K. if I use the sticks?" I repeated.

"Of course it is," she replied, grinning as the implications of what I was saying sank in. "They belonged to my sister over on Norfolk, God rest her soul. She won't be needing them any more."

I stumped over to the short flight of half a dozen steps, hooked the handles of the canes over my forearms, took hold of the railings, and hoisted myself up the steps, one leg at a time. Piece of cake! We went down the long hall to the living room, where I sat down and removed the short braces from my legs to show Nell the amazing difference they made to my mobility.

I slept well that night!

❖

14

The 240Z screamed around the corner on two wheels, burning rubber as it desperately attempted to straighten up before bouncing off the embankment on the wrong side of the road. It hit the sloping wall of shale and loose rock, ricocheted back into the middle of the gravel road, spun round through 360 degrees and kept going, spinning the back wheels as it hurtled on its unknown date with destiny. I had no idea where it was going, but wherever it was, I was along for the ride. I was sitting in the driver's seat, but I was not driving. Looking down, I was horrified to discover that my legs were completely gone. The dusty road stretched out before me, long and straight, like the railroad track across the Nullabor Plain.

There was nothing in front of me, nothing behind me. Not a car or a house or a tree or a bush or an animal of any kind. Just the road. Suddenly, even the road disappeared! There was nothing!

The sleek little two seater hurtled through space and time and began tumbling, end over end. I was not wearing my seat belt and my head was being pounded on the low ceiling of the car every time it turned over. I began to cry, not wanting it to end like this. I had not come this far to disappear off the end of the earth without a trace!

It got very dark!

I was trembling uncontrollably, sweating profusely, and staring at the outline of some strange object straight in front of me. It seemed vaguely familiar, but I could not quite make it out.

My eyes adjusted to the dark and the faint, dim shape of my own face stared back at me from the mirror mounted above my bedroom dresser.

God! Was that really only a dream? I usually slept very soundly and normally was not bothered by bad dreams; but that had been so real! For the rest of the night, I lay on my back as I had done for so long in the hospital, my hands clasped behind the back of my neck, semi-dozing and thinking about the implications, if any, of the dream. By the time dawn's gray light began to tint the room with pale shadows, I knew what I was going to do.

As we talked over coffee that morning, Nellie asked me what I was planning to do with my day. I stared out the back door at the bustling activity on the waters of the harbor, and without batting an eyelid, proceeded to tell her.

"I am going to buy a car," I said as calmly as possible, still not believing my own words.

Nellie had just taken a sip of her strongly brewed coffee. She sputtered and choked, nearly took a bite out of her cup, which was still perilously close to her lips, and almost swallowed her teeth.

"You're going to WHAT??" she screeched, her voice rising about ten octaves on the last word.

"You heard me," I replied. "I am going to buy a car. I have been adding up my meager funds and I think I have enough in the bank to put a deposit on a car. Think of it! We will be able to go shopping in style again. No more having all those people staring at me every time I get on a bus. I will be truly free again. I can even think about going home for a while."

"You're crazy!" she responded in genuine alarm. "What's more, if you think I'm getting in a car with you, you're double crazy! I think I'll call the hospital and tell 'em to come get you and lock you up. Lord! The thought of it! If the general public out there discovers that YOU are behind the wheel of a lethal weapon . . . "

She left the sentence unfinished, as if the consequences were too horrible to imagine.

I began to chuckle.

She mistook the meaning behind the devilish sound, and began to chuckle with me.

"Ha, ha! Very funny. Some joke!" she said, pouting.

"Oh, I wasn't joking," I replied, increasingly amused by my own thoughts. "I was just thinking about what the guys at the Academy will say when I turn up back there driving a car, and get out on walking sticks and irons, to go take up where I left off and complete my commercial pilot's license training. They won't believe it!"

This time, she dropped her cup, which shattered on the floor, spreading coffee and shards of china over a liberal portion of the kitchen floor.

"WHAAT??!!"

Her voice climbed into a high-pitched shriek, and her face turned bright red. The coffee was spreading over a wide area of the floor, and we both got up simultaneously to get the emergency equipment. She took a brace of mops from the nearby closet, handed one to me, and as we started from opposite sides of the room to clean up the mess, she stared at me in horror, thinking I had gone completely troppo!

"Please tell me you really are joking," she pleaded, with a tone of desperation in her voice. "I really don't need this. I'm not very strong, you know."

"Bull!" I rudely replied. "You're as strong as an ox and almost as heavy!"

I ducked awkwardly, almost losing my already precarious balance, as she took a swipe at me with her now saturated mop, splattering the refrigerator with the soaked-up contents. I dropped my own mop and retreated down the hall towards the front room, with Nell in hot pursuit, weapon held high for the next strike. She was faster than I, as I hobbled along on my irons and sticks, and I soon felt the heavy, wet splat of the mop as it came into stinging contact with my rear end, ejecting me forcefully out the front door, and almost causing me to lose my balance and fall on my already badly punished face.

"O.K., O.K., I surrender," I said with feeling. "I'm sorry. I didn't mean it."

She stood there in threatening posture, holding the mop ready for another wallop. "You didn't mean it about going flying again?"

"No! I didn't mean it about the ox."

"Never mind the bloody ox! What about the other thing with the car and the flying?"

"I'm sorry, Nellie. I did mean it about the flying. I am going back."

She lowered the mop with a huge sigh of resignation.

"You'll never give up, will you?"

"Nope. Not until I have beaten this thing," I replied, pointing to my legs, "and got my wings," I added with determination.

"Come on back inside," she said. "I'll clean up the mess and get us some fresh coffee. I need it, even if you don't."

"Good idea," I replied, eager to please, after the shock I had just inflicted on her.

We spent the rest of the morning discussing my plans for the future.

I was going to shop for a car that very day. It would have to be an automatic transmission, of course, as I did not have the control in my legs to operate a clutch and a brake simultaneously. In fact, I did not know whether I even had the strength or movement to effectively and safely control an accelerator and a brake. Perhaps she was right. Maybe in my fierce determination to put things right in my world, I really was becoming a threat to society in general. Well, we would not know until we tried, would we?

An hour later, I stomped out the front gate towards the bus stop. Forty minutes after that, I was perspiring freely as I clumped up and down a short stretch of busy Parramatta Road in the western suburbs.

Used Car Row!

Pennants fluttered in the gentle summer breeze. Billboards and neons and signs of every description and size beckoned me in to a hundred different lots. Cars and trucks of every brand, style and color were tempting me with windshields ablaze with offers that I could not refuse.

Each time I spotted a possible entry in the stakes for my business, I was set upon by a swarm of used car salesmen, bedecked in their checkered sports coats, garish yellow ties, and dazzling, phony smiles, all trying desperately to convince me that they were THE Honest Joe of the used car trade. Most of them turned away to chase a more likely sucker as soon as they realized that I was handicapped.

Oh, how I hated that word! Dammit! I was NOT handicapped. At least, not permanently. I would show them who was handicapped!

My legs were beginning to chafe where the low irons were strapped to them. My knees were shaking with the effort of keeping them bent, thus taking my entire weight, which they were still not strong enough to support.

I was starting to feel foolish, staggering up and down this busy highway, obviously not in any condition to be out by myself for so long.

Frustration was setting in, and I was about to give up — at least for the day — when I spotted her, tucked away at the back of a lot, her British Racing Green dully reflecting the sun off the long, sleek, curving snout. I stepped awkwardly over the low chain-link fence on to the white pebble gravel of the lot, and actually made it to her side without attracting the attention of one single Honest Joe. Her windshield was almost covered with white greasepaint announcing that she was "$7600. Very clean. No rust. $1500 down."

Good grief! $7600! Could I ever pay that off? Even if I had a job, which I didn't. I did not even know if I could GET a job. Any job, let alone flying airplanes! Would they let me buy her, knowing I was unemployed? Would they think to ask? Of course they would, unless I could pay cash, which I couldn't.

I gently rubbed my hand over the still shiny paint work of her sleek hood. I crunched my way over the gravel, my sticks sinking and sliding in the loose surface, until I came to her right hand door.

I opened the wide door, looked all around for the Police, and slowly and carefully let myself down into the low-slung, comfortable, tan-colored leather bucket seat. The grainy wood wheel and shiny aluminum spokes with the holes in them felt smooth and right to my grip and touch. I placed my left hand on the large, wooden T-bar of the automatic shifter, depressed the release button with my thumb, and moved it easily out of Park, through Reverse, Neutral, Drive, Second and Low, and then back up to Park again.

My right foot rested comfortably on the pedal. I found I could control the movement fairly easily. I tried lifting my left leg to place that foot on the brake. This was more difficult, but not impossible. Could I do it quickly enough though? I tried. My left leg was still weaker than the right. I would never be able to do it in an emergency. I tried transferring my right foot from the gas pedal to the brake. This was easier, and had the double safety feature of removing the real danger of my still not totally controllable reflexes from applying pressure to the wrong pedal at the wrong time.

A crunch on the gravel outside warned me that Honest Joe had spotted my unescorted intrusion.

"She's a beauty, all right. Would you like to take her for a spin?"

Would I! I looked up at him. He did not have a checkered jacket or a yellow tie. In fact, he looked almost human. He even pretended not to notice the canes leaning against the side of the car, or the irons on my legs.

"Would I!" I found myself repeating aloud.

"Close the door," he said. "Do you mind if I come along to show you some of her finer points?"

At least he asked.

"No. Not at all," I replied. "It's probably better that you do," I added under my breath.

He came round to the left side, opened the door and slumped into the other bucket, handing me the keys as he did so. He loosened his sober blue tie with his left hand while extending his right to me.

"Whew! Sure is a hot one. John Martin's the name."

"Rod Lewin," I returned, taking his hand, surprised to find a warm, firm, shake. Not like the limp, dead fish shake of Honest Joe at all!

"Just start her up and ease through that gap there on to the driveway," he said, indicating a narrow space between the side wall of the sales office and several other vehicles to our right.

I started her up.

The twin, double-barrel carburetors hissed as they sucked air and then fuel. She fired on the first crank and throbbed with power, the twin exhausts burbling throatily behind us. My stomach curled into several large knots. I could not tell this man sitting confidently beside me that I had not driven a car for nearly six months, and that I had not driven at all since becoming a paraplegic. Good God! What was I doing, for Pete's sake? Risking this stranger's life — and my own — on a selfish whim to prove something to myself.

I reached for the ignition key and almost turned it off. John Martin looked over at me, wondering why I was stalling. Did I want to test drive this beauty or didn't I, I could almost hear him thinking. I left it running.

I grabbed the T-bar, shifted her into Drive, and with my right foot placed firmly on the brake, cautiously and gingerly maneuvered her out of the lot and on to the driveway, nudging her up to the edge of the highway. As soon as there was a reasonable gap in the traffic, I took my foot off the brake and planted it heavily on the gas pedal with much more pressure than I had intended, thanks to my uncontrollable foot.

The 240Z took off like a startled jackrabbit, and amidst screeching, smoking tires, hurtled down Parramatta Road with John Martin hanging on to his seat belt and me hanging on to the wheel for dear life. He grimaced at me with a glazed stare and an open mouth. I did not know whether he was trying to speak, or was simply in a state of deep shock.

However, I quickly had the Z car under some measure of control, and soon we were running safely, if somewhat jerkily under my heavy and not totally effective control. The knack quickly came back to me, and I found that the single foot operation was both manageable and safe in the heavy Sydney traffic.

I fell in love with the 240Z instantly, and spent the rest of the test drive trying to think up suitable and plausible lies to tell in order to convince the man beside me that he should give me this car for a deposit, with no guarantee of any further payment. As I turned back into the driveway of the used car lot, I remembered last night's dream and hoped that the rest of it would not become a reality as well. I parked her in the drive and we both got out. John Martin waited patiently as I retrieved my canes from the space behind the seats and struggled up the sloping slab of concrete to the sales office.

"If you don't mind me saying, you drive remarkably well, considering your . . . ah . . . condition."

"Thanks. I didn't think I did too badly; for the first time, anyway."

"For the first time . . . ?" he repeated incredulously. "First time since when?"

"Why, since I learned to walk again. I was a paraplegic for four months, but I'm O.K. now."

"I . . . see," he said, obviously not seeing at all. "Well, come into the office and we'll talk. I assume by your reaction that you are interested in making me an offer on the vehicle?"

"An offer?" I repeated with amazement. "Oh. Yes, of course. Let's get in out of this heat." I had been out of the real world for too long, and had forgotten that you don't accept the sticker price as final on a used car.

Soon we were dickering in earnest, and we finally settled on a price of $6800 with a $1000 down. As he began to wade through the reams of paperwork this type of thing always seems to involve, he casually asked me the big question.

"Now, Mr. Lewin, how would you like to pay the balance. In cash with a month to pay, or by time-payment?"

"Ah, time-payment, if you don't mind. Can you get it for me through your loan company, or would you prefer that I go to my own bank?"

"Oh, I think we can arrange it through our finance company. Let me start filling out the necessary forms for a loan."

I sat and fidgeted awkwardly as he asked me the thousand and one personal questions that were on the application for a loan. Then came the next big one.

"Employer?"

"Ah, unemployed. At the moment! You see, I am still recovering from my accident, and I really do need a car in order to be able to get to any job I do have."

"I see," he said glumly, suddenly losing his enthusiasm.

He sat for a few moments, rocking back and forth in his chair behind his desk.

"Tell you what I'll do, son" he said, leaning conspiratorially toward me and speaking in a barely audible whisper, "I'll take a chance on you. I'll let you have the car for the deposit and a month to pay. In the meantime, I'll be working on getting your loan approved, if you can get a job in that time. If you can't, well, you will have had the car for a month anyway. Maybe we can work something else out by then. How's that sound?"

"It sounds too good to be true," I responded warily. Honest Joes don't do you favors out of the goodness of their hearts.

Half an hour later, however, I had almost literally signed my life away and was beginning to seriously doubt my own sanity.

John Martin got up from behind his cluttered desk, handed me the copies of all the binding papers I had signed, then held out the keys to the 240Z with a flourish.

"She's all yours, son. I really do wish you all the luck in the world. Let me know as soon as you get a job so we don't have to send the dogs after you. Ha! Ha! I'll see you in a month."

I ignored his reference to having to repossess the car. I was too elated by my new-found ticket to freedom to be disturbed my what might happen thirty days from now. Something would turn up so I could keep her. It had to!

Shaking his hand and thanking him profusely, I stumped out of his office and down the concrete steps to the driveway, still not quite able to believe I had escaped with the shirt on my back AND the car.

There she stood! Green and shiny and sleek — and all mine! Well . . . almost all mine. But I was not going to think about that now. I hobbled over to her, opened the right side door for the second time, threw my sticks into the back, oozed into the warm leather seat, and just sat there for a few moments, marveling at the amazing turn of events over the last two days. Here I was, sitting in the warm Sydney sunshine in my very own sports car, about to drive away on a brand new adventure. Looking back, I think that moment was the beginning of my new life.

Driving out of that used car lot a happier man than I could ever remember, I cruised around Sydney for hours and hours, visiting all my old favorite places and enjoying every minute it.

The time simply flew by, even as I sat in traffic jams in late afternoon rush hour, playing with all the knobs and dials of my new toy. I was oblivious to everything around me, except the car.

At last, I decided that I had to go back to Nell's place. I knew she would be worried by now. She already thought I was out of my mind. Wait till she saw this little beauty!

I drove the long way home. Taking the North Sydney Expressway exit from downtown, I soon found myself crossing the harbor on the famous 'Coathanger'; the Sydney Harbor Bridge. Ferries plied back and forth far below, carrying commuters home to their bayside suburbs from their city offices. The huge laughing clown mouth of Lunar Park yawned open, allowing hundreds of pleasure-seekers to pass into the cavernous interior of the well-known amusement park. I came off the bridge on the North Shore, and drove briskly along the Pacific Highway through St. Leonards.

My former home for such a long time, the Royal North Shore Hospital, passed on my right, and I felt more than a twinge of guilt as I drove past the bus stop which I had used every day, until just recently, on my way to and from the therapy sessions with Julia. Was it only yesterday that I had been in that very place for the last time? For the last time! They had known! They had known even before I consciously admitted it to myself that the day was fast approaching when I would exchange the hospital therapy for my own brand, and when that day came, they would not see me again. Well, they were right! They would know by now that today was the day.

I was a long way from complete recovery from my paralysis, but for some time now, I had realized that I could do at home most of the strengthening exercises they were giving me for my legs. I kept returning to the hospital, I think out of a sense of duty to Doctor Yeoman and Julia, more than for any real practical purpose. Now I must discipline myself to rigidly stick by my own exercise program at home, until my legs were back to being as strong as they were going to get, given the permanent damage to parts of my spinal cord.

Turning off on the road that connected the highway to Victoria Road, I was soon running down the final stretch over the Lane Cove Bridge which spanned dozens of small coves and backwaters which made up the inner reached of this incredibly beautiful harbor. Up the hill and I drove into Drummoyne, the suburb that had been a second home to me for the past five years — ever since I had known Barb and her mum.

I rounded the post office corner, passing the bus stop where I had experienced my first attempt at public transport, and then I was in the quiet back street which had been a haven and shelter to me when I had no place else to go. I would be ever in Nell's debt for taking me in when my own home and family were so far away and out of reach. Well, they were not out of reach any longer!

Nellie was standing by her mail box at the front gate when I rounded the corner on the opposite side of the street. I honked the twin sports horns as I did a sharp U-turn and pulled up outside the house. She did not recognize the car of course, and even though she knew I was out hunting for one, she did not know me either until I got out of the 240Z and came hobbling around the blunt, stubby tail on my two sticks.

"Well, what do you think of her?" I asked proudly.

"Good grief!" she replied, still shocked at the fact that I had actually gotten out of the car.

"What do you call THAT?"

"Why, Nellie, of course!" I said with a straight face.

"Oh, funny boy! You know what I mean! What IS it?"

"It's a car, don't you see."

I could tell by the strange, bluish tinge around her tightly pursed lips that I was beginning to slightly exasperate her, so I let her off the hook.

"O.K. It is called a Datsun 240Z. Six cylinders, two seats and lots of get up and go. And it only cost me a thousand bucks! Well, for now anyway."

She came forward and peered into the cozy cockpit, noted the absence of seats in the back, and sniffed contemptuously.

"Four-wheeled motorbike! If you think I'M getting in that thing, you're off your rocker."

Sadly shaking her head, she turned and waddled back up the garden path toward the house, speaking to me over her shoulder as she went.

"Come on inside and I'll get you a cup of tea and something to eat. God knows, it might be your last meal if you're going to drive that thing again," she finished huffily.

❖

15

"I am leaving soon, Nellie."

"I know," she replied sadly.

''Where will you go?'' she asked, smiling and trying to hide the tears in her eyes.

She must have known for a long time that I was becoming more and more restless with each passing day. The car was my escape. I had to be moving again, trying to find my true destiny. Where was fate taking me? Here I was, out of hospital, out of work, and out of money. No prospects for the future, and no earthly idea where to go from here.

We had sat talking long into the evening the day I returned with the car.

"I am going to head north," I replied thoughtfully. "I am going back to the Academy first, finish my course, then when I have got that whipped, I can go home for a while."

"I guess it's about time you did, Rod," she said, sniffling. "I would love to have you stay here, of course. You know that. You have been wonderful company for me. But your folks must be getting tired of just talking to you on the phone. They have not seen you since you got out of hospital. They'll be thinking you don't want to see them."

"They should know better than that," I said rather defensively.

"It's just that I CAN'T go home until I finish what I set out to do. I am NOT going home a failure. I HAVE to get my wings first."

"Nobody would think you are a failure. Just look at what you have achieved so far. You have already beaten the odds by walking again, when the so-called experts said you never would."

"I know, but I still have to get my Commercial Pilot's License. I have to get a job now, so I can pay for the car, if for no other reason. And it has to be a flying job. That's what I have my heart set on. That's what I have been through all this for."

"When will you leave?" Nellie asked, already knowing the answer.

"Tomorrow," I replied, rising to bid her goodnight. "I'll see you in the morning, Nellie."

"Will you want breakfast?" she asked hopefully, trying to stall the inevitable as long as possible.

"Of course! Do you think I would leave you without one more time partaking of the worst scrambled eggs, the greasiest bacon, and the thickest coffee in Sydney?"

"Get out of here!"

That night before I went to bed, I packed lightly as usual, taking as few clothes as I thought I would need. I placed my golf clubs beside the door where I would not forget them, wondering if I could ever play the game again. I instantly dismissed that ridiculously negative thought. Of course I would play again. If I could fly airplanes, I could play golf!

Last of all, I neatly folded and packed my Academy uniforms. I left behind the blue cotton windbreaker with the dried blood stains splotched darkly over the front. I did not need that to remind me of my last flight at the Academy. The note pencilled in my log book by the Chief Flying Instructor would forever be reminder enough.

In the remarks column, where there would normally have been written something like "solo upper air work and simulated emergencies," there were three devastating little words: "Driven to hospital."

Well, now I would bloody-well drive myself back again.

I had already telephoned the management at the Academy and warned them that I was returning. They had been pleased to hear from me, and had told me that provided I could prove myself competent to handle the rudders and brakes on the aircraft, they could see no reason why I could not graduate with the next class at the end of March.

I slept well and awoke the next morning refreshed and ready to set out on my first big adventure since my admission to hospital. By the time I got to the kitchen, Nell had a huge breakfast of bacon, eggs, grilled tomatoes, toast and coffee already prepared and waiting for me.

"I want you to get all that down, too," she said. "You never know when you will eat again. Possibly never, if you really intend to take that green monstrosity outside on a two hundred mile drive, no doubt at breakneck speed."

"Don't worry, Nellie. I'll be fine. I promise I will drive carefully. I owe too much money on that 'monstrosity' to take a chance on wrecking it."

"All right, then, but I want you to call me as soon as you get safely to the airport. I don't want to find out second-hand that you are back in hospital. O.K.?"

"I promise," I replied, sincerely.

Thirty minutes later we were standing at the front gate saying good-bye. Nellie was trying very hard not to cry. She crushed me in a huge embrace, practically winding me.

"You be careful, now, and keep in touch. We'll all be thinking of you every minute, you know."

"I'll be careful. And Nellie, say good-bye to Barb for me," I said. "Tell her . . . tell her I love her and if she ever needs me, I will be there. I would probably still be in a wheelchair if it wasn't for her."

"I know. I'll tell her. But she already knows that. She will be sorry she didn't see you before you left."

"It's better this way," I said sadly. "So long Nellie. Take care. I love you, too."

With that, I pulled away from her, turned as quickly as I could on my sticks and irons, and hobbled to the edge of the sidewalk. I stepped down to the street and clomped to the driver's door of the 'Z'. I stood there a moment, gazing around at the familiar surroundings and the sunlight sparkling on the brilliant blue water of the harbor behind the house, raised my hand in final salute, and slid into the bucket.

The powerful engine fired on first turn. I let it warm up a moment, then with a final wave to Nellie through the passenger door window, I carefully transferred my right foot from the brake to the gas pedal and let the sleek green machine carry me off on my brand new adventure. Nellie's hand was still waving furiously as I rounded the corner.

I did not see her again for another four years.

Five minutes later, I was on the main road heading north-west to the highway that would take me on the long drive back to the past where I left off my life. The outside temperature was over ninety degrees. I drove with the two door windows fully open. A blast of hot air rushed through the cockpit, burning my eyes and ripping at my hair, but I was as excited and contented as I could ever remember.

I was FREE again. Australia, here I come!

The Sydney traffic rushed by me. I still could not believe that I was actually sitting in my own car once more.

My previous car was sold to help me finance my flying course, which had taken just about every last cent I had, except for a contingency fund, now almost exhausted as a result of my unexpected stay in hospital and the expenses of normal living once I had been released.

A couple of months ago, I did not think I would ever be driving again, yet here I was cruising north out of Sydney at a comfortable seventy miles an hour. The beautiful mountainous bush country of the north shore flashed by. Yellow wattle, blue gums and other scrubby trees and brush of every color and variety lined the narrow highway. The freshly paved asphalt surface of the road made the tires hum so that even the 'Z' sounded happy to be free of the confines of city life.

I settled into a steady routine with my right foot doing most of the work of running and stopping the car. My left foot continued to be stubbornly weak and slow to respond to commands so I left it for the most part lying idly on the footrest conveniently provided for that purpose.

As I headed north on the New England Highway, the traffic gradually petered down to a trickle and soon I was almost alone on the road. I breathed deeply of the hot, dry wind lashing my face which was already browning again with exposure to the sub-tropical sun after months of being hidden indoors at the hospital. The burning air singed my nostrils and the blinding glare turned my eyes to watery slits, but I was in Heaven. I simply could not recall the last time I had felt this good!

The bitter memories of Barbara's second rejection faded in direct proportion to the increasing distance between me and the beautiful city where we had shared so many good times.

I vaguely wondered if I would ever see her again, knowing deep down that I probably never would, but at the same time, dreaming of the day when she would step back into my life once more, flashing that mischievous, crooked smile I loved so much.

Then, suddenly the image of her was gone, as if she had never existed. I could not even remember her strangely attractive island features. I sat scowling at the road ahead for a few moments, disturbed by her ability to penetrate my new-found inner peace. Then the thought was gone, and I was once again thinking of the times ahead; of the determination and work and strength and courage it was going to take to begin where I left off, this time with the extra burden of being still partially handicapped, to complete the course, gain my commercial pilot's wings, and find a flying job which paid well enough for me to live in reasonable comfort AND pay for the car.

After I had been driving for about an hour, I stopped at a roadhouse to take a break, gulp down a chocolate milk shake which only made me more thirsty, and buy some gas. I had discovered to the dismay of my vanishing funds that the 240Z was even thirstier than I.

Back on the road again. The sun was high overhead as we settled into cruising speed once more. Another two hours should see me in the small coal-mining and wine growing community of the central Hunter Valley where the Academy was ideally situated. Good flying weather nearly all year round, except on cold, rainy, lousy September days, that is.

That depressing memory prompted a string of misgivings and doubts to race through my mind. What if I can't pass the medical check? What if I have not got the strength in my legs and ankles to use the rudders and brakes? What are all those other new students, mostly much younger than I, going to think of an old cripple invading their hallowed ground and taking up precious time in their airplanes?

WHAT IF I CAN'T FLY ANY MORE?

RUBBISH!!

If I can walk, I can fly!

And I have already proven to them that I can walk. Maybe a little clumsily on these confounded sticks and irons, but I CAN walk!

The country subtly changed from the rugged bush hinterland north and west of Sydney to more open, gently rolling land which was mostly under some kind of cultivation. Before I realized where the time had gone, we were coasting through the small hamlets of the scenic Hunter Valley. Three hours and forty minutes after leaving Nell waving at her front gate, I drove down the long, narrow main street of the main township in this fertile valley.

On the north side of town, I drove through the brick and white-chain portals of the Academy gates and up the curving gravel drive to the buildings neatly grouped around a parade ground, at one end of which was a cement dais. A tall, white flag pole stood before the dais. The Southern Cross flapped lazily at the top of the pole in the gentle afternoon breeze. I pulled up outside the neat, functional brick building which housed the Flight Operations room and the Management offices. I reached into the back for my sticks, opened the car door, and very self-consciously heaved myself out of the seat and on to my feet where I stood for a moment, taking in the familiar surroundings under the glare of the noon-day sun.

The air was too hot and turbulent at this time of the day for any productive student flying, and the instructors usually preferred to wait for an hour or so after the midday meal to allow the students' stomachs time to settle, in order to minimize the possibility of wearing their lunch in the hot, close, confines of the small trainer cockpits.

I was thankful for the fact that there was not a soul around as I hobbled over to the main door of the administration building. The sound of voices raised in laughter and merriment, mixed with the clatter of pots and pans being bashed about, drifted across to me from the mess hall, fifty yards to the right of where I stood.

Awkwardly, with my left cane draped over my arm, I opened the door and rose the one step into the air-conditioned interior of the flight operations room, the heart and main reason for existence of the entire establishment. The room was empty. Log books, charts, aircraft clipboards and other aviation related paraphernalia littered the central console. Plastic-covered documents adorned the walls, and computer terminals relaying student and aircraft scheduling information flickered on overhead monitors in each corner.

The clacking sound of a typewriter reached me through a door on the opposite side of the room, leading to the offices of the management and their staff. I followed the sound down a long corridor until I came to an open door. The girl behind the machine was not familiar to me. She had obviously been employed since my departure five months before.

"Afternoon, miss," I said, leaning heavily on my sticks in the doorway of her office.

"Hello," she replied with a polite smile, her gaze following my canes down to the hinged heel supports on my shoes at the end of my braces. "Can I help you?" she inquired with genuine interest.

"I hope so," I replied. "I'm here to do some flying. I wonder if I could see Mr. Flint. He should be expecting me."

"You're here to ... do some FLYING?" she repeated in astonishment. "Ah, wait one moment, please. I'll give him a buzz. I think he's in his office."

She hit an intercom switch on her desk and spoke into the mike, all the while staring at me as if I was from another planet.

"Mr. Flint? There is a gentleman here who would like to see you. His name is . . . just one moment, please. What IS you name?"

I smiled at her.

"Rod Lewin."

"Thank you. His name is Rod Lewin. May I send him along?"

Jim Flint's reply boomed through the speaker.

"Rod Lewin? By all means. Send him down. He knows where to find me."

I smiled again, thanked her, and turned awkwardly in the narrow doorway, then stumped down the corridor to the Academy President's Office. Jim Flint, the creator and owner of the first integrated commercial flying academy in Australia, sat behind his huge, paper-littered, mahogany desk wading through the mountainous pile of red tape generated by the workings of such an establishment. He stood, grinned and extended his giant hand as I knocked on his open door.

"Come in, come in, Rod! Have a seat," he said as he came round the desk to pull out one of the comfortable leather guest chairs for me. "How have you been? I must say, you look tremendous! Are you ready to take to the air again?"

"That's what I'm here to find out," I replied, laying one cane beside my chair and leaning forward on the other with both hands as I sat dawn.

"Well, we're ready to give you the opportunity, if you are. When would you like to start?"

"Immediately, if I could. I have everything here with me for an extended stay. If you can organize a bunk for me, I'd appreciate it. Preferably in a room with someone from the class behind mine, so that I am not a total stranger to them. My presence may not be quite so disturbing to somebody who is at least familiar with my history."

"Trust me, son," Jim replied, not unkindly. "Everyone on this campus is familiar with your history. You MADE history. But leave it to me. I'll see to it. I think there is a spare bunk in one of Green Flight's rooms. If not, I will have some rearranging done. Anything else?"

"Yes. I would like to meet the current Academy Captain. I don't want him, or anyone else, thinking that I am here to try to muscle back into my old position, particularly under the circumstances," I said, whacking my steel encased legs with the cane. "I just want to take up where I left off with my training, finish the course, and get back out into the working world as soon as possible. Are my written exams still valid, do you know?"

"Of course. They are good for one year after you passed them, until you obtain your license. Then they are permanent. All you have to worry about is getting your feel for the aircraft back. And I am sure that will not be any problem for you, from what I have heard about your recovery so far."

"Only one way to find out, I guess," I replied with confidence.

We chatted for a while about my stay in hospital, what I intended to do when I left the Academy, what had happened to some of my former classmates and instructors, so forth. When the small talk had petered out, we both stood and shook hands again.

"Thanks Jim. I appreciate your time. It's good to be back. I'll see you later."

180

"Good luck, Rod. Let me know if there is anything else I can do for you."

I turned and stumped out of his office and back along the corridor. As I passed his secretary's door, she called to me.

"Oh Mr. Lewin! Mr. Flint asked me to find you a room. I have located a spare bed in room 16, block C. There are two Green Flight students in that room at the moment. I believe they have been there since about the end of August last year, so you may know them."

"Thanks miss . . . er, what's your name? I guess I will be spending a bit of time here, so we may as well get to know each other."

"Yes, of course. Helen. Helen Shafer. I'm Mr. Flint's personal secretary. And everyone else's secretary, for that matter. If any of the students, instructors or other staff want anything done in the way of extra-curricular paperwork, they usually come to me. You may feel free to do the same."

"Why, thank you . . . ah, Helen. My name is Rod."

"I have heard of you," she replied demurely. "Who hasn't, of course. Around here, practically everyone mentions at some time or other the 'big crash.' As you know, I was not here then, but apparently it was the worst accident in the Academy's history. Your plane's engine and propeller are in one of the classrooms, and what is left of the plane itself is down in the hangar."

I found myself blushing uncontrollably. I know she did not mean any offense, but right at that moment I could not help feeling I was being held personally responsible for damaging the Academy's good reputation as well as destroying one of its expensive aircraft.

"I see!" was my intelligent reply. I could think of nothing more to say to her, other than to thank her again. Then I turned and clumped out of the building, quite distressed for some reason that I could not fathom.

It had not occurred to me at all that my name would be immortalized here as the Academy's first almost fatal accident. When the word got around that I had returned, I would have to learn to deal with constant stares, comments, both to my face and behind my back, and questions about the accident, by boys who had not yet discovered the meaning of the word 'tact.' I had already been subjected to a rigorous session of questions by Department of Aviation accident investigators who visited me in hospital shortly after I regained consciousness following my spinal operation. Now it was painfully obvious by Helen's comment that I was going to have to go through it all again to satisfy the curiosity of students and instructors alike. Oh well. Life wasn't meant to be easy.

I got back into the 240Z and moved it the short distance to the familiar barracks. It was the same building in which I had previously been billeted, just two doors down from my old room.

A touch of deja-vu surged through me as I opened the 240's stubby trunk, lifted out my suitcase and golf-club bag, and hefted them one at a time to the concrete verandah outside the room. As I did so, I made a rather joyful discovery. Without realizing what I was doing, I had hooked my left cane over my forearm, lifted my (admittedly light) suitcase in my left hand, and hobbled over to the verandah using only my right cane. Only as I placed the case on the ground did it occur to me what I had just done. I had walked with only one cane; and I had been lugging a suitcase at the same time! I immediately set out to prove what I had done, and clomped back and forth up and down the verandah using one cane, first in the right hand, then the left.

As I arrived at my room once more, the door opened and a familiar face poked out, no doubt to see if there really was a runaway horse on the verandah.

"Jeff Collins, by God!" I remarked in utter astonishment at the coincidence.

He was a close friend of one of the fellows in my flight, and had applied for entry to the Academy just a little too late to be in our class. He had therefore been selected for the following one, known as Green Flight. They were about six months behind my original Blue Flight, and were due to graduate at the end of the month. With any luck, I would be with them.

"Good grief! If it isn't the 'old man,' " he rudely replied. "Thought you were dead!" he added with a grin.

Like I said, no tact!

"In the famous words of Mark Twain," I replied, vigorously shaking his hand, 'rumors of my death have been greatly exaggerated.' How the hell are you, Jeff?"

"Be better when we get out of this place," he said, indicating the establishment in general with a sweep of his hand.

Typical of youth, I thought, feeling my age. They don't like anything but the flying. Cannot stand the discipline or the morning drill sessions or the classroom work. Just the flying! When they get out into the real world, they will quickly wish they were back in the security of 'this place.'

But I could not tell him that. After all, he was over ten years younger than me.

"Come on," I said. "Surely it isn't that bad. I seem to remember that we had a few good times here, before my untimely departure."

"Yeah, we sure did. As a matter of fact, we haven't had many tours of the vineyards since you left."

"Very funny," I scowled.

Jeff took my bag inside and threw it on the lower of the spare double deck bunks. I got my golf bag, tossed it over my shoulder, and hobbled into the room, using only one cane. I still could not believe that I could get around on one stick, and that it had not even occurred to me to try it before this!

I sat on the bunk Jeff had indicated and gazed around the familiar surroundings. The only window in the room was in the back wall of the building, opposite the door, and facing on to the parade ground and the single narrow runway beyond. The Piper Warrior trainers were parked as neatly as I remembered them, waves of shimmering heat rising off the polished paint-work of their aluminum skin.

A double bunk, a two place desk, and two chairs placed against each side wall were the only pieces of furniture. The walls were dull, olive green, there were some plain drapes on the window and brown nylon carpet, thin with wear and splotched with stains on the floor. The room was otherwise bare except for the meager possessions of Jeff and the other student. There were normally four to a room, but these two fellows had a bit more room to spread out until I had shown up. I hoped they did not resent my presence.

I opened my suitcase and hung my uniforms and other shirts and trousers on the open hanger bar between the end of my bunk and the wall, and tossed the rest of my stuff in one of the drawers beneath my bunk.

Home again!

Jeff and I sat chatting for a while, mostly about the exams he had just taken — the same exams I had passed the day of my crash.

It suddenly occurred to him that I might be hungry. He had not yet eaten, so he suggested we go over to the mess hall to grab a bite. I reluctantly agreed, after some persuasion. He knew why I was balking, and so did I. I did not want to face the best part of one hundred and fifty students and a dozen or more instructors all at once! I would have much preferred to meet them one or two at a time, but at least this way, the trauma would quickly be over. They would get to see me and then forget me — I hoped.

We walked out into the bright sunlight and slowly ambled over to the mess hall, Jeff matching his pace to my own stumbling gait. He commented several times on my remarkable ability to walk, considering the relatively short time since the accident. It might be a short time for him, but for me it seemed a lifetime had passed in the last few months!

As we arrived at the steps leading up to the hall, the sound of voices grew louder and my stomach churned harder. I balked again at the bottom of the steps. Jeff grabbed my left arm partly to support me and partly to drag me up to the sacrificial alter. I clumped slowly up the half dozen wooden steps and stopped, panting, on the wide verandah at the top. Now only a flyscreen door separate me from the racket inside.

I did not want to go in there! I did not want all these kids to laugh at this stupid, crippled old man who was already a failure in their young eyes, and who dared to return to their sacred ground in this horribly handicapped condition! Jeff read my mind.

"C'mon, Rod! They won't bite! They've already had lunch," he grinned.

I glowered at him and turned to retreat back down the steps. He gently took my left arm above the elbow and led me to the entrance. He pushed the screen door open and we stepped into the room. The din was tremendous. Voices raised in laughter and friendly argument, utensils of all kinds clattering in the kitchen, silverware scraping on plates. The familiar aroma of the kind of food the students loved, franks and beans and fries and burgers and all that wonderfully bad stuff, struck me like a physical blow. Suddenly I was very hungry.

For a moment after we entered, the racket continued.

I stood in the doorway leaning on one cane, with Jeff still firmly gripping my left arm against any attempted flight. I gazed about the room, looking for any other familiar faces, not really wanting to see one. The news of our presence quickly passed from one table to the next, and the noise subsided. The room was suddenly deathly quiet. Even the pots and pans ceased to rattle in the kitchen.

❖

16

Every face was turned in our direction. Though I tried very hard to prevent it, I could still feel my face turn hot with sickening apprehension. My stomach was all butterflies again and I began to tremble.

Jeff broke the horrible silence.

"Gentlemen, for those of you who do not already know him, I would like to introduce Rod Lewin to you. No doubt you have all heard of him. Rod has returned to the Academy to finish his course, which as you know was interrupted by his crash in Charlie November Romeo. That accident left Rod a complete paraplegic. You would not know it to look at him now. Let's welcome him back!"

For a moment, the silence continued unabated. Then a spontaneous applause erupted around the hall. Every one of those boys jumped out of his chair and began wildly clapping and whistling. When the outburst had died down, they left their places and began to come up to me in small groups to shake hands and introduce themselves. Some of them led me to one of the long tables, where I managed with little difficulty to sit at one of the benches. In a few minutes, everything was back to normal, the din had resumed, and I was temporarily forgotten. Jeff went to the cafeteria style serving line, piled two plates high with assorted excellent high fat and cholesterol junk food, and returned to sit beside me. The trauma was over.

I was just one of the boys again.

Several of the lads, including some of the instructors, came over to sit at our table for a while, talking about old times and asking me questions about my stint in hospital and how I went about regaining the use of my lower limbs.

Not one of them asked if I thought I could or should fly again. They simply assumed that I could. In the typical innocence of healthy youth, where the body is taken so much for granted, it never really occurred to them just what I had been through. I came to understand that they thought of my braces and cane as a temporary setback, like wearing a cast after breaking a limb in a football game. That quiet confidence was a tremendous boost to my own doubts about my ability.

The lunch hour wore on and they gradually drifted out of the mess hall and back to their classrooms or over to the operations building for pre-flight briefing. Soon Jeff and I were alone in the hall. The cooks cleaned up the mess around us as we sat there finishing our dessert and coffee.

"See? It wasn't nearly as bad as you thought it would be, was it?" Jeff asked with a grin.

"I guess not," I replied reluctantly. "I really don't know what I was expecting. I suppose I am still very self-conscious about these blasted irons and the cane. But I am relieved that they took my return so well. I kind of thought they would resent it, for some reason. You know, a blemish on their record, an old man trying to recapture his lost youth and making a complete botch-up of it in the process, something like that."

"Forget your age, why don't you! You're only thirty! I know a couple of the guys in your own flight used to rib you about it. But this isn't 1940 and we aren't fighter pilots in the Battle of Britain. You are not 'Old Man' Douglas Bader. Although you could be, the way you made your comeback like you did. I think you are more concerned about your age than they are. So just forget about it. O.K.?"

"And as for the accident, that could have happened to anyone. In fact, if it had happened to any one of us, we would probably be dead, or still para-lyzed. So don't let that bother you either. Just get in there and start flying!"

187

"Thanks, Jeff. I needed that," I replied earnestly.

We got up and wandered out of the hall and back to our room.

Jim Flint had told me I would not be programmed to fly until tomorrow, but in the meantime, there was no reason why I could not jump in a spare trainer and test my strength on the brakes and rudders.

Jeff's classroom work was completed now and he was not scheduled to fly today, so together we strolled over to the flight line behind our barracks and picked one of the Warriors which was secured and not ready for flight.

It was Charlie November November. I had spent many hours in this very aircraft and it might just as easily have been this one that I took up on that fateful day. Memories of that awful day flooded back into my mind, and I hesitated as I raised my left foot onto the step protruding from the right side of the fuselage just aft and below of the trailing edge of the right wing root.

The sunlight reflected off the shiny stainless steel of the caliper connected to my left shoe. A cold shiver began at the nape of my neck and ran down the length of my steel spine. Sharp twinges of pain surged through my back. Did I really want to do this? Was flying the only thing in the world I simply had to do? I would never get to become a professional pilot in my condition. So what was the point of going on with it?

BLOODY COWARD!

I gritted my teeth, angry at myself for those ridiculous negative thoughts. Of course I was going to be a professional! I had not come all this way just to give up the first time I set foot on an aircraft again.

Grabbing the handhold on top of the cabin, I hauled myself up until I was standing with my left foot on the step and my right foot on the black, gritty surface of the wing root walkway. I leaned forward, unlatched the door, opened it wide and lowered myself into the tiny cockpit, sliding over to the left seat as I did so. There was no cover over the canopy and the hot sun was shining straight through the perspex which was crazed in places by continual exposure to the elements. The temperature in the cabin must have been over one hundred degrees and I began perspiring immediately, despite the second cold shiver I felt when I sat in that seat.

Jeff climbed in behind me and slid down into the right seat, leaning my cane against the side of the fuselage as he did so. I opened my storm window and we left the only door wide ajar to get some cross breeze through in a vain effort to lower the temperature.

I delayed the real purpose of entering the aircraft by unlatching the seat belt which was wrapped around the control wheel to prevent the control surfaces from flapping about in any wind. I then carefully scrutinized every dial and instrument, recalling its position and purpose. Finally, when I could think of no more delaying tactics, I raised my feet one at a time and placed them on the rudder bars, with the tips of my shoes resting on the toe brakes.

The parking brake was set. To set or release it required considerable toe pressure to be applied to the main brakes before the park brake handle could be pulled out and locked.

I looked across at Jeff, who was sitting there perspiring quietly.

"Well, come on then. Don't just sit there! Lets see some action," he bellowed in mock frustration. Or maybe it was real frustration, considering the temperature.

"O.K.," I replied. "Here goes nothing."

And that was precisely what I got.

"Well?" he repeated, his voice rising again. "Release the bloody brake, why don't you?"

Obviously he could not tell the difference between my previous sweat and the increased amount as a result of my effort. But you would think he could see the changing color of my face!

"I'm trying," I grunted. "I did say here goes nothing. That's what I'm getting. Nothing."

"Well, push harder then," he said unsympathetically.

I grabbed the front of my seat cushion with both hands. I sat up straight in the seat and pushed my feet against those toe brakes with all my might, practically pushing myself through the seat back with the effort. My eyes bulged, my faced contorted and turned an even deeper shade of red, and the veins stood out on my temple. Still nothing!

I realized that I had been holding my breath. I let it out in a huge gasp and panted heavily. Jeff was looking at me with a strange expression on his face. He said nothing this time. Just sat there. All right, I said to myself. ALL RIGHT! We are going to release that BLOODY brake if it kills us!

Taking another deep breath, I grabbed the seat again, and PUSHED!

Nothing!

I could feel the weakness in my feet and ankles. The braces were doing all the work, supporting me when I walked. However, there was no allowance for movement of the kind I was now demanding. The irons were holding my feet rigid, as they were designed to do.

I attempted something different. Instead of trying to push with my toes only, I put the balls of my feet on top of the brakes. Then I pushed, using the entire length of my legs for leverage. Click! It worked! The brake handle released and moved forward. Lord! What an effort. I was trembling, sweating and swearing profusely and profanely.

"About bloody time," was all my esteemed co-pilot could say.

I nearly reached over and throttled him. There was nothing wrong with the strength in my hands!

Panting heavily, I sat there and regained my composure as I tried to figure out exactly what I had done to achieve the required result.

Jeff broke into my reverie with another little gem. "Now re-set it," he said simply, an evil smirk playing around his perspiring lips.

"Re-set it?" I repeated stupidly.

"Whatsa matter? You deaf?" he rudely replied.

He leaned away toward the door as I reached for his throat with two clawing hands.

"Just kidding," he said, grinning.

"O.K., I'll re-set the bloody thing."

I again placed the soles of my feet at the very tops of the pedals, took a death grip on the front of the seat cushion with my left hand, and pushed as hard as I could, using the entire length of my legs for leverage. At the same time, I took hold of the park brake handle with my right hand. When I felt the pressure build under my feet, I pulled on the handle and released the trigger. I did it. Nothing to it!

"Very good," Jeff said, clapping his hands. "See? It's easy, isn't it?"

"Easy for YOU to say," I puffed.

I sat there sweating and panting and fuming, not daring to move lest I accidentally do this child some grievous bodily harm. Fortunately, we both knew that he was only joking, trying to help and encourage me by means of the 'dare' method. He must have heard stories from hospital and realized that was the most effective way of getting me to accomplish the impossible. With great effort and considerable pain in my back, I performed the maneuver several more times, just for practice.

Press and release. Press and release. Finally, I felt I had the hang of it.

We had been sitting in that steaming cockpit for nearly an hour by the time I had had enough. Jeff did not have to be asked twice to remove himself from the right seat so that I could get out.

As I crawled over the right seat and out the door, it occurred to me that the last time I tried this, I had to be carried out on a stretcher. That unhappy thought gave me extreme satisfaction with the last hour's work. I slid out on to the burning surface of the wing and scorched my hands on the black walkway.

From a squat, I stretched my right leg out and down and placed it on the step, then with a firm grip on the cabin hand-hold, I pulled myself up and stepped to the ground, retrieving my cane from beside the fuselage at the same time.

"A good afternoon's work," I triumphantly remarked to Jeff.

"Yeah. Not bad for an old fella," he replied, ducking as he spoke, to avoid being brutally struck by my cane as it whistled past his backside.

When it failed to connect, I lost my balance and almost fell flat on my face. I had put a great deal of momentum behind that swipe. He turned and put up his hands in surrender.

"Just kidding!" he squawked apologetically, backing away from me as I raised my weapon for a second attempt.

"I should bloody-well think so, after that fine speech about me forgetting my age," I retorted in mock anger.

"I really didn't mean it, Rod."

"Well, buy me a beer and I'll forgive you. Let's get in out of this heat. I don't suppose you keep a supply of stubbies in that fridge I noticed at the end of your bunk?"

"It just so happens I do have one or two left over from the weekend. I guess seeing neither of us is flying till tomorrow, it will be O.K. Good idea, in fact."

Together we strolled back across the parade ground to our barracks, and along the shady verandah to our room. Jeff's other room mate was there when we arrived. His name was Pete Marney, and although I did not know him well from the last time I was here, he had introduced himself to me a while ago in the mess hall. He must have read our minds, because as we entered the room, he tossed each of us a cold beer.

"Here's to your return, Rod," he said, raising the frosty stubby to his lips. "Best of luck!"

"Here, here," Jeff added, downing a huge gulp from his own bottle.

"Thanks, guys. I appreciate it. I sure am glad to be here again."

The rest of the afternoon passed quickly. Neither of them had any further classes and had only a few more flying lessons before they had completed the course. We lounged on our bunks, relaxing in the cool shade of the room, and passed the time talking mostly about flying and what we were going to do when we finished up and got out of here.

At about six-thirty, we drifted back to the mess hall for an early dinner. This time, there was no reaction to my entry apart from the odd glance as the three of us stepped through the door. I was greeted with normal, friendly hellos as we lined up for our supper. My presence was now just a fact of life once more. I was home! For a few weeks, anyway.

After supper, the three of us were joined by several of the other fellows and we took a long stroll down the perimeter fence of the runway, picking grapes from the vines poking through the fence as we did so. A glorious, crimson and orange sunset tinged the high cirrus clouds with magnificent hues as we returned to the barracks. The fellows were strung out along the fence, mostly holding themselves down to my slow, rolling gait on my one cane. On that beautiful afternoon, I reflected that God was certainly in His Heaven and all was right with my world once more.

As we were about to cross the approach end of Runway 16, the north end of the strip closest to the buildings, we saw a single bright light out on a long final. We all stopped to watch the last of the students coming home from his final session for the day. He must have been one of the Green Flight students about to graduate, because he put that Warrior gently down right on the numbers with a gentle squeak of the tires, rolled a hundred feet or so, then turned and taxied back to the parking area adjacent to the parade ground opposite where we were standing.

Tomorrow that would be me, I thought as I clumped across the runway and back to my room.

I went to bed early that night, and lay for a long time listening to the idle conversation of Jeff and Pete and the occasional visitor who dropped in from time to time. Sleep did not come easily. I tossed and turned for ages, wondering about how I would perform tomorrow. I worried that I might have forgotten everything I had learned in the seven months prior to my accident. Would it come back to me? Could I repeat today's performance with the brakes? Could I use my feet properly on the rudders to control the yawing moment of the aircraft?

A hundred other doubts and fears tormented my semi-conscious mind. The one thing that did give me a measure of satisfaction as I rolled about was the fact that I was able to do just that. My upper legs were now strong enough to follow my body as I moved in the bunk, even if my feet still dragged uselessly as if they were not a part of me. I finally drifted off into a fitful sleep and awoke at six the next morning, reasonably refreshed and ready to face whatever the day might bring.

After showering, I shaved and dressed in my carefully pressed uniform which consisted of a standard white aviation shirt, blue tie and gray trousers. I slid my Blue Flight stripes over the shirt's shoulder epaulets, even though there was no class presently assigned with that color. My own Blue Flight had long gone, and most of my former classmates were now out in the working world of General Aviation. One or two of them had even had the right combination of good fortune and academic ability to be accepted by a major airline. Those lucky few were now set for life, and would probably make captain on one of the big jets long before they reached my present age. Oh well. At least I was back in the ring, trying to do something about it. But why didn't I make this decision ten years ago, instead of what I had done? How many of us have asked that question — and how many times — during the course of our lives?

Stumping over to the mess hall for breakfast, I felt the butterflies again flapping about in my stomach. This time, I knew, it was not anything to do with facing the crowd in there. It was what was going to come afterwards that was bothering me.

I gulped down several gallons of black coffee, along with a generous helping of greasy fried eggs, limp, fatty bacon, over-stewed tomatoes and baked beans; I sopped up the suspicious looking residue with a piece of burnt, over-buttered toast, had another cup of coffee for good measure, then waddled out of the building wondering why I insisted on punishing my body that way. I knew I had to eat well to fly well, but less quantity and more quality in what I consumed might be far better for my state of mental alertness.

It had been so long since I had flown that I failed to remember the painful result of an over-indulgence of liquid prior to sustained aerial maneuvers. Before the morning was out, I would long for the automatic venting system of the in-stomach catheter which I had hated so much in hospital in the early days of my confinement. If I still had it installed, I could have jettisoned through the storm window!

I hobbled over to the operations building to examine the day's flying schedule and find out what was in store for me, and when.

Inside the main hub of the academy, I stood leaning on my cane, gazing up at one of the television monitors portraying the day's events. This morning was a far cry from the empty lunch-time room I had encountered yesterday. The place was a bustling hive of activity!

The operations room was full of students studying charts and filing flight plans, while every small briefing room and alcove was occupied by instructors and students in one on one sessions covering the planned maneuvers which would be covered during their particular training exercise. I had been through all this before, so I knew exactly what they were feeling.

My own name flashed before me on one of the lines on the screen.

"R. Lewin: Instructor — J. Forrest — revision and general handling."

Oh my GOD!

I was suddenly very thankful that I had that voluntary session with Jeff yesterday. They were showing me no mercy!

First day out, and they were sticking me in with the Chief Flying Instructor; a man whose outward appearance and general disposition did nothing to inspire confidence in a student who was already nervous and anxious about what new terrors he must face in the course of trying to learn how not to die in an aeroplane. I guess they figured there was no point in wasting the time of a junior instructor, who could be of better use elsewhere, if it was quickly discovered that there was no hope of my coping with the basic rudiments of taxiing, braking and using the rudders in the air.

My stomach already regretted breakfast, and its condition was not improved by the brief message flashing on the screen.

I looked again to see what time I was to receive my baptism of fire. Under the first line displaying my name, I read "0900 to 1100 and 1400 to 1500." Dear God! Two sessions with him in one day. It seemed they did not want me taking up any more of their valuable time than was absolutely necessary. Well, that was all right by me, too. I had no great desire to spend the rest of my life here.

I glanced at my watch. Eight forty-five. Fifteen minutes to pull myself together and psychologically prepare for the forthcoming mental and physical test of my ability to fly an airplane again. My whole future career depended on the outcome of the first few minutes in that aircraft with the man whose word could make or break me.

Stumbling out of the room, I retreated to my own quarters, where I spent the remaining minutes going over my aircraft checklist, trying to re-memorize the pre-start and pre-takeoff items which the C.F.I. would be sure to expect me to know. With my heart in my throat, I returned to the operations room on the stroke of nine o'clock and waited; and waited! The knots in my stomach grew tighter and tighter.

At nine twenty-five, John Forrest stepped into the room from his own office a few doors down the hall. He was a big man, about six feet three inches tall and very broad. Balding on top, with gray-brown hair on the sides and back of his head. He had a huge hooked beak of a nose, which reminded me of a bird of prey. He spotted me standing by the door gazing out at the line of aircraft and came over to me in three giant strides.

Shoving out his huge paw, he greeted me with a curt "Good morning, Rod. Are you ready to show me what you can do?"

No mucking about or wasting time on the niceties with this guy. Straight to the point! It was this same lofty personage who had written those three horribly descriptive and final words, "Driven to Hospital," in my log book.

"Uh . . . good morning, sir," I stammered. "I . . . uh, think so."

"Very well, then. Let's get on with it, shall we?"

With those few brusque words, he strutted past me and out the door, making for the parked aircraft, his head down and hands clasped behind his back. Once again he reminded me of a carnivorous bird searching the ground for a suitable lunch.

Damn nice of him to ask me about my general health, I thought, staring after him with slit eyes and dreading even more the next hour or so. I picked up the log book and maintenance release for the aircraft we were to use. The registration number was Charlie November Mike, the sister ship of the one I had sat in yesterday afternoon. By the time I caught up with his lordship, who was already standing impatiently by the aircraft, I had embarrassed myself several times by tripping over my own feet in a wasted effort to impress him with my mobility. I came to a stumbling halt to be greeted by a stony, unblinking stare down that long, curved beak.

I swallowed several times from a combination of shortness of breath and acute apprehension at what this man had in store for me. He continued to stare at me. If he thought I was afraid of him, he was absolutely correct.

"Uh . . . would you like me to do a full pre-flight inspection?" I timidly inquired.

"Of course. That's what you would normally do, I hope. I want you to show me everything you know, just as if this was a check ride for your license. Indeed, you may consider the entire session a pre-license test for that very purpose."

I swallowed again. Thanks for nothing, mister. What about a bit of helpful instruction after months away from flying, not to mention all I had been through in the interim. One thing was sure; even if I wanted or expected any, I was not going to get any sympathy or leeway from this man. He moved back a few feet away from the aircraft so he could watch my every move. Oh well, I thought, I would show him that I knew how to do a pre-flight, if nothing else. Shoving my checklist in my belt, I got on with the job.

First, I stepped up on to the right wing using the method I had discovered was easiest for me yesterday. Reaching into the cockpit, I pulled up the flap handle until the wing flaps were fully extended. Then I slid to the ground again, retrieved my cane and commenced limping around the plane, performing all the necessary (and some unnecessary) visual checks of wing and tail surfaces for cracks or damage, nuts and bolts and connecting rods for correct tension and play, elevators and ailerons and rudder for freedom of movement and normal travel.

With considerable discomfort, I managed to bend down under the wings to check the tires and brakes for wear. I found the only way to do this properly was to struggle to my knees like a camel and crawl about under the plane, dragging my rigid, steel-encased feet in the gravel. This was no problem, after the long hours and days of practise in hospital. It was, however, extremely painful as the hard, hot surface of the tarmac bit into my bare hands and through the thin fabric of my trousers into my unprotected knees. While I was down there, I remembered to check the pitot tube and fuel drains so that I would not have to repeat this awkward maneuver for the benefit of his eminence.

I struggled to my feet and hobbled around the front end of the aircraft, checking the fuel contents and making sure the caps were secure when I replaced them. I lifted the engine cowlings and peered around all the tubes and wires and ducts and harnesses, checking for leaks or cracks or breaks or loose connections.

As I did all this, it occurred to me that this bastard standing behind me might have deliberately disconnected something to see if I discovered it. With that pleasant thought in mind, I searched even more vigorously for something amiss, but found nothing out of place. Finally, before closing the cowl, I checked the engine oil and hydraulic fluid. Then I buttoned it down and went over the propeller with my fingertips, carefully inspecting it for nicks or gouges along the leading edges and the tips. When this was done, I limped around the right wing to stand at the step, ready for boarding.

"Anything else?" his nibs asked, raising his bushy brows and pinching the bridge of his beak between thumb and forefinger.

"I . . . uh, don't think so. Did I miss something?"

"What about the alternate static source?" he inquired without malice.

"Oh," I replied weakly, stepping up to the small, circular probe flush with the fuselage on the right side just in front of the stabilator. I checked it to make sure the probe's tiny holes were free from dirt or insects.

"Very well. Let's get aboard, shall we?" he said, apparently satisfied with my pre-flight.

Today was no cooler than yesterday, and I began to perspire immediately I crawled into my seat. I knew that it was not entirely due to the heat, however.

John Forrest folded his giant body into the right seat after me, leaving the door ajar to keep the temperature down in the nineties until we had the engine running.

"All right, let's have the pre-start check," he said unceremoniously.

I took my check list from my belt and began reading through it aloud, performing each task as I called it out. I expected him to chastise me for using the check list instead of calling it from memory, but apparently he had no objection to my referring to it. The checks were finally complete, the battery switch was on and the engine was primed ready for starting. I turned on the rotating beacon and shouted the customary warning through the storm window.

"Clear prop!"

This was to ensure that no unobservant fool had decided to stand with his head under the propeller the moment I decided to crank it. The engine turned four or five times, then burst into life with a familiar roar. I felt the adrenaline already pumping through my body, and the tightness in my stomach returned with a vengeance. I carefully went through the after-start check list, once again performing each item as I read it out, shouting over the blast of the engine. As I completed the check, Forrest picked up the microphone.

"I'll handle the radio. You just fly the aeroplane," he said perfunctorily. Then he keyed the mike and made the standard taxi call. Our airfield was uncontrolled, so he had only to advise other traffic in our area that we were taxiing for take-off.

"All academy traffic, Charlie November Mike taxiing runway one six for take-off," he shouted. He released the transmit button and then turned to me.

"O.K. Let's see if you can still fly," he said caustically.

At that moment, however, I was not worried about flying. I was exerting every pound of pressure I could muster just to release the bloody brake!

"Well then! Let's go!" he bawled, his hawk-like eyes glittering at me impatiently.

I readjusted the position of my feet atop the toe brakes, took a firm grip on my seat cushion with both hands, and pushed with the entire length and strength of both legs against the pedals. Click! Ah, music to my ears, I thought as I heard and saw the hand brake lever release and move forward of its own volition when the brakes came off.

At the same time, I gently nudged the throttle lever slightly forward. The engine note increased fractionally in response, and we trundled to the edge of the parking area adjacent to the threshold of runway one six. As we moved slowly ahead, I surreptitiously applied pressure first to one rudder pedal, then the other, in an effort to verify that I could in fact control the direction of the aircraft with my feet; indeed, the only way to steer a light aircraft on the ground. This was routinely done anyway to ensure that the nose-wheel steering was operating correctly and connected to the rudder in the proper manner.

Forrest apparently ignored this subtle movement, no doubt under the impression that I was merely carrying out a standard item on the before takeoff checklist.

I quickly ascertained that there was no problem in exerting the required strength to move the rudder pedals on the ground, and since there was less pressure required in the air, due to the obvious fact that the nose-wheel was not subject to the same load of the aircraft as when on the ground, it was plain that I was going to have no difficulty once we were airborne.

It seemed that my only headache — apart from my co-pilot — was going to be getting the brakes set and released. I had to build up sufficient strength in my legs to overcome this minor obstacle. At the threshold of the runway, I again struggled to exert enough pressure on the toe brakes to set the park brake lever. I could not be sure, but it seemed to be a little easier that time.

I ran the engine up to the customary twenty-five hundred r.p.m., checked out the magnetos and the carburetor heat, then backed it off to idle speed and finally returned it to one thousand r.p.m., and finished off the before take-off check by asking my taciturn observer to close and lock the door, which I checked for good measure to impress him with my thoroughness, then closed my own window.

Once again, I placed the soles of my feet on top of the toe brakes and applied every ounce of my strength to release them. It was either getting easier, or I was becoming used to the pressure required. I finished off the check list by briefing Forrest on my take-off decision speed and my actions in the event of an engine failure on take-off, gave him the expected instructions on how to release himself from his seat belt and the aircraft if we crashed, then taxied the airplane onto the runway.

He keyed the mike and advised any traffic that we were entering the runway, and we took our position for departure. I slowly and evenly advanced the throttle to full power. The Lycoming engine bellowed and we lurched forward like a startled snail. Gradually we picked up speed, and I found myself automatically, and quite unconsciously, controlling the slight yawing tendency with my feet firmly on the rudders.

There was one terrifying moment for both of us when my left foot slipped off the pedal, causing my heavy right foot to apply excessive pressure to the right rudder. The airplane's nose abruptly swerved to starboard, and we headed unerringly for the boundary fence separating the runway from the neighboring vineyards.

Forrest's feet immediately went toward the rudders, but I beat him to it, amazingly enough, and had my left foot back in position and the aircraft under control before he could take over. I noticed a strange pallor on his face as he turned toward me. His mouth was open, no doubt in an attempt to royally castigate me, if not cancel the exercise completely. However, no words came out, and his jaw snapped closed as quickly as it had opened and he turned to face the front once more.

With the aeroplane again under control and heading straight down the runway, we were airborne moments later without further incident. I put us into a gentle left bank and headed out over the Academy complex toward the training area from which I had not returned on my last flight.

We arrived in the aerobatic area about ten minutes later, and Forrest instructed me to show him the usual standard maneuvers of stalls, steep turns, incipient spins and slow flight. He then put an instrument hood over my head so that I could not see outside the aircraft, covered up some of the flight instruments with suction pads, and had me recover from several unusual attitudes on partial panel. He took control of the plane, pulled it up into a steep climbing turn to the right, then dived it and let go of the controls, telling me to take over and recover. I managed to get us back into straight and level flight without putting us into a flat spin which surely would have further imbued this man with my aviating prowess!

After one or two more attempts to have me throw up, he conceded defeat, and asked me with slightly less hostility to take him home and show him some circuits and landings.

When he had got me all calmed down and in a nice, relaxed frame of mind, the bastard did it to me! I was flying happily along gazing out my left side of the canopy when the engine died. My heart leapt into my throat and my stomach, never really convinced that we were safe, tied itself into another huge, knotted ball. Jerking my head back to the instrument panel, my eyes immediately discovered the cause of the engine failure. Forrest had waited until I was not looking and then reached forward and closed the mixture control, causing the engine to instantly quit from fuel starvation.

The propeller windmilled uselessly in the airflow, and the silence was deafening! History repeats itself. We were at about one thousand feet when it happened. The nose of the aircraft immediately went down, and I instinctively set her up for the correct glide speed.

Forrest calmly said, "Now show me your emergency actions, find a suitable field, and demonstrate your power off approach technique. Let us hope, for both our sakes, that it is considerably better than your last one."

Bastard! I'd show him, all right! My right hand automatically went to the mixture control to try to correct the obvious problem. Forrest knocked it away.

"Don't touch the power until I say you can!" he ordered vehemently.

All right! I'd show him. I was repeating myself with monotonous regularity, I thought, as I curled my lips, bared my teeth, and fought my terrible fear as the past came rushing back to haunt me.

For a few moments, I was struck motionless with terror at the thought of the pain and the months of frustrating immobility I would have to go through all over again.

NO! This is only an exercise! The engine WILL start again. It HAS to! Then I forgot about the past. My hands went about their duties with no conscious command, turning off the electrical and fuel switches and trimming for the glide, at the same time searching forward and side to side of the nose for a suitable landing field. I quickly found one that was clear of trees and other obstructions — including, and especially, power lines — and appeared to be firm, smooth ground. It was just to the left of, and almost immediately below, the aircraft.

I was going to be way too high, so I commenced a steep left turn to enable me to descend and keep the field in sight at the same time. When I knew I could make it in, I started getting out the flaps, one stage at a time.

Lower and lower we went. My stomach was cramping so badly, I thought I would be sick.

It looked good! We were going to make it.

No! Still too high. Get the flaps all the way down.

Sideslip! More yet!

Three hundred feet to go.

Two hundred.

One hundred feet above the BLOODY ground!

Pull UP, damn you, the cowardly organism inside me was shouting.

"Go around!"

His lordship did not have to tell me twice.

My left hand flashed to the switches I had turned off in preparation for the crash, then back to the yoke. My right hand hit the mixture to full rich, then the throttle to full r.p.m., then blurred around the panel re-activating the other vital switches necessary to keep us in the air. My left hand reached down to the side wall under my left knee and double-checked that the fuel valve was turned on. At the same time, I yanked the control wheel back with my now free right hand and trimmed for the best angle of climb speed to clear the trees which were now rapidly approaching from the far end of the meadow.

The engine bellowed, the tachometer quivered on the red line at twenty-seven hundred r.p.m. Flaps up, I reminded myself, operating the manual flap handle between our two seats one stage at a time. The Warrior sank slightly as I milked up the flaps, but then we were zooming away in a steep, steady climb. The scrubby trees and underbrush flashed past beneath us, seeming to reach up for our fixed wheels as we roared over the end of the field. Then, we were free of the dangerous proximity to the ground, climbing away and setting heading for the welcome sight of our own airstrip.

"Very rusty, but it was at least survivable, assuming that you had not turned us over by striking some unseen hole or obstacle on the ground, that is. I would call it a fair attempt," his nibs generously allowed, as we flew home in the bright morning sunlight.

I know what I would like to strike, I thought, my mind filled with dark and unkind words about this man. I said nothing, however, as I gritted my teeth and stared across at his unfortunate profile, noticing for the first time the tiny, broken blood vessels which wound their way across the top of his left cheek and over the bridge of his predatory beak.

I was not being very complimentary myself, I thought. After all, he might be a real nice guy under the armor of hostility. His de-briefing and report on my file and in my log book would tell the true tale.

We flew home in silence.

He had me do two touch-and-go circuits, then told me to full stop on the third one. The first two landings were acceptable, though a trifle hard. I botched the third one by bouncing us, but the Warrior settled lumpily and forgivingly back to earth and I found the toe pressure required to brake to a stop while keeping the airplane straight at the same time was not nearly as great as that required to set the park brake. I was getting there!

As we rolled to a stop, I placed my left foot atop the pedal and, as I had learned, used the entire length of my outstretched leg, to boot in full left rudder and brake, turning us to taxi back up the runway to the parking area. I turned round and stopped between, and several feet in front of, the same two aircraft that had flanked us before we departed, went carefully through the before shut-down checks, including setting the park brake once more, then drew the mixture back to idle cut-off. The engine died and the prop slowed, flicked through the last few compressions, and stopped.

John Forrest unlatched and opened the door, and got out without a word. I turned off all the switches, secured the controls, completed the shut-down check, and followed him, retrieving my cane and the aircraft documents from the back seat as I did so.

"See me in the briefing room in fifteen minutes. We will go over the areas you need to work on," was all the Chief Flying Instructor could manage to say as he turned and strode back toward his office. My thoughts of him were rather unkind at that moment!

He had left me to push the Warrior back into its slot between the other two aircraft by myself! I hobbled round to the nose of the plane, hooked my cane over my right arm, and pushed on the spinner. And pushed! And then angrily remembered that I had set the parking brake. Cursing vehemently, I returned to the cockpit, climbed back in with practised ease, and again went through the extreme effort of releasing the brake by the method discovered earlier. Panting with exertion, I jumped down, limped heavily to the front of the aircraft once more, and with great difficulty and much sweating and swearing, managed to push the plane back into its allotted space.

Once more unto the brake, dear friends . . .

Bloody parking brake would be the death of me!

Little did I realize at that angry moment that the simple exercise of setting and releasing the parking brake, combined with the long-term effect of dancing on the rudders, would serve to strengthen my hamstrings and ankle muscles more quickly than any other physiotherapy that I could have undertaken to achieve the same result. My return to the air would provide the final therapy I needed to enable me to at last free myself of my handicap.

As I limped over to the administration building, I greeted some of the other cadets heading for the flight line. By the time I got there, the fifteen minutes his eminence had so graciously granted me to recover from my ordeal had already expired. I entered the briefing room, sat at a table in front of the blackboard, and awaited his unwelcome return. Five minutes later, Forrest stepped into the room with a steaming mug of coffee in his hand. I would not have accepted one from him on this hot morning even if he had offered, which he didn't, of course!

He sat on the edge of the table and sipped at his brew for a few minutes, pensively gazing out the window toward the flight line. Finally his unblinking, lizard-like stare came to rest on my forehead, which he seemed to study as if it was a totally foreign object.

"Well Rod, considering your handicap, you did quite well," he began.

Thanks for nothing, I thought.

"However, before I sign you off as completely ready for your check ride, I want you to have one or two revisional sessions with one of the other instructors. When he considers you are ready, I will personally conduct the check ride, and if satisfactory, I will report you physically sound for the requirements of the Medical Section of the Department of Aviation. They may still want one of their examiners to give you another ride. You will certainly be required to undergo a special check when you attempt your first multi-engine rating."

I nodded. I could think of no earth-shattering reply to his monologue, so with great difficulty, I kept my mouth shut.

"Now then," he continued, "as to your efforts today. You are obviously having difficulty coping with the brakes and rudders. Not unusual under the circumstances."

I felt my face boil with anger.

"You seemed to be coping with this problem much better by the time we taxied in, so you will no doubt be able to overcome this. Your general flying was quite safe. Turns were coordinated well and you did not seem to have any worries with the rudder pedals in the air. Unusual attitudes were well recovered, although much too slowly for my liking. Your judgment on the engine failure left much to be desired. You should have 'S' turned down to that field to keep it in sight instead of that three-sixty

205

degree turn. You do NOT perform steep turns at low altitude under any circumstances, and especially with no power. You were too high for the entire approach; perhaps a natural reluctance as a result of your accident, but something which must be overcome if you are ever to learn to face the same situation again, and survive."

I sat there ashen-faced, enraged at the bastard for ripping into me like this. Five months since I had flown, all that time just learning to walk again, and he was criticizing the successful outcome of the very exercise which nearly killed me before. Maybe he had been afraid himself. He certainly would not admit it to me, though.

"Your circuits and landings weren't too bad," he continued, "but they will need more work, too. That's about it. I will check on you in a few days to see if you are ready for the actual license ride. All right?"

He actually smiled at me. More like the salivary grin of a starving vulture, but it was a smile, nevertheless. He obviously did not expect or require any questions or comments. Rising from him perch on the table, he strode out of the room, coffee mug still firmly gripped in his hand.

I was left with an empty, hollow feeling in my stomach, which was admittedly a change from the tangle, knotted cramp it replaced. He had made it sound as if I was a just-soloed novice with another eight months of training ahead of me. Well, the hell with him! I'd show him what I could really do the next time I saw him! I promised myself that I literally would not rest until I passed that final check ride with him.

Returning to my room, I threw myself onto my bunk to contemplate the next few days of tortuous training. Was it all worth it? What a ridiculous question! I had just flown again for the first time since becoming a paraplegic and being told I would never regain the use of my lower limbs. Why the hell was I feeling sorry for myself just because one insensitive man criticized my ability? After all, that was his job, was it not?

The unmistakable aroma of fried food wafted in through the door of my room, reminding me that it was lunch time already. I was starving after the energy I had expended in the last few hours. I got to my feet and hobbled over to the mess hall, quickly forgetting my encounter with the Chief Flying Instructor.

As the week wore on, my flying abilities became more and more polished under the watchful and patient eye of my old instructor, Chris, who had requested that he be assigned to me to assist me with my re-indoctrination. I was very grateful to him for this, and I was also pleased to be back in the cockpit with someone whose abilities and instincts I admired and trusted implicitly.

My feel for the aircraft returned swiftly and with amazing ease. By the end of that week, Chris pronounced me fit for the check ride. He took me up for a two and a half hour cross-country simulated license check, on which he observed all my navigation skills, together with my general handling and normal and emergency procedures. He concentrated on my engine failure and forced landing routine. I told him of the incident with Forrest, and frankly admitted my absolute terror when he had caused the engine to quit.

"I guess that's a perfectly natural reaction, after what you have been through as a result of an engine failure," Chris said sympathetically, "but it's something that you simply must overcome, or you will never be any good in the cockpit. You know, probably better than anyone, that the difference between a good pilot and a dead one is always being prepared for the worst to happen, and to know what to do about it when it does."

So we practiced engine failures; over and over again; every time I least expected it. Soon, I had completely overcome my fear of the sudden, horrible silence when the engine quit. I instantly and automatically went through the emergency cockpit procedures while unconsciously setting the aircraft up in the correct attitude to reach the field I always had picked out in my mind at every stage of the flight. There was always some road or paddock or meadow that was big enough and flat enough to accommodate a Warrior, if the approach was correct. I practiced so as to make damn sure the approach was always correct!

"By George, I think you've got it!" Chris exclaimed, after tiring of the game ,which by now had become second nature to me.

I managed to pull off a perfect 'greaser' landing when we touched down back at the strip. As we taxied to the ramp, I noticed that the operation of the brakes and rudders was becoming decidedly easier. When I brought the plane to a stop, I found that although I still had to place the soles of my feet on top of the toe brakes and apply pressure using the length of my legs for leverage, it seemed that the effort required was not as great as it had been.

As we jumped down from the wing, Chris turned to me with a grin.

"Well, mate, I think you're ready for the big one with his nibs. I'm not even going to send you out for some solo practice. The last time I did that, you disappeared on me."

As my face fell about six feet, he hurriedly added, "Just kidding, Rod. I don't think even old buzzard-beak will be able to fault you now. I am going to program you for your check ride tomorrow, while you're still hot. Now let's go get something to eat."

17

The following morning at ten a.m., I stood nervously waiting by Charlie November November. The day was clear and hot. My palms, like the rest of me, perspired profusely. I had completed the pre-flight inspection and now there was nothing to do but wait for John Forrest to arrive.

This was what I had been preparing myself for since the day of the accident six months ago. My fate rested in the hands of the Chief Flying Instructor! If I screwed anything up this morning, I could kiss my flying career good-bye.

I glanced down at my hands and noticed with dismay that they were trembling. C'mon, Lewin. Get a grip on yourself! After all, he IS only human, despite rumors to the contrary. Do the bloody job properly, and he can't fault you. It's as simple as that! But what if...? Shuddup! Talking to myself was definitely not a good sign!

Any further self-recrimination was abruptly terminated by the arrival of my lordly examiner-of-airmen, crunching his way across the gravel, hands tucked behind his back, searching the ground for insects to crush.

"Good morning, sir!" I greeted him cheerily, trying my best to get off to a good start with him.

"Morning, Rod. Let's get on with it, shall we? I assume you have performed the pre-flight already?"

"Yes sir. I . . . "

"Very well, then. I know you can do that properly! Let's find out what you cannot do."

Bloody dingo!

He fidgeted impatiently as I scrambled with my usual difficulty into the cockpit, then he followed me in. We sat there in the scorching heat as I ran through the pre-start checklist. When I had finished, he simply said, "Let's go!"

I fired up the engine, and we were away on the longest two hours of my life. Apart from telling me to show him specific maneuvers at certain points along the route, he spoke not at all during the entire exercise, except to tell me he wanted me to deviate from my flight plan and return to base via another route, which just happened to pass over some very mountainous terrain with absolutely no place to land on the thick, densely forested slopes.

It didn't take a genius to guess why he had chosen this route. And I was proven right very shortly. At least this time I was expecting it. Suddenly his left hand snaked out and pulled the mixture lever all the way back into idle cut-off! We were about three thousand feet above the highest terrain when he did it. My brain immediately surged into emergency gear and before either of us knew it, we were set up for the glide, and had all the switches in the correct positions. There was only one minor problem. We had no place to go!

John Forrest just sat there, arms folded, in stony silence, watching and waiting.

The only sound was the whistling of the airflow as it passed over the surfaces of the aircraft. The silence was almost unbearable. I circled in a gentle turn like a giant condor as we glided down, lower and lower, searching for a suitable place to put the plane down.

There was no such place!

If this had been a genuine emergency we would be landing in the tops of the trees. Suddenly, through the thick leaves and branches below, I thought I saw a narrow gap in the foliage. A splash of reddish yellow caught my eye, then was gone.

There it was again! A barely visible dirt road winding through the bush. I lined up on the straightest stretch I could find. The wingtips would probably be taken off in the descent below the treetops, but we should be able to land reasonably intact. I got the flaps out and steepened our approach to keep a close watch on the evasive track.

At two hundred above the foliage, the engine roared as his grace returned the fuel supply to me. I shoved the throttle up to maximum, hauled up the flaps, and pulled the Warrior up into a maximum rate climb, readjusting the trim as I did so. Forrest remained silent, with arms folded and eyes staring straight ahead. We landed at the Academy exactly two hours and thirty-three minutes after we had departed. As we taxied into the parking area, he opened the door and stepped onto the wing, jumping to the ground a moment after I had stopped the engine.

"See me in my office in ten minutes," he said with about as much emotion as a professional hangman.

He began to stride away, then half-turned back to me. He almost smiled.

"By the way," he said grudgingly, "you passed."

He strutted off without another word.

I did not care! The few words he had spoken, despite their tone, were music to my ears. They meant the successful culmination of eight months of hard study, followed by six months of agony, frustration and hopelessness. I had won! By sheer determination and plain pig-headedness, I had beaten the odds! Oh, I still had the tell-tale braces on my legs. I still limped with a cane like a drunken sailor. But these things I could eventually overcome. I was as sure of that as I was sure that I was going to walk again the day my parents told me I would.

The thing was that at last, I had my Commercial Pilot's License. There was no holding me back now!

I secured the aircraft, patted it on the nose like a faithful old dog, and hobbled over to the administration building. The heat of the midday sun burned down on my bare head, causing rivulets of sweat to run through my hair and down my forehead and face.

Halfway across the ramp, Chris came running up to me and began excitedly pumping my hand, almost tearing my arm out of its socket.

"I just heard from the old man," he said with a huge, infectious grin. "Congratulations, Rod. Congratulations! You have probably made aviation history here today. Certainly in this country. Perhaps the world!"

Tears welled in my eyes, despite my efforts at nonchalance. "Thanks, Chris," was all I could manage to choke in reply.

He took my arm and we walked over to the 'old man's' office together. I knocked on his open door. He was sitting at his desk, filling out a ream of paperwork on top of which was prominently displayed the green, hard-backed wallet which contained the blue-bordered pages of my new license. He looked up as I knocked.

"Come in, Rod. You too, Chris," he added, as Chris turned away. "Sit down, both of you. I'll be with you in a minute."

He continued to busy himself at the paperwork for several minutes longer, then put down his pen and clasped his huge hands together and placed them squarely on top of all the red tape.

"Well, Chris, it appears that you have done an outstanding job with him," he said, speaking directly to Chris as if I was not present in the room. "His ride today was a vast improvement over the last one — and a million times better than his last solo," he said, referring to the near fatal flight six months before.

I squirmed uncomfortably in my seat.

He looked at me then, and his face actually softened into a semblance of kindness. "As for you, Rod, I must admit that when you returned here, I did not expect you to be capable of safely controlling an aircraft — at least, to commercial pilot standards, anyway. You have, however, demonstrated that you can do just that. Therefore, as a designated examiner-of-airmen appointed by the Department of Transport, I am presenting you this license, with some reservations, I must admit. Do not do anything to make me think I have made a terrible error of judgment."

We both stood, and he handed me the license, shaking my hand reluctantly as he did so.

"Congratulations, Rod," he added, indicating that the interview was ended.

"I . . . uh, thank you, sir," I stammered in awkward reply, "thank you very much!"

I turned and stumbled out of his office, my head spinning and my eyes watering. I thought I was going to pass out with the emotion of the moment. Chris took my arm again and led me back to my quarters, where we spent the next half hour rejoicing, and re-hashing what Forrest had put me through on the check ride. Chris left shortly after that, to go up with another student.

As I lay on my bunk in the semi-darkness of the room, still clutching the proof of my official recognition as a commercial pilot, I reflected on all the adversities that had brought me to this moment. The end of the beginning was over at last!

The next week dragged on forever, as I loafed around waiting for the rest of the students in Green Flight to finish their course and pass their check rides. The following Saturday was the big day. Fortunately for me, heavy rain was pouring from a leaden sky that day, so the Academy management decided, for the benefit of the students' guests, to dispense with the march-out onto the parade ground for the ceremonial presentation of wings. I was not looking forward to making an ass of myself by having to hobble out, while twenty-five other fellows in full uniform marched smartly, in perfect step, arms a-swinging, in ranks of three, to come to a perfect military heel-clicking halt before the dais.

Instead, we all gathered just prior to the appointed hour of three p.m. in the cavernous recreation room, which had been cleared of all games equipment by students of one of the junior flights. A mobile dais had been set up for the occasion, and we all formed up before it in ranks of three and were stood at ease by the Academy Captain, who had replaced me when I did not return from my near-fatal flight.

As soon as we were in position, the guests were invited into the room from an adjoining ante-room where they were being entertained by the instructors and staff.

At precisely three o'clock on the afternoon of March 19th, exactly six months to the day since my near-fatal crash, Jim Flint, accompanied by the Chief Flying Instructor, entered the room with their special guest, the Governor of the State of New South Wales, who was to have the honor of presenting the wings. He was an old Royal Australian Air Force man, and had a special interest in the Academy. As they mounted the dais, we snapped smartly to attention.

Well, most of us snapped smartly to attention. I just about knocked myself and the cadet next to me over in my attempt to get my steel-bound legs together in a reasonable facsimile of smartness! I stood swaying on my one cane, trying to regain my balance. Glancing sideways, I noticed that my neighbor was clenching his teeth in silent agony. I looked down and saw, to my horror, that my cane was now firmly planted on his left foot!

Jim Flint opened the proceedings with an address to the assembled crowd, then invited the guest-of-honor to present wings to the graduating students. The Governor gave a short speech of his own, then began calling out the names of the cadets in alphabetical order. As each graduate marched up, the Chief Flying Instructor passed a pair of gold wings, displayed on a purple velvet pillow, to the Governor, who in turn pinned them on the white uniform shirt of the cadet before him, shook his hand, and said a few words to him. As each cadet returned to the ranks, the guests applauded him.

When my name was called, I stepped out of the front rank, where I had been deliberately placed to make my exit and re-entry less difficult, and stumped up to the dais with my usual rolling gait. It was immediately and embarrassingly obvious from the moment I stepped forward that the crowd was well aware of my presence and my achievement. They loudly applauded me all the way to the dais, ceased while His Excellency pinned on my wings and spoke to me, and then applauded me even more loudly as I limped back to my position.

I almost made it, but the other graduates began to join in the applause before I could get to the safety and anonymity of the ranks. The noise grew to a crescendo, then finally died away. My quest for wings had earned me much more than a three inch gold pin. I had gained the respect and admiration of my fellow students — my peers. They continued to clap as I stumbled back into line and turned my now bright red face to the dais.

As the din of the applause gradually subsided, the next cadet's name was called. He stepped forward, and I thankfully blended back into the ranks once more. When all the cadets had been presented with their wings, the assembly broke up and the crowd of guests mingled with the graduates, talking and eating and drinking the refreshments provided by the management.

I found that I was a celebrity. There was no escape. Just when I got through answering one barrage of questions about my recovery and return to flying, somebody else would corner me and ask me the same questions all over again. It was five o'clock before I finally managed to slip out of the room and back to the seclusion of my quarters, where I fell onto my bunk to ponder what the future held in store for me now.

❖

18

The following morning, I bid good-bye to my new-found friends at the Academy, and drove out the gates for the last time, savoring the freedom of the road and the exhilaration of speed in my 240Z once more. I was in a euphoric mood as I headed north for Brisbane. Having at last won my wings, I was now free to get on with my life and find myself a niche in the aviation world. There was still a nagging feeling of loneliness and emptiness somewhere in the back of my consciousness, but I pushed it down and thought of nothing but the road ahead, seeing my parents and sisters again, and the opportunities waiting for me around the next bend.

Three hours after I had departed the Academy, I made a gas stop and got some coffee to keep me going. Then I drove until I could no longer keep my eyes open and the 'Z' started drifting dangerously. It was past nightfall when I finally gave up and pulled into a motel by the highway. I don't remember hitting the bed. I awoke the next morning, refreshed and ready to continue my six hundred mile drive north to the city of my birth.

I had a good breakfast, delivered to the room in traditional Aussie motel style, and washed it down with strong coffee and orange juice. After showering, I dressed comfortably, checked out and hit the road once more.

Late that afternoon, I entered the outskirts of Brisbane, and half an hour later I was coasting up the familiar cedar-lined street that held thousands of boy-hood memories. It had been a long time since I had seen this street and these wonderful houses in which lived my friends and neighbors of years past.

As I reached the end of the street, I did the usual one-eighty degree turn and pulled up under one of the scrubby cedars outside my parents' house. I had not told them that I was coming home, so I did not know whether they would be there or not, but as I braked to a stop, I saw the familiar yellow Toyota station wagon in the driveway, and my heart leapt in eager anticipation of seeing my folks again.

I honked the tinny sounding sports horns of the 'Z', opened my door, strugled out of the low slung seat, and hobbled round the stubby trunk. As I stepped up onto the sidewalk, my mother opened the front door and came running up the front path, dabbing at her eyes with a handkerchief as she cried her customary welcome. That precipitated a flood of tears from my own eyes. We hugged tightly and walked arm in arm down the path and onto the front porch as Dad came out to see what the commotion was about. He had no doubt been downstairs in the garage, where he spent most of his spare time, tinkering with some broken appliance or gadget.

The three of us hugged together and we went inside to the kitchen. Dad brewed the coffee and Mum served up huge chunks of my favorite rum-laced fruit cake, and we sat there catching up on everything that had happened to me. Mum began preparing dinner early as usual, and the three of us continued to chat about my days at the Academy and my plans for the future. At precisely five-thirty p.m., as had been her practice for the last thirty years, she served up dinner. It was my favorite roast beef, in honor of the unexpected return of the prodigal son.

After dinner, we sat around for hours, just getting to know each other once more. I phoned my two younger sisters, who were both married and lived quite a distance from my parents. One lived on a cattle ranch about three hundred miles west of Brisbane with her husband, three kids, and an unknown number of cows, bulls, horses, kangaroos and other assorted animals. The other lived with her husband on five acres of natural bush way over on the other side of town, where they played nursemaid to

217

almost as varied a menagerie. I promised them that we would all get together as soon as possible.

The next few weeks were some of the happiest I ever remember. For the first week, my folks and I went to the famous Gold Coast about sixty miles southeast of Brisbane, where we stayed in a beachfront unit and surfed and sunned and generally had a wonderful, relaxing time. Nobody seemed to notice or care about the calipers on my legs, and soon my own self-consciousness wore off, and I ignored them as if they did not exist.

Early in the first morning on the Coast, I hobbled across the street and onto the beach, where my shoes quickly filled with sand, bogging me down. I sat in the warm, fine, white sand, removed the calipers and shoes and dragged myself down to the water's edge. After a few hesitant minutes, I plucked up the courage to drag myself all the way into the roiling surf. Once there, I found I was completely at home. My upper legs were strong enough to kick normally, so it did not matter that my feet dragged. I could swim almost as well as I had always been able to.

I swam out far enough from shore to get a good ride back in on the surf, then let the huge blue and white waves carry me to the beach. Time and time again I swam out and let the waves carry me back, until I was absolutely exhausted. Finally, I dragged myself up the beach again, where I had to re-don my calipers to walk home.

This was entirely too much of an inconvenience, so that afternoon, I visited the local hospital and borrowed a couple of old wooden crutches. From then on, when I was going swimming, I left the calipers and shoes off and used the crutches only to get me down to the water. This was an awkward process, as my feet were still dragging uselessly. I found the easiest method was to put both crutches in front of me, lift both legs up high enough to clear my drooping feet off the ground, then forward, then down. Sometimes my toes and feet curled under in the uneven sand, and I tripped myself up on several occasions, but I finally got the hang of it.

I swam hard every morning before the beach got too crowded, and sometimes again in the evening. It quickly became obvious that this was precisely the therapy I needed to strengthen my weak ankle and hamstring muscles. The tremendous resistance of the water as I moved my legs up and dawn was having a noticeable effect on my lower limbs.

After a week of hard swimming, I saw and felt the difference in my ability to control the movement of my feet. I could actually lift my feet almost to a horizontal position, and although they became weak again after a few steps, I did not have to lift my legs as far to prevent my feet from turning under. This turn of events was extremely encouraging. I decided that I would continue to swim every day.

When we did return to Brisbane, I got into the habit of visiting a nearby public swimming pool every morning, and followed the same routine I had developed in the surf. Dad would come with me, pace me in the water, and keep pushing me even when I thought my legs were going to fall off with pain and fatigue.

After several more weeks of this strenuous exercise, I found that my feet were almost controllable. There was muscle on the back and sides of my lower legs where before there had been only atrophied skin and bone.

I had also been experimenting at home with walking without the calipers. With the increasing strength in my feet and lower leg muscles, I thought it might now be possible to walk unaided. I found that I could just get by without the calipers. However, I had to revert to using two canes. I had to lean heavily on them, and my rolling walk was so slow and awkward that I found it was as yet impractical to try it in public. I did not want a repeat performance of my antics in Sydney. After all, this was my own town; people knew me!

There was one encouraging sign of improvement. A couple of days after returning from the coast, I decided to try walking without the support of the one cane I had been using. I donned the calipers and, using the walls of the hallway at home for moral support, I stumped up and down the house, flinging my arms in all directions for balance. My folks were horrified, of course, at the imminent threat of untold damage to the house and its precious contents. Mum made many unkind remarks, but the experiment was a success.

From then on, apart from the calipers on my legs and their supporting braces on my shoes, I walked completely unaided. Oh, I rolled around like a drunken sailor all right, and once I was even apprehended in downtown Brisbane by a police officer who would have arrested me for being 'drunk and disorderly' had I not lifted my trouser legs and shown him my braces. He then apologized profusely, and with great embarrassment hurried away without a backward glance!

In the weeks that followed, although I was still very contented to be home, I grew increasingly restless to be on the move again. The nagging worry persisted in the back of my mind that John Martin, the trusting car dealer, would soon be sending the repo men after me, despite my parents' offer to cover the payments until I could find a job.

I pushed down this yearning for a little longer, as I had decided that I would not go anywhere until I could walk without the use of the calipers.

My feet and ankles were becoming stronger by the day now, and it would not hurt me to stay for a while longer. After all, I did not know when I would see my parents again, once I left home this time. I did not know where I was going, so how could I know when I was coming back?

Three weeks after I had begun to walk without a cane, I tried once more to walk without the calipers. The daily swimming had been of such a tremendous help to my lower limbs that I now felt confident that I should be able to walk unaided at last. My parents stood by, watching in horrified dismay as I sat down and removed my calipers and shoes. I unscrewed the nuts which held the supporting braces in place in holes drilled through the heels of my shoes. I replaced the shoes on my feet, noticing for the first time that my toes did not curl under nearly as much as they used to.

I gripped the arms of the chair and hoisted myself to my feet. For a few moments, I stood there, trembling on the brink of my greatest triumph. I was very glad that I was here at home for my parents to see the final outcome of my long, frustrating, personal battle against my paralysis. They had been of tremendous help and encouragement through the entire ordeal, even though they were not actually present for much of it. Now at last, they could witness my final victory.

I leaned to the right, barely keeping my balance without the cane to lean on, lifted my left leg high enough to counter the residual foot drop, and put my left foot forward. So far, so good. For a second or two, I teetered on the brink of unbalance. I decided the only way to counter it was to put my other foot forward. I took a deep breath, leaned forward and stepped out with my right foot. Slowly but surely, I limped up the hallway, throwing my arms about for balance as I had when I discarded the second cane. By the time I made it to the end of the hall, I was as exhausted as I had been that day in the hospital when I first walked with the calipers. I leaned against the wall panting, but entirely satisfied with the result of six months effort.

My mother stood there weeping uncontrollably, dabbing at her eyes with her ever-present handkerchief. They both came to me and the three of us embraced emotionally. There were no words that could express what we were feeling just then.

I had won! With the unceasing assistance, understanding and encouragement of many people, I had finally beaten the odds and won the greatest battle of my life. Doctor John Yeoman, in his wisdom and experience, had once told me that despite the skillful surgery he had performed on my back, I would never walk again. Flying, of course, was simply out of the question. Well, I HAD walked again! And flown again! Yes indeed! I had finally won!

When I regained my breath, I staggered back to the lounge and sat down in the same chair from which I had started. There was still a lot of work and frustration ahead of me. It would be a long time before I felt completely comfortable on my own two feet, but I had come so far now, that the little distance left to go was nothing. I still went to the pool every day. With the combined effort of the swimming and the walking, my legs became stronger by the hour. I also got into the habit of using my left foot on the brake in the car now, which helped a great deal as well.

The stronger my legs became, the greater was the desire to move on up the track, searching for a flying job. I had been out of work since I signed up at the Academy more than a year ago. Now, with my Commercial Pilot's License, it was time for me to try to find a job, and finally do what I had always wanted to.

I was strongly tempted to return to Sydney. I tried to justify that temptation by arguing to myself that there would be more opportunity for a flying job down there. But I knew in my heart that there was only one reason why I really wanted to go back, and so I resisted the urge and decided to head in the opposite direction.

Accordingly, a week after I began walking completely unaided, I broke the news to my parents.

"I think it's about time I started looking elsewhere for a job," I said hesitantly. "I have knocked on every door at every airport around Brisbane, and there is nothing available; at least, nothing for someone in my condition. I'm going to head north up the coast and see what I can find. Don't worry, Ma. I'll be just fine. I'm a big boy now. I can even walk."

My mother cried as usual, but understood completely.

"I know, mate. We have been expecting it for a long time. Ever since you came home, I have been dreading the day you would leave us again. But I know you must. Just remember that your home is always here, no matter what happens."

"Thanks Ma. Thanks Pa. I'll be back. And I'll write often. Don't worry."

They helped me pack that night, and the next morning, after Dad had filled my belly with a huge pile of scrambled eggs, bacon, toast and coffee unequaled by anyone but Nellie, I sadly loaded my bag, flight kit, and golf clubs into the short trunk of the 240Z.

We said an emotional good-bye amid another stream of waterworks courtesy of Mum. I reluctantly pulled away from them and slid down into the driving seat of the car. I was hard pressed not to cry myself. I did not know when, or indeed if, I would ever see them again.

They stood on the sidewalk with their arms around each other's waist, waving and wishing me good luck. I hit the starter. The engine bellowed, I put her in 'Drive,' waved through the passenger window, and drove away on my search for . . . I did not know what I was searching for. All I knew was that I would find it.

❖

19

My heart was light and my belly was a-flutter with excitement and anticipation as I drove through the northern suburbs of Brisbane on that bright, sub-tropical morning, but at the same time I felt a deep sadness at leaving my folks again. Every time I said good-bye to them, doubts and misgivings filled my mind, making me wonder if I was doing the right thing. What was I searching for? Would I ever find it, or was my restless heart just a kindred spirit to the wayward wind?

One thing I did know: I had fought the greatest personal battle of my life — and won! Nothing could ever beat me again. No matter how frustrated I became in the future with any undertaking, I knew I could always beat any challenge, if given the chance.

The earth and sky were clean and clear from a downpour of heavy, cleansing rain during the night. The 240Z seemed to sense the excitement within me, and with the solid concrete pavement of Highway One under her wheels, she surged ahead, sniffing at the slipstream with her long, green snout. It had been many years since I had driven north on this main artery from Brisbane to the tropical towns and cities of idyllic North Queensland, flanked on the ocean side by thousands of islands separating the shore from the Great Barrier Reef. I had forgotten what a magnificent coastline this really was!

We wound through the natural bushland, past the Glasshouse Mountains, so named in 1770 by Captain James Cook, the English explorer, as he observed them from the deck of his tiny ship the *Endeavour,* because of their glasshouse appearance as the sun reflected off their steep, rocky slopes.

After several hours of driving, the country gradually and subtly changed from densely timbered mountainous bush to rolling flatlands, mostly covered by fields of sugarcane which stretched for nearly a thousand miles up the coast. On the ocean side of the highway, enormous breakers pounded the white, sandy shoreline for a hundred miles north of Brisbane.

As I drove further north, however, the huge surf died down as a result of being pushed further and further out to sea by the intrusion of the Reef. The southern end of this extraordinary phenomenon, considered by many scientists to be the eighth wonder of the world, lies abeam the city of Gladstone, and stretches more than one thousand two hundred miles north to the very top of the east coast of the Australian continent. The deep blue of the ocean changed to lighter colors of turquoise, reflecting the shallow, sandy waters surrounding the islands of the reef. A renewed sense of wonder and awe filled my consciousness. I breathed deeply of the salty air, sensing that my future happiness and contentment lay somewhere ahead on the waters of the Great Barrier Reef.

At every major town I came to, I stopped at the municipal airport, inquiring if anybody needed the services of a pilot. The answer was always the same.

"Sorry. We don't need anyone right now," or "Sorry. We just hired someone the other day," or "Sorry. You don't have enough flying experience to satisfy our insurance requirements."

It was a long, frustrating day. But I had expected nothing less, and was not deterred by the negative results. I stopped late that first evening at Rockhampton, about four hundred miles north of Brisbane, found a good motel, dined well in the restaurant, and slept like a log.

The next morning was fine, clear and hot as usual. I visited the Rockhampton airport on the way out of town, with the same result as yesterday. Not at all discouraged, I jumped back into the 240 and continued my journey up the coast, enjoying every minute of the drive, and marveling at the changing scenery, the screeching of wild cockatoos and galahs, and the magnificent coastal views of shimmering blue water, fine white sand, and verdant tropical islands.

I stopped for a counter lunch in one of the many fine old hotels in Mackay, checked the airport afterwards, with no luck, then drove north again. Cane fields lined the highway almost continuously in this area. The stuff stood about ten feet tall in places, and it was like driving through a living, swaying, green and yellow maze.

About two hours later, still deep in sugarcane country, I passed the outskirts of the town of Proserpine. The highway forked just outside the town. The left branch became Main Street, Proserpine. The right fork was the highway. I decided to pass the town, as I had already visited the airport about ten miles back.

Two or three miles further along the road, I came to another intersection. The huge green sign announced 'Airlie Beach and Shute Harbor.' A large white arrow pointed off to the right, indicating a narrow road, winding through more cane fields. The instant I saw that sign, I had the eeriest feeling of deja-vu. I could not remember the last time I had traveled this road. Perhaps I had indeed passed this way some time in my earlier years. In any case, before I was consciously aware of it, the wheel was turning and the car was heading down that narrow road towards the coast.

The main highway had been tracking steadily inland since leaving Mackay, so I was at least ten miles from the ocean now. The cane fields gave way to bush again. Eucalyptus trees and thick brush lined the road and covered the low hills through which it wound.

Shortly afterwards, I came to the outskirts of a small community. A sign indicated that the name of the place was Cannonvale. I slowed to the posted forty kilometers per hour as I drove past a tiny police station, a few stores and a gas station, and there, just as the road made a sharp right turn, was the sparkling blue water of the Whitsunday Passage.

The gentle waves of the protected waters inside the reef lapped at a small, pebbled beach. Battered wooden palings of an old shark-proof swimming enclosure protruded about fifty yards out into the clean, clear sea. Small boats bobbed on their moorings in shallow water around the enclosure.

I drove very slowly along the narrow, curving road, enjoying the view as I followed the coastline. Seaside houses, bungalows and cottages climbed up the hill on the shore side of the road. Another lovely little beach came into view around a left hand curve, then the road sloped up a steep incline. Houses on the right, blue, blue water on the left. At the top of the rise, a clear, unpaved area on the left side of the road gave me a chance to stop and admire the view.

And what a view it was! I will never forget the first time I saw that magnificent panorama! It lives in my memory still, like a color slide I can flash before my eyes at will.

Immediately below and behind me were the two beaches I had just passed. I was standing on top of a small headland. The road wound down the hill to my right. In front of me lay the northern islands of the famous Whitsunday Passage, also named by the industrious Captain Cook as he passed through the area in 1770 on the ancient English sabbath known as Whit Sunday.

All around the headland, as far as the eye could see, was the bluest, clearest, calmest water I had ever seen in all my years of traveling the world! Below and to the right lay the town of Airlie Beach, once a sleepy seaside village, now a vibrant tourist town, the gateway to the Whitsunday Islands with their many resorts and beautiful beaches.

I struggled out of the seat and limped round the car to stand on the grassy headland and gaze out at the islands in the passage. A gentle breeze stirred the grass and rustled the eucalyptus leaves of a lone gum tree on the hillside. The tang of the salt air was exhilarating, and I felt an inner peace I had never before experienced. Somehow, I knew then that this was going to be my home for the foreseeable future.

Shielding my face with hand against the glare coming off the brilliant blue sea, I squinted down to my right toward Airlie Bay. Hundreds of sail and power boats of every size and shape rode at anchor beyond the point below. The half-moon beach was lined with palm trees and littered with semi-naked bodies baking themselves in the tropic sun.

What an incredibly beautiful place!

It was totally unlike the Gold Coast I had visited with my parents a few weeks before, where high rise apartment buildings lined the edge of the ocean for twenty miles. This town I now admired from above had not one high rise building! It had obviously been planned that way, as most of the structures appeared to be new, but with no more than two levels. I could see the entire length of the main street from where I stood. It was not more than half a mile long, flanked on both sides by shops, motels, and restaurants. The oddest thing instantly attracted me to the place. I noticed that there was not one single traffic light, parking meter or neon sign in the whole town.

This had to be Paradise!

I let my eyes sweep around the magnificent vista one more time, took another deep breath of the hot, salty air, then hobbled back to the car to continue my exploration. My legs were still too weak to move quickly, and occasionally, my knees gave way or I tripped over my feet, causing me to stumble.

I drove into Airlie Beach and drifted slowly down the main street. Dozens of boutiques and travel agencies and restaurants lined the narrow thoroughfare. Before I knew it, I was out the other side of the town. Thick bush and scrub closed in around the road immediately as the town ended at another small cove, where a number of boats were pulled up on the sandy shore for repairs. Houses and shops became fewer now, and the road once again wound through densely wooded flatland. About five minutes driving brought me to the base of a large, scrub-covered hill. The car surged up the rise, as if anxious to see what was on the other side.

As we crested the summit, still surrounded by thick scrub, I began to catch glimpses of a lush, green valley below. At the bottom of the incline, the road took a sharp turn to the right, and it became immediately apparent that the valley through which I was now driving lay between two ranges of scrub-covered hills, roughly paralleling the coastline. I began to see patches of blue water through the trees to the left of the road. There was a sheltered bay at this end of the valley. A dirt track led off in the direction of the water, but I decided to explore it later, when I had discovered where the main road led me.

Behind tall grass to the left of the road, the center stretch of the valley ran parallel to my direction of travel, and appeared to have a flat, hard surface, covered with short grass. In fact, it almost looked like an airstrip! Thirty seconds later, my suspicions were verified. I came to an intersection which could quite easily have been missed had it not been for a prominent red and white sign pointing off to the left and bearing the words "Air Whitsunday — The Great Barrier Reef Airline."

I braked and turned hard left onto a narrow asphalt track. It was less than a hundred yards long. The first half had the same thick scrub on either side. The last half was cleared and lined with tall coconut palms, their bases surrounded by well manicured grass, on both sides of the track. It ended in a circular parking area, to the left of which was an attractive little hewn-log terminal building. The airstrip stretched about two thousand feet to the left, and about one thousand to the right of the building, then abruptly ended in more thick bush.

There were no aircraft in sight, and nobody appeared to be about. The building was empty and locked. A hand-printed note on the sliding glass door announced, "If terminal unattended, please come to office through trees on other side of parking area."

I got back in the car, turned it around the way I had come, and immediately noticed another parking area to my left, almost hidden by the trees. A dirt walking track led off into the bush. I again parked the car, got out and limped a short distance through trees and scrub until I arrived in a small clearing. In the center of the clearing was an old, unpainted aluminum trailer with another Air Whitsunday sign emblazoned across the front in red and white letters. Around the trailer were wooden benches roughly cut from the very trees that had been chopped down to make the clearing. Off through the trees, about fifty yards behind the trailer and almost hidden by the bush, I could just glimpse the outline of another structure which appeared to be a residence.

I approached the trailer with excitement mounting in my stomach. The door and windows were open and screened to allow the cooling ocean breeze in and keep the hostile bugs out. The sound of girls' voices and laughter came from within. As I knocked on the side of the flimsy structure, the sounds tapered off, and a moment later, the screen door opened and one of the girls appeared.

"Hi! What can I do for you?" she greeted.

"Hello," I replied, smiling back. "My name is Rod Lewin. Actually, I'm looking for work. I was just driving by and I noticed the airstrip and my curiosity got the better of me."

"Come on in," she said.

As I ducked my head and ungracefully hoisted myself up the one high step into the 'office,' she spoke again.

"I'm Annie," she said, stubbing out a cigarette, and, pointing to the other girl, added, "and this is Di."

"Hi there," said Di, flashing a huge, infectious grin at me. "Did you say you are looking for work?"

"Yes, flying," I replied simply.

"Well," Annie replied thoughtfully, "there's nobody here right now who could help you with that. All the boys are out at the reef, aren't they Di?"

"That's right," she replied. "But Kevin in on his way back in. He should be here in about twenty minutes. Did you say you're a pilot?"

"That's right," I replied, rather self-consciously.

"Well, it just so happens that Kevin is in fact looking for another pilot. I'm sure he would like to talk to you. Why don't you have a cup of coffee and wait around for a bit. He won't be long."

"Thanks very much!" I replied, scarcely able to believe what I was hearing.

Annie plugged in an electric jug, opened a giant economy size tin of instant coffee, and scooped a heaped teaspoon full into a white enamel mug.

"Milk and sugar?" she inquired.

"Just milk, thanks," I replied. "Who is Kevin anyway, and how many and what kind of aeroplanes do you have?"

"Kevin Bowe," Di replied. "He and his wife, Sue, own Air Whitsunday. We fly tourists to the outer reef for reef-walking, snorkeling, diving, or you can stay overnight on a big boat out there if you like. The planes are Lake Buccaneers. We have three of them at the moment, but we're just about to take delivery of two more. That's why he is looking for another pilot."

"That's wonderful!" I replied, barely able to conceal my enthusiasm and excitement. "Sounds like a pilot's heaven. I sure hope he will talk to me. I don't have any experience with landing on water, though," I added with a worried frown.

"That's O.K.," Annie said. "He likes to train his people himself, before they have picked up any bad habits. It can be very dangerous, taking off and landing in the open sea — especially in and around coral reefs. Kevin is a master at it. He has been doing this for years, so he knows all the tricks of the trade."

"I guess he would have to," I replied thoughtfully, conjuring up a mental image of a tiny aircraft being dashed to pieces on the coral or breaking up in huge ocean swells.

Annie made my coffee from the now boiling water in the jug, and added a dash of fresh milk she took from the trailer's tiny refrigerator. As she handed me the mug, she said, "Why don't you take it and sit outside on one of the benches. It's a lot cooler out there."

"Good idea," I replied, standing and lowering myself awkwardly down the step. She was right. It was stifling in the van, with only one tiny fan circulating the already hot air.

As I hobbled to the nearest bench, she commented on my limp.

"Did you hurt yourself?"

"You . . . could say that," I stammered. She correctly interpreted my hesitation as embarrassment.

"I'm sorry. I didn't mean to pry."

"Perfectly all right," I replied with a grin. "Actually, my legs are still a bit weak. I was paralyzed after a plane crash, and I am just now learning to walk again more or less normally."

"My God! Are you serious? And you want to FLY again?"

"That's what got me out of bed and on my feet again," I said.

"Well, I've got to hand it to you. You would not get me back in a plane after something like that."

"I guess I am just basically pig-headed," I said with a grin. "I just wouldn't let something as trivial as paralysis stop me from doing what I always wanted to do."

I was just about to raise the steaming mug to my lips when I heard an unfamiliar sound. It was vaguely reminiscent of the buzz of a chainsaw; a very BIG chainsaw! It grew louder by the second.

"That sounds like Kevin coming in now," Annie remarked casually.

I stood and peered through the trees towards the strip as the harsh cadence grew louder by the second.

"Do you mind if I go take a look?" I inquired eagerly, placing the coffee mug on the bench beside me. "I'd like to see him come in."

Annie laughed and, with hands on slender hips, replied, "You bloody pilots are all the same. Can't resist watching a plane take off or land. Come on! I'll run you down. It'll be quicker."

She strode toward a little blue Mazda coupe parked beside the trailer. I took another glance in the direction of the approaching aircraft, decided it would indeed be quicker to ride the hundred yards or so to the strip, and followed her to the car.

Thirty seconds later, we were standing on the grass outside the tiny terminal, shielding our eyes against the glare of the hot, bright sun as we searched for the speck in the sky which would soon materialize into an aircraft. There was little wind, so it was at first difficult to determine from which direction he would approach. The rising sound was soon isolated as coming from the south end of the strip, where the valley seemed to end in thick brush. The line of hills on the right curved around to the left, and the hills on the left side of the strip ended as abruptly as the valley.

"What's down there?" I asked Annie.

"That's Shute Harbor," she replied, still searching the endless blue sky. "It's the main boat basin on this stretch of coast. Good, deep water surrounded by islands and those mountains, so it is completely protected and storm-proof. There are a few patches of coral that you have to know about, though."

"There he is!" she cried suddenly, pointing at a distant black spot high over the distant trees.

Within seconds, the sound grew into a high-pitched crescendo and the black spot became recognizable as an aircraft. The distinctive lines of a Lake Buccaneer, with its rear-facing two hundred horse power engine and pusher propeller, mounted on a pylon high atop the fuselage, came into view on a steep approach. The landing gear unfolded from under the wings and out of the nose as I watched.

With the wheels almost clipping the high grass of the overrun at the end of the strip, he came in low and slow and pulled the power off with a crackling, backfiring burble just before the gear touched the ground. Small puffs of dust flew from the main wheels, the nose wheel touched gently, and then he was slowing to a stop. He brought it to a halt just a few yards north of the terminal, in a landing roll that must have been only a few hundred feet, turned, and taxied back to the terminal with a burst of ear-shattering power from that noisily exposed engine.

Seconds later, the engine died and the right side of the perspex canopy was lifted from within, exposing the front two occupants. The right seat passenger stood and, placing his right leg over the cockpit coaming onto a small step on the side of the fuselage, literally dismounted from the aircraft as if he was getting off a horse. The back of his seat was pushed forward by the pilot, whereupon two more passengers, both attractive girls in their early twenties, disembarked in the same manner. They were all scantily clad in typical Aussie beach style, and wore beat-up old canvas tennis shoes on their feet.

A moment later, the cockpit opening was reversed when the pilot lifted his side of the canopy, closing the passenger side. He jumped out of the aircraft, ignoring the step, landed lightly on his bare feet, and followed his passengers. He appeared to be in his early forties, although it was difficult to tell, as his face was completely concealed by a huge, bushy, black beard. His brown eyes were bright and mischievous. He was dressed in a pair of brown shorts and a creamy beige uniform shirt with the Air Whitsunday logo embroidered over his left pocket. A salt-stained red ball cap, emblazoned with the same logo across the front, was perched jauntily on the front of his head, shading his eyes. When he took it off to wipe the perspiration from his eyes and forehead, a thatch of thick, ocean-matted black hair flecked with early gray was revealed.

Kevin Bowe escorted his passengers to the terminal, chatted and joked with them for a few minutes, then handed them over to Annie. Before she led them inside to interest them in some of the souvenirs on sale, she introduced me to Kevin.

"Kevin, this is Rod Lewin. Rod, meet Kevin Bowe. Rod's a pilot looking for work. I took the liberty of telling him you may be interested in talking to him, Kev."

"Sure. Thanks, Annie," he said, pulling a huge black pipe from his shirt pocket as he shook my hand. "Let's get in out of the sun. The salt is really sticking to me today," he added, leading me onto the shaded concrete verandah of the terminal, where we sat on wooden benches.

My limp did not go unnoticed.

"Hurt your legs?" he inquired casually, as he stoked that black briar.

"Sort of," I replied as nonchalantly as possible.

He did not reply, and was obviously expecting me to enlarge on my explanation, which was understandable. He would not consider hiring anyone who was going to be a threat or liability to the operation of his aircraft or the lives of his passengers. So I explained briefly the circumstances surrounding the crash, and my subsequent recovery from my injuries.

"Hmmm," was his eloquent reply when I had finished the abbreviated story.

He sucked on the pipe clenched firmly between his teeth, scratched that great black beard, and remained silent for what to me seemed like an interminable period. I thought for sure the interview was going to end in disappointment, as had all the others so far.

"Had any water experience?" he asked suddenly through his pipe-filled teeth.

"No. I . . . I'm afraid not," I said hesitantly.

"Hmmm," he muttered again.

After another long pause, he said, "Tell you what. I don't have any more rides scheduled today. Give me a few minutes and then we'll go see if you have what it takes to be a good water pilot. No guarantees, mind you. Just a trial flight — for both of us. O.K.?"

"Yes SIR!!" I replied, jumping unsteadily to my feet in my eagerness to show Kevin what I could do.

"Why don't you go familiarize yourself with the plane and the panel layout. I'll be along in a few minutes."

With that, he turned and disappeared into the terminal, leaving me trembling with excitement and disbelief at my change of fortune.

I limped over to the red Buccaneer, registration number VH-AWI, and stood by the side of the cockpit, gazing around at the dials and knobs and levers. Most of them were familiar to me. They were just in different positions. The throttle and mixture and propeller controls, for example, were on the overhead panel, between the two canopy halves. There were things like a water rudder handle and a bilge pump switch which were foreign to me.

I put my left foot on the step, took a firm grip on the coaming and hoisted myself up, raising and swinging my right leg inside the aircraft at the same time. It was indeed similar to mounting a horse! I thought it would be difficult with my weak legs, but my arms, made extra strong by months of relying on them for the majority of my support, took most of the weight as I grabbed the central handgrip.

Swinging my left leg over the side of the cockpit, I fell into the low, hard, vinyl-covered seat. Sand and water were everywhere inside the plane. Flecks of corrosion dotted parts of the panel, particularly the heads of the screws holding the instruments in position.

My right hand automatically reached for the overhead throttle, which was an upended T-shaped lever mounted between the propeller and mixture knobs. Its position felt comfortable under my hand, despite the unusual location, and it moved forward and aft easily. There was a small, plastic friction wheel on the right side for adjusting its freedom of travel. My eyes roved over the interior of the aircraft with mounting excitement and anticipation, as I dreamed of flying it on and off the ocean with practiced ease.

Kevin Bowe returned unnoticed by me to the side of the Buccaneer, where he stood silently for a few moments, reluctant to interrupt my reverie.

"Well, what do you think of her?" he asked with a grin that flashed through his beard, chuckling at the fact that he had startled me almost out of my wits, which were of limited capacity at the best of times.

"Beautiful!" I said enthusiastically. "How does she handle the rough water out at the reef, though?"

"That depends totally on the skill of the pilot," he answered truthfully. The aeroplane is very strong and soundly built. But it won't take abuse. Come on! I'll show you!"

With that, he threw the canopy over to expose the right half of the cockpit for entry, jumped in as easily as he had previously jumped out, strapped on his belt, and reached across me with his left hand to turn the starter as he gripped the mixture knob with his right. The engine was still warm. The prop turned through a couple of blades, then an ear-splitting roar threatened to deafen me immediately, as the two-hundred horse-power Lycoming burst into life right over my head.

Kevin pushed the mixture knob forward and adjusted the throttle to give a steady one thousand r.p.m. idle speed. The whole airframe shook and shuddered with the vibration of the high mounted engine. The noise was awful, but I could not think of a more wonderful sound right at that moment.

I was where I belonged at last!

Quickly scanning the instruments with eyes and hands, Kevin turned to me and said, "She's all yours. Taxi up to the end of 32. Watch the steering. It's a free-castering nose wheel and it takes a bit of getting use to."

I put my feet on the rudders, rested the tops of my shoes lightly on the toe brakes, and reached up to take the throttle in my right hand. Gingerly at first, I moved the lever forward. The engine note rose, and the aircraft inched forward, immediately deciding to turn left of its own volition. I countered with right brake and the nose came round to maximum deflection in the opposite direction. We slowly weaved our way up to the end of the runway, with the nose wandering from side to side apparently at will. When it came time to turn in the direction of takeoff at the end of the runway, the fickle beast refused to budge in the manner requested, and Kevin had to get it around for me. The fact that my feet and toes and ankles were still very weak did not help matters at all.

"Don't worry. You'll get used to it," he grinned.

He waited patiently as I ran through my usual pre-takeoff drill.

"Whenever you're ready," he said when I looked at him for the go signal. "Full throttle for take-off. Back off to the normal twenty-five squared on throttle and prop for climb power. Don't forget to get the gear up as soon as you have a positive rate of climb. Let's go!"

We went!

The engine bellowed with a shattering roar, the aircraft shook defiantly, and then we were rolling down the grassy slope of the runway.

Before I realized it, we were airborne. I remembered the gear lever, selected it to the 'up' position, and then we were climbing away to the north, straight toward the trees and scrub covering the mountain I had driven over not an hour before.

As we rose effortlessly into the hot, still air, the most magnificent vista was spread out below me. A secluded palm-lined beach, lapped gently by wavelets of calm, blue water, lay at the base and to the right of the hill. The dirt track I had noticed from the car when I reached the bottom of the slope led off to this pretty little cove. I could not believe my eyes! The whole area was even more beautiful than I had at first suspected from my vantage point on the hill overlooking Airlie Beach.

Off to our right were dozens of green islands, set like emeralds in a sapphire sea. Kevin leaned toward me and shouted over the racket of the engine that most of them were uninhabited. There were only seven islands in a group numbering more than seventy which had resorts built on them. The rest were national or state parks where camping only was allowed. Construction of new buildings on these islands was strictly prohibited.

We rounded the hill to our left, and there was Airlie, spread out before us, the sleek hulls of hundreds of boats and their stainless fittings glinting and gleaming in the harsh afternoon sunlight. The blue of the water was absolutely incredible!

I settled comfortably into flying the aircraft. It was a stable and easy plane to fly, and I decided that if I could handle the water work, this was the plane — and the life — for me.

After Kevin had spent a few minutes showing me the spectacular points of interest on the islands and the mainland, we turned and flew back around the hill, over the top of the airstrip and then over Shute Harbor itself, another breathtaking piece of scenery from the air.

About five miles southeast across the protected water of the harbor lay another island, thickly covered in dense rain forest. It was known as Long Island, and ran almost parallel to the coastline forming a narrow, sheltered passage about a mile wide between the island and the mainland. Kevin shouted that this was where he did most of his training, because the water was generally much calmer here than at most of the other islands, which were exposed to an ocean swell.

We flew down the passage and turned back to the north to point into the light breeze. Our altitude was about one thousand feet and the hilly terrain on both the island and the mainland rose above us on both sides.

"I want to see if you have a natural feel for this," Kevin yelled. "I'll follow through with you, but I want you to try to put us on the water. Remember, the most important part of your pre-landing check in an amphibian has to do with the gear. Always ask yourself if you are landing on ground or water. Do you want your wheels down or up? It may sound silly, but many people, me included, have forgotten from time to time. It can be both costly and extremely embarrassing! It's not so bad for the aircraft if you land on the ground with the wheels up. But it is very bad for the aircraft, and very dangerous, if you hit the water with them down. You could tear the wheels off completely, and you will certainly buckle the main wing spar to which they are attached."

I looked at him with rising apprehension.

"What happens if you do land on the ground with them up?" I shouted back over the din.

"The hull is built strongly enough to withstand the constant pounding of water, which can be just as hard as land at any kind of speed. If you make a nice approach, all you will do is scrape a bit of paint off the keel, and maybe bend whichever float she comes to rest on when you stop. Much less damage than the wheels digging into water at sixty knots! Apart from the damage, there is the danger of cartwheeling, or waterlooping, which would do substantially more structural damage to wings and floats."

As he finished this frighteningly vivid description of disaster, we were descending to the final approach. Now he became silent, and we both began to concentrate on my first attempt at alighting on water. While he had been talking I was getting the aircraft configured for landing. I had reduced the power and gotten out the flaps, which had only two positions; either up or down. Simple.

I reduced the airspeed to about seventy knots as we approached the sparkling water, flared as in a normal aircraft, and held her just off the surface as the speed washed off. I brought the nose up to counter the deteriorating speed, and at something like sixty knots, with the power right back and in a perfect attitude, she rushed along with her keel barely off the water.

A moment later, a most delightful and satisfying sound filled my ears over the popping of the idling engine. The keel kissed the calm water with a long, lovely, swishing sigh, the hull came in next with a slight bump, bump, bumping over the ripples generated by the gentle breeze. Then, as she slowed and settled, a huge bow wave came up along both sides of the plane, and she was completely in the water, resting on her boat-like belly with her wings held off the surface by their own floats fixed beneath them.

Kevin reached up and pulled the mixture, shutting down the engine, and then there was absolute silence except for the lapping of the wavelets against the hull and the songs of the birds in the bush all around us. We sat quietly for a moment, then he threw open the canopy on my side, allowing me to feel the sensation of sitting low in the water with the peace and quiet around me. I reached over the side and dragged my hand through the clear, unpolluted blue water which was only about eighteen inches below the cockpit coaming.

If he was looking for a new convert, he had one! I did not need any more convincing. This was it! This was for me.

"Not bad at all," he allowed.

"You could have kept the nose down just a little longer to let her speed wash off by the drag of the water. That way, she settles with less of a bow wave than you got then. But that was good. How do you feel?"

"Fantastic!" I replied with undisguised enthusiasm. "This is great! Do you mean to tell me you actually PAY people to do this? What a GREAT job!"

"Oh, you'll earn your keep, all right. There will be days when you wonder why you ever thought this was fun, believe me. Wait till you get three other heavy people in here with their bags in the hold, and you have to get out of a four or six feet swell with the wind blowing like hell! Like any job, it does have its drawbacks, but yes, it is mostly a lot of fun."

"You will have a lot of training, though, before you are let loose in anything but ideal conditions. Anyway, let's see how you handle a take-off. We'll go back to the strip, let you shoot a landing or two, then well talk about the job for a while."

He was going to give me the job!

20

Kevin started the engine again and we taxied around on the surface for a few minutes so that I could get accustomed to the feel of steering the plane in the water. The water rudder dropped out of the bottom of the main air rudder, the bottom of which was itself a couple of inches under the surface. This allowed excellent maneuverability, but the extra drag required much more pressure on the rudder pedals than I was used to, and before long, my weak legs and feet were aching and throbbing with the effort. The heat of the day brought out the perspiration on my face as I struggled to get the hang of it.

"Any problems?" Kevin inquired gently, as he noticed my difficulty.

"Not really. My legs are still pretty weak and it makes me work, that's all. I'll manage. In fact, it is probably the best therapy I can get."

"O.K. Pull up the water rudder. She will swing into wind, if there is any. When you are ready to go, just give her full power and at the same time, pull the stick back into your belly as far as you can. When the nose is right up, you will feel her want to come up out of the water. That's the time to push forward on the stick to get her into a horizontal planing position. That's the attitude you want, so you can skim along the surface till you have flying speed. Let's try it!"

"All right," I replied excitedly. "Here we go!"

I held my feet firmly on the rudders, pushed forward slowly and steadily on the throttle, and brought back the yoke as far as it would come. The engine bellowed, the nose came up, and another huge bow wave threatened to engulf us. It washed down the sides of the plane. We were light, and she reared her nose up and fairly leapt onto the surface of the water. I pushed forward on the yoke, and we were instantly planing across the rippling wavelets. What a sensational feeling! A boat that flies!

Kevin shouted to let him have the controls. I took my hands and feet away from the throttle, yoke and rudders. He reduced power to about fifteen hundred r.p.m., enough to keep the aircraft from getting airborne. Then he showed me how to do high speed turns on the water. A little pressure on the rudder and yoke to lean into the turn, just like a motorcycle. She came round easily, one float barely skimming the surface.

We turned left, then right, then left again, all over the narrow straits between the island and mainland. What a glorious feeling! The exhilaration of being able to run and maneuver like a high-powered speedboat, yet have the ability and freedom to take to the air any time we chose to.

Kevin handed the controls back to me and I tried a few turns myself. I was ecstatic! This was where I belonged, all right.

"Let's go home," he shouted.

Home! This was my home now. It sure beat the pants off The Royal North Shore Hospital in Sydney, which seemed like a galaxy away now.

I turned her easily back into wind. The rudder pressure required in the planing attitude was just like in flight, and much less than when in the water.

With the throttle forward in the full power position, we were airborne in seconds, finished with the sparkling water for now. We flew low over the surface all the way back to Shute Harbor, where we climbed just high enough to clear the boats and the scrub behind the harbor at the approach end of the airstrip. I got the landing gear and flaps out, reduced the power once more, and flared over the tall grass, just as I had seen Kevin do on his earlier approach.

Moments later, we lightly thumped onto the ground. The arrival was not nearly as good as Kevin's had been, but that was to be expected. I used the toe brakes with the full pressure of my legs and feet, as I had become accustomed to doing, slowed us down, and turned to taxi back towards the terminal. I did a much better job of taxiing than I had before, and we trundled up the slight grade in a more or less straight line. As we approached the terminal, I reached for the mixture and reluctantly shut her down.

"What a wonderful experience!" I shouted, forgetting that the terrible din overhead had ceased.

"You really liked it, huh?" Kevin asked with his infectious grin, as he restoked the black briar.

"Liked it? Are you kidding? I loved it!"

"Well, I think we may be able to use you. Let's go over to the house and have a couple of beers while we talk about it. O.K.?"

My eyes lit up with genuine excitement, a small part of which, I had to admit, was definitely attributable to the offer of some free amber refreshment. The terminal was locked again, and there was no sign of Annie, so we wandered back up the track, through the parking lot, and past my car.

"Yours?" Kevin inquired through teeth clenched around his pipe.

I nodded and said, "Yeah, if I can keep up the payments on her."

"Nice job," he remarked as we continued our stroll up the narrow track through the trees.

As we approached the trailer, Kevin put his head in through the door and spoke to the girls. "I'll be over at the house if anyone wants me," he said.

"O.K. No worries, Kev," said Annie, who was busy putting some brochures and advertising material together.

Di was working on some accounts and bookwork. She looked up and spotted me behind Kevin. "How did you like it?" she asked, with a broad, white grin.

"I am a definite convert!" I replied. "It's the most wonderful experience in flying I have ever known."

"Well, hope we see more of you. See you later."

"Bye," I said, as I stepped aside to allow Kevin to lead me through the trees beyond the trailer.

About a hundred yards behind it, and well hidden by the trees and bush, was the structure I had wondered about before. It was Kevin's house. Built of split logs and natural timber, it blended perfectly with the surroundings, and was almost invisible from any distance more than fifteen or twenty yards.

As we walked into the room, we were greeted by Kevin's wife.

"Hullo darling. This is Rod Lewin. He's going to be working with us, I think. Rod, this is my wife, Sue."

"Very glad to meet you," I said, shaking her extended hand.

"Hi Rod. Welcome. I hope you will like it here."

"I love it already. This really is a beautiful area."

"We like it. It sure beats the city rat-race! I hope you aren't a night-life person. If so, you will probably get bored around here."

"Are you kidding? I don't care if I never see another city as long as I live."

"Good. Well, I have some work to do with the girls, so I'll see you later."

"Bye. Nice to meet you."

"Like a frothy top?" Kevin asked, as Sue went out and headed up the track to the trailer.

"Love one!" I replied, already tasting the cold, bitter, ale which was about to caress my lips.

Kevin went to the fridge at the bar, pulled out a couple of Brisbane Bitter stubbies, flipped off the tops, and handed one to me.

"Make yourself at home," he said as he eased into an oval, carpeted pit in the middle of the lounge room floor, and sat on a bench built into and all around the side wall of it.

I descended into the strange hole in the floor, carefully clutching the cold, dark bottle of beer in eager anticipation.

"Cheers," he said, tipping the 'stubby' to his lips.

"Cheers," I replied, doing likewise.

Kevin took a long pull of his beer, then spoke at length. "Well, Rod, like I said before, I think we can use you. I will need to go through the formality of seeing your logbook and license, of course. And I can't let you officially start for a week or so yet. I have to go to Brisbane with Rod Johnston, my brother-in-law and partner. You will meet him and our other pilot and partner, Peter Bull, when they get back from the reef shortly. Anyway, as I was saying, we have to go to Brisbane to pick up a couple more Buccaneers which have just arrived from the States. They are packed in crates, and in pieces, and I want to personally supervise their assembly and fly them back up here. Probably be a week before we get back.

"While you're waiting, you can set yourself up in an apartment, settle in, and get to know the area and some of the people. You are welcome to hang around our hangar which I'll show you shortly, and learn what you can. And I'm sure Peter will be happy to take you out to the reef any time he has a spare seat. How's that sound?"

"Sounds too good to be true!" I replied earnestly. "I have been through so much in the last few months. I wanted to fly so badly! And now it seems I have stumbled on something I did not even know I was looking for. Thanks for offering me the job. You won't be sorry."

"I know that. I think it will work out just fine, for all of us."

We talked through another two or three beers.

Just as I was about ready to leave, the air was once more filled with the crackling buzz of returning Buccaneers. Kevin suggested I wait a little longer, so that I could meet Rod and Peter. Less than ten minutes later, the two pilots, dressed in the same casual garb as Kevin, strolled onto the patio and into the lounge.

The first one was about my height, but as thin as a rake with medium length black hair and a huge black moustache. A cigarette dangled precariously from his lips as he made a beeline for the bar and opened a stubby. The second was more heavily set, with curly, dark brown hair about the same color as my own. He joined us in the pit and waited for his companion to toss him a beer.

"Rod, Peter, I'd like you to meet our new pilot. Another Rod, believe it or not. We may have to give him a nickname, to avoid confusion." Kevin said with a chuckle. "Rod, meet Rod Johnston and Peter Bull."

We shook hands all round, and soon we were all merrily chatting and I was listening in rapt awe as they told of their day's adventures.

During a slight lull in the conversation, I interjected, "Is this standard procedure?" indicating the empty beer bottles now littering the bottom of the pit.

"Sure!" Rod grinned around the cigarette permanently adhered to his lips. "Every afternoon after work, we adjourn to Kev's place to wet our whistles. It gets mighty hot out on that reef all day with nothing to drink, ya know! A man could die of dehydration!" he cackled through his frothy moustache.

"Besides, it's one of the perks of the job," he added with a wink, removing his cigarette just long enough to swallow half the contents of his stubby without drawing breath.

"Don't you believe him!" Kevin chimed in. "We all take our turns. I can't afford to keep everybody in booze permanently. At least, not the way these guys lap the stuff up."

"Pete," he went on, "I told Rod about our upcoming trip to Brisbane. I'd like you to take him out to the reef a few times while we're away. Familiarize him with the area, the bomies and other danger zones, etc. Give him a bit of practice at taking off and landing inside the lagoon, if the water is O.K. for it."

"Sure. No worries. I'll show him the ropes. He'll be ready to put on line by the time you get back."

"Well, don't go too far with the training side of it. I want to initiate him to the various water techniques myself."

"O.K. I'll just ease him into it, show him how to read the water, so forth."

"That's the ticket," Kevin replied, satisfied.

I was already feeling slightly heady by the time the other two arrived. It had been a long time since I had consumed so much beer in one sitting. By the time I had worked through two or three more with Rod and Pete, my head was positively reeling and I knew it was time to quit.

"Listen guys, I want to thank you for the hospitality, but I do think it's time for me to run. It's getting on toward dark and I have to find myself a place to stay, you know."

"You're welcome to stay here the night," Kevin said with genuine concern.

"Thanks anyway Kevin, but I think I'll push off. I have to find a permanent place to live and I might as well start looking now. Do you have any idea where I might find a good, clean apartment where the rent is not too high?"

They all thought for a few moments, then Rod said, "You might go back to Cannonvale and have a look at a block next to the Ampol garage. It's on Shute Harbor Road — that's this main road you came down — almost right on the beach. I noticed a 'For Rent' sign on the front of the building as I drove past the other day. Looks like a pretty new place, too."

"Thanks. I'll try it. Back to Cannonvale, you say?"

"Yeah. You must have driven right by it to get here. Just before where the road takes a sharp right turn at Cannonvale Beach."

"Oh. I know where you mean. On the other side of Airlie Beach. I remember. Thanks again."

With that, I rose unsteadily to my feet, shook hands with them all, and, not without difficulty, climbed up out of the pit and hobbled toward the door.

"What did you do to your legs?" Rod asked bluntly, as he noticed my unsteady gait and my legs, which were almost as thin and bony as his own.

"Get run over by a truck?" he chuckled, not unkindly.

"No. An aeroplane," I replied, feeling the familiar hot blush rising to my temples.

"Oh. Sorry. No offence meant," he said, embarrassed at his lack of tact, which I admitted to myself, almost matched my own.

"That's O.K. I don't mind. It's ancient history now. See you all later."

"Bye Rod," Kevin said, still sucking on his ever-present pipe. "See you in a week or so."

"So long," said Pete, raising his beer in salute. "Come on down to the strip tomorrow. I'll see if I have a spare seat for you."

"See ya later, Hoppy," Rod grinned around his dangling cigarette.

"That's it!" Kevin exclaimed, slapping his knee. "That's what we'll call you — if you don't mind, that is. It suits you perfectly. Remember the old radio serial, 'Hop Harrigan,' about a pilot who walked with a limp after a plane crash? That's you, Rod!"

"Well . . . it doesn't bother me," I replied hesitantly, wondering if they were pulling my leg, so to speak.

Apparently they were not! I have been 'Hop' or 'Hoppy' ever since.

I bid them all good-bye once more, then stumbled back through the trees, past the trailer and down the track to my car, where I sat for a long time with the windows rolled down, listening to the melodic sounds of the bush. The breeze rustled in the gum trees. Wild cockatoos and rosellas screeched, and crows cawed incessantly. All this was music to my ears. There was no sound of human intervention. I was at home at last!

The combined effect of the heat of the dying sun and the half dozen stubbies I had consumed caused me to doze off right where I sat. When I awoke half an hour later, absolute silence surrounded me. Twilight had fallen in the valley. The mountains surrounding the airstrip were silhouetted against a starry sky, barely visible above through the tops of the gently swaying gum trees. I remembered that I still had no place to sleep tonight, unless I stayed in the car, the cramped quarters of which did not exactly appeal to me. I reached for the key and started her up, flicked on the headlight switch, and with an unintended spin of the back wheels, drove up the access road, turned right onto Shute Harbor Road a moment later, and headed back the way I had come earlier in the afternoon.

Shortly afterwards, I turned into the driveway of the apartment block Rod had mentioned. The 'For Rent' sign hung prominently on the end of the brick building which faced the road. A light shone upstairs towards the back of the building. I ascended the dozen concrete steps, limped a short distance across a wooden verandah, and knocked on a screen door. A lady in her late fifties came to the door.

"Sorry to bother you, ma'am," I said. "But I noticed the sign on the front of the building. I am new to the area and I am looking for a place to stay. Do you mind if I take a look at your unit for rent?"

"Not at all," she responded kindly, despite the lateness of the hour.

"Come on. It's the two-bedroom unit downstairs. I'll show you around."

"Thank you. I appreciate it."

We went back down the steps and approached the unit in front of which I had parked. She opened the sliding glass door and we stepped into a large living-dining-kitchen area, comfortably furnished with a table and six chairs in the kitchen area and two sofas and lounge chairs in the living area. A set of polished wooden steps secured to the right wall of the unit led upstairs. At the top of the stairs was a bathroom and a little further down a short hall were two bedrooms. The second one opened on to a wide, wooden deck with a view of a rocky, sheltered bay which I had not seen from the road. If I had not already been satisfied that this would do nicely, the view convinced me.

"I'll take it," I said happily, forgetting in my eagerness to ask what the rent might be. Fortunately, it turned out to be more than reasonable.

"Wonderful!" she said. "Let's go upstairs and I will get you a lease agreement. The rent is payable two weeks in advance."

"O.K. How long will it take to get a phone in?"

"Oh, only a couple of days. The jacks are already in place. All you have to do is apply at the Post Office. Or, if you are in a real hurry, you can go into Proserpine to the Telecom Office and apply in person. They're pretty good around here."

Thirty minutes later, I was settling into my new home, weary but very, very contented. Within two days of leaving Brisbane, I had found a job and a place to live. And both were situated in the heart of Paradise! I had no supplies as yet, so that evening I went out and discovered an excellent Chinese restaurant in Airlie Beach, one of many fine dining places I was to locate over the next few weeks.

After a satisfying meal, I wandered up and down the one main street of the town, walked over to the beach, sat in the cool, course sand with my back against a palm tree, and gazed out over the calm, boat-filled bay, gleaming in the light of a nearly full moon. I wriggled my toes in the sand, still amazed at my ability to perform this simple act after the months of frustration and anguish I had been subjected to. There was just one more thing that would make this beautiful evening perfect, and that was a companion to share it with. I was very lonely, but I still had hopes that Barb would finally choose me over her new love.

As the evening wore on, fatigue from the day's long drive caught up with me. I returned to the apartment, made up the large, double bed in the master bedroom with some sheets my mother had thoughtfully packed for me, and collapsed into them. The night was hot and humid, so I reached over my head to the ceiling fan switch and turned it to a medium setting. That was my last conscious action on my first night in Paradise.

Sunlight streaming through cracks in the bedroom curtains awoke me early the next morning. I rose, showered and dressed in the standard tropical garb of

247

shorts, T-shirt and boat shoes, then went out in search of breakfast. The town was already alive with tourists, even at eight a.m., and every sidewalk cafe, restaurant and snack bar was doing a brisk trade. I selected a place that looked appealing. It was furnished with wicker chairs and tables covered in elegant pink cloths, fine silver and a surprisingly inexpensive blackboard menu. The tables were practically on the sidewalk, which allowed a good view of the street activity. After an excellent breakfast of very fresh, locally grown tropical fruit, bacon and eggs and all the trimmings, I headed back out to the airstrip, hopeful of getting my first aerial look at the Great Barrier Reef.

The tiny terminal was a hive of bustling activity when I arrived. Apparently Air Whitsunday was not the only user of the airstrip. An Air Queensland twenty seat Twin Otter commuter plane was parked on the grass outside the terminal. People milled about, coming and going, while airline agents organized their tickets and baggage.

I recognized Annie in the thick of the crowd, and went up to her to find out when I might be able to hitch a ride with Peter.

"Hi Rod," she beamed at me as I approached her. "Or should I say 'Hoppy.' I hear congratulations are in order. Welcome to the team."

"News travels fast around here," I responded with a grin.

"You'd better get used to that," she said. "This is a small town."

"Yeah. That's right. I'll have to remember to keep my mouth shut. I have a habit of putting my foot in it."

"Don't worry. Everybody does that. That's what makes life in a small community interesting."

"Kevin said I might be able to ride out to the reef with Peter some time today. Would you know when I could go?"

"Come on inside and I'll check the schedule. I know there is not much on for the next few days while he and Rod are away. Let's have a look."

"Yes. Here's one at ten-thirty with only two people on it. We will have to check their weights when they arrive, though. You and Peter are both fairly big guys. If the two passengers aren't pretty light, you probably won't be able to go. Those Buccaneers are the devil to get out of the water with a heavy load! Believe me, I know. Peter scared me out of my wits one day, trying to get off rough water at nearly high tide with two other big bods on board. Never again!"

"That bad, huh?"

"Are you kidding? Wait till you get enough experience to try it. And then you will have to do it. It's not much fun."

"Thanks Annie. Just what I needed on my first day on the job."

"Sorry. Didn't mean to scare you. Anyway, I have to help check these passengers for Air Queensland. We are agents for them. If you want, you can wander up to the hangar. Pete is up there with the plane. It's just through the trees behind the house."

I squinted off in the direction she was pointing, and saw the reflection of sunlight on galvanized iron siding at the Shute Harbor end of the strip, so I ambled off in that direction.

"Thanks Annie. I'll see you later."

"O.K. If I can help you with anything, don't hesitate to ask."

"I won't. Thanks."

I was halfway up the strip towards the hangar when I heard the unmistakable roar of a Buccaneer engine firing up. A few minutes later, Peter came trundling down in my direction. He stopped beside me and brought the throttle right back to idle so we could hear each other.

"Morning, Hoppy. Find yourself a place all right?"

"Yes thanks. That place Rod recommended turned out to be just perfect. Almost right on the water and practically brand new."

"Good. Did you check with Annie about the schedule?"

"Sure did. Apparently there is an opening at ten-thirty, depending on the other people's weight."

"O.K. Should be no problem. I've got a couple of scenic flights to do first. I'll see you then."

"Looking forward to it," I replied eagerly, waving as he gunned the engine and continued to taxi down towards the terminal.

I continued my walk up to the hangar where I met some of the mechanics. There was another Buccaneer in the open-sided structure. It was practically in pieces, with both wings and the engine removed completely. The two mechanics, John and Theo, chatted amiably with me about the inner workings of the aircraft, as they continued their never-ending maintenance program on the Air Whitsunday fleet. Before I realized where the time had gone, it was almost ten-thirty so I said good-bye and limped as fast as my weak legs would carry me back to the terminal about two hundred yards away.

When I got there, Peter was already showing the two passengers to the aircraft. Fortunately for me, they were a young married couple — honeymooners by the look of them — and were both very light. Peter showed them how to climb into the back seat, then grinned at me and said, "All set?"

"You bet!" I replied as I climbed into the right hand seat.

When I was settled in, he threw the canopy over so he could get into the left side. The engine roared again, the young lovers in the back held hands tightly as if they did not expect to live through the experience, and away we went. The breeze was still blowing out of the north, so we taxied up to the same end of the strip which Kevin and I had used yesterday. Peter cursorily performed the pre-take off check as we were rolling up the slight slope to the departure end. Then, with the now familiar vibrating, shattering, ear-splitting roar, we plunged down the grassy strip directly toward the mountain at the end of it. Before we were halfway down the runway, we were airborne and climbing away in a gentle right turn towards the islands and, fifty miles out to sea, the reef.

The view was nothing less than spectacular! I thought that I would never tire of admiring this incredible scenery. The morning was clear and hot, as usual. The deep blue water sparkled in the shimmering sunlight and rippled under the light breeze. As we passed low over the first island we came to, Pete shouted that its name was Daydream. It was a tiny place, perhaps a half mile long with a resort on the south end and a gravelly beach protected from the north wind. The other end of the island was more exposed, but had a good, yellow sandy beach at the foot of a rugged hill.

A few minutes later, we flew past a large, heavily timbered, uninhabited island presenting the appearance of a giant three-pronged anchor, with two calm inlets separated by the central prong and facing roughly southeast. This island was appropriately called Hook Island. What a great boat anchorage! We were flying at about one thousand feet now and the view was fantastic!

About one mile to the left of Hook Island was a small coral atoll known as Langford Reef. The tide was receding, exposing a sandy beach at the south tip. A couple of yachts were anchored off the beach, and semi-naked sun worshippers were frolicking at the edge of the shallow, clear, turquoise water.

We descended in a steep diving turn to roar low over the folks on the atoll, waggling our wings at them as we zoomed past. They waved back, then we were gone, on to the next island a couple of miles northeast of Langford. This was Hayman Island, one of the larger, older, and more expensive resorts. It had a beautiful, crescent-shaped beach facing out onto a bay of crystal clear water, protected by an encircling reef. The entire resort was concentrated between the beach and a steep, rocky, sparsely treed hill immediately behind it. A small, narrow gauge railway line ran from the end of a long wooden pier, which stretched out into deep water where boats could dock without danger of being holed by the nearby coral. Hayman had recently been completely modernized, and it was now a truly magnificent world-class resort.

Peter circled it a couple of times, banking left and right so we could all get a good look, then we roared off into the glare of the mid-morning sun. Before us lay open ocean. Not a glimpse of land anywhere ahead. Just a cobalt gleam on an empty, copper sea, sparkling under the bright yellow orb high in the eastern sky. Fifty miles to go before we sighted that section of the Reef in which we would be alighting.

The two in the back looked around apprehensively as we left the last of the islands far behind, no doubt wondering if their pilot knew where he was going.

"How long to the reef?" asked the young man, trying to sound nonchalant.

Pete turned and shouted back at him with a reassuring grin. "Oh, about fifteen minutes, I'd say. I'll point it out as soon as we approach it. You can see it for miles, from the air. It's very beautiful."

Almost exactly fifteen minutes had passed when he again turned in his seat and pointed excitedly ahead.

"That's where we're going! You can see the changing water color. See where it goes from deep, dark, blue to a lighter turquoise shade. That's the edge of Hook Reef. We cross over that and land in a lagoon beyond it known as Hardy Reef. You will see it all in a minute."

Moments later, we roared over the most spectacular sight I have ever witnessed in my entire life. The water changed color almost instantly, and then we were staring down, eyes wide in amazement and wonder, at the magnificent view of coral reef stretching away for miles and miles on both sides of the aircraft; twelve hundred miles, in fact. The hue of the water was absolutely unbelievable! Light, delicate pastels of every shade of green and emerald and turquoise, were separated from the deep blue ocean by unending reaches of coral of infinite patterns and designs and colors. We came around in a tight turn and zoomed low over the southeast corner of the lagoon.

Look there, Pete shouted. "Tiger sharks! Six of them. Real beauties. About twelve or fifteen feet long."

"We . . . we're not landing near there, are we?" shouted the girl, speaking for the first time since we had taken off.

"Don't worry," Pete grinned. "We're going back up to the other end of the lagoon where we have our moorings. We are never bothered by sharks up there. Well, not the dangerous ones, anyway. Occasionally we romp with four feet shark in the channel, but they won't hurt you."

"Oh, joy!" said the young man.

Seconds later, we passed low over a large motor vessel which was moored, incredibly, INSIDE the lagoon! People sunning themselves on the top deck waved as we made a swooping pass at deck height, then zoomed into a climbing turn to set up for the tricky approach over the exposed coral to land inside the protected waters of the lagoon.

Pete slowed us down, got the flaps out for a steeper, slower approach, fed in just enough power to take her barely inches over the treacherous coral which would easily have shredded the thin aluminum skin of the hull, and, just inside the deadly reef, put us down in the calm water. The keel touched the water with that long, satisfying swishing sound which I would come to love. He expertly kept her on the step until she had run out of speed, then eased the stick back to the neutral position. She settled in the water with a fraction of the huge bow wave I had induced yesterday, then we were turning toward a pink mooring buoy about fifty feet from the edge of the coral we had just so narrowly missed.

An open, glass-bottomed boat swung lazily at the end of a long painter attached to the buoy. We idled up behind the boat, Pete chopped the mixture at precisely the right moment, and we drifted forward to gently bump the stern of the boat with the rubber nose of the tiny amphibian.

Peter had opened his side of the canopy as soon as we settled in the water. He jumped out onto the nose of the plane, then into the back of the boat, took a mooring line lying in the water beside the boat, and secured it to the nose cleat of the plane. Then he helped the young couple out through the open canopy, along the nose and into the boat. I followed last, almost throwing myself into the warm, shallow water of the lagoon as I did a balancing act on the front of the plane. I hardly had land legs yet, let alone sea legs!

When I was safely in the boat, Pete let the plane go, and it drifted back to the full length of the mooring line, where it rolled gently from float to float in the light breeze. A couple of tugs on the starter rope of the Honda outboard and it fired up in a sputtering, coughing chatter, belching blue oil smoke. He let go the line and we were putting over to the inside edge of the reef.

Moments later, he stopped the motor, ran forward and tossed a light anchor onto the top of the reef. The boat swung and came to rest with a gentle crunch against the exposed coral. A kaleidoscope of incredible colors immediately assailed our disbelieving eyes. We put on the canvas tennis shoes provided by Peter. It was easy to see why these were necessary. The vividly colored coral was razor-sharp and would cut our feet to ribbons if they were unprotected.

We spent a fascinated hour wandering the surface of the reef as Peter, who turned out to be a knowledgeable and expert guide, showed us various specimens of multi-colored coral and sealife. When the young couple drifted off on their own, he began pointing out dozens of different species to me in more detail. This was going to be part of my new job, and I would be expected to be familiar with them and be able to answer with reasonable confidence the questions put to me by my passengers.

A little later, Peter handed us all snorkeling equipment which was stored in the boat, and we made our way over to the outer edge of the reef, which was actually the side of a deep channel between the lagoon and Hook Reef. I had great difficulty walking on this razor-edged stuff, and several times I tripped and almost fell on the sharp, uneven surface. My legs were simply not yet strong enough to cope with this kind of unexpectedly rough treatment.

However, when I reached the outer edge and slid into the cool refreshing water, I was back in my healing element, light and ethereal, breathing through my snorkel and staring through the glass of my mask with pure disbelief at the incomparable beauty which confronted me. Rays of soft yellow sunlight lanced down into the clear water, dancing on the impossibly numerous varieties of colored fish and coral and other sealife.

A giant moray eel poked its ugly fanged head out of a hole in the almost vertical underwater coral cliff beside which I was swimming. I rolled with my face to the surface, coughing and spluttering on the mouthful of salty water I had involuntarily inhaled when I sighted the brute. Moments later, though, I had my face back under the surface, just in time to see a huge sea turtle lazily paddle right by me. He turned his head toward me and I could almost see him sniff his disgust at this unwarranted intrusion.

Shortly after the turtle disappeared, one of those 'small' reef sharks Pete had mentioned decided to investigate me. I decided that discretion was definitely the better part of valor, and hurriedly attempted to retreat from the water. This was easier said than done, however. Climbing back on to the top of the exposed reef from the channel, which was actually about a foot lower than the surface, would have been a difficult task for two good, strong legs. In my haste to evacuate the water, I left enough shredded, dangling pieces of bloody skin on various jagged outcrops of coral to keep my unwelcome friend occupied until I was safely out of his reach.

Peter laughingly watched the performance and assured me that he, the shark that is, was in fact harmless. Well, I'd have to take his word for it! I was not getting back into the water right now, no matter how beautiful and enticing it was. I was already practically bleeding to death. Those scrapes caused the first of literally dozens of scars which now adorn my feet, ankles and legs, as a permanent reminder of those wonderful, care-free days on the Great Barrier Reef.

The incoming tide was beginning to wash across the top of the reef when we finally left it and motored back to the plane. Peter explained that the protected lagoon disappeared under six or eight feet of ocean at high tide, causing huge swells to flow across it.

"Makes takeoff a bit hairy," he commented casually, when asked the significance of this by the naive young man in the back seat.

Peter, I discovered later, had a definite flair for understatement.

I helped him secure the boat, then I struggled back into my seat in the plane. He followed me in, let us drift back to the end of the mooring line, started the engine and then released the line.

"Don't ever let go of the rope until you're sure the engine is running," was his sage advice. "It's not comforting for the passengers or yourself to be drifting helplessly towards the reef with no power to save you; and believe me, Kevin would not be amused. I know!"

"Seems like very sound advice," I replied, shuddering involuntarily at the thought of us being pounded to pieces on the treacherous coral.

We taxied around in circles for a few minutes to let the oil temperature and pressure rise into their safe operating arcs, then Peter tucked her as far back near the inside edge of the lagoon as we could safely get, closed and locked the canopy, pulled up the water rudder, and hit the throttle. The engine bellowed defiantly. Pete pulled the yoke far back into his stomach, as Kevin had shown me yesterday.

The difference in performance today, however, was quite astounding. I could see now why Annie had been so concerned about the weight of the passengers. The nose of the aircraft came up sluggishly. She seemed to inch forward in the water, and a tremendous sheet of spray engulfed us. White water washed over the nose, canopy and wings. I thought we were being driven under the surface. I don't know what the poor young couple in the back thought. They sat there stiffly, tightly clutching each other. Their faces were a strange white pallor and their eyes were bulging like those of frightened cattle. It seemed to take forever to get the plane up on the step.

Peter performed a strange ritual with the yoke, pushing and pulling it forward and back until the plane began rocking in response. Plumes of white spray still deluged down upon us. Finally, she began to rise out of the water. Then she was up and slicing down the watery path between isolated patches of coral in the lagoon.

There was a slight swell running by this time, and a small chop, generated by the light breeze, also ran under her keel. No comforting swishing sound this time! Pete held her down to skim the surface with the hull. A terrible din, reminiscent of a steel trash can being pounded by a thousand baseball bats, assaulted our already aching ears. We bumped through the water with ever-increasing speed. At sixty knots, Peter hauled gently back on the stick and she came away cleanly. The awful racket ceased, leaving only the roar of the engine at full power to deafen us.

And this was in relatively calm water! I could see what Kevin meant about having to earn my pay on some days! This was no game for an inexperienced pilot to play at. There was a definite art and technique to getting these craft out of the water.

Double sighs of relief from the back reminded me that I was not the only slightly apprehensive person on board. I could see that a careful and comprehensive passenger briefing was an absolute necessity in this job.

Turning to look down at the water just as we broke away, I was horrified to see a complete coral barrier across our takeoff path pass not six feet under the keel. I stared across at Peter, opened my mouth to say something, then thought better of it. I didn't want to know! He must have read my mind.

"Standard procedure, chum. Not a lot of room in here. Got to keep her down to build up speed, then yank her off just before the reef. There are longer runs, of course, but when the wind is blowing from the northeast, we have to use this one."

I nodded stupidly. Strangely enough, I did not find it comforting to know that we could only be smashed to pieces on the coral when taking off in one particular direction. I again attempted to speak, then let it go. Like I said, I didn't want to know!

We zoomed over the "Reef Encounter" once more; the name, I discovered, of the large overnight vessel moored in the lagoon. I promised myself that at the first opportunity, I was coming out here to spend a day or two, and do some serious scuba diving. Perhaps even a night dive, which Peter said was absolutely spectacular.

We climbed away and headed west, back to the airstrip via another route so that he could show us some more islands and resorts. As we set course, we could just make out the distant green of the islands on the horizon. Twenty minutes later, we approached the south side of Hook Island. As we passed through the narrow gap appropriately named Hook Passage, between this island and Whitsunday Island, the largest in the group, Peter pointed out the famous Underwater Observatory, jutting out on a spit beside a narrow, sandy beach.

We circled for a few minutes, then we were flying past a large, sheltered bay on the north side of Whitsunday Island. Dozens of boats lay at anchor in the pretty cove, surrounded by natural bush and rain forest. This entire island was a national park and not one single building marred its silent, peaceful beauty.

"You'll be doing a lot of pickups in there," Peter said.

"It's one of the most popular and safe harbors for folks who rent boats to spend the night. They call us on the radio and organize trips to the reef. We'll teach you how to approach the back of a boat and transfer passengers without tipping them in the drink."

"That would be helpful," I replied with a hint of sarcasm, wondering if I had not taken on more than I could hope to handle with this job.

A few minutes later, we were flying low over the last of the islands which we could see on the journey back from the reef. This one was named South Molle and was one of the more popular resorts for young people and honeymooners.

As Pete pointed it out, the two in the back pricked up their ears and got excited. They craned their necks to look down at the resort.

"That's where we are staying," the girl shouted, gazing down through the perspex back window.

"Oh really?" Peter replied, with a gleam in his eye. "Would you like to be dropped off there instead of having to wait for the ferry to take you back from Shute Harbor?"

"You bet!" said the young man enthusiastically.

"O.K. Hang on!"

We roared low over the water to check the swell direction, which Pete said could be quite tricky here sometimes. It seemed to be fairly calm, so we came in low and slow around the point on the southeast side of the island, turned north in front of the beach, and touched down easily, paralleling the shore across a lazy swell. Just as we thought we were safely down, a huge swell lifted us out of the water and dropped us back in with a spine-jarring crunch and a plume of white spray. We bounced a couple more times, then Pete pulled the stick back and put the tail in the water for a full stall landing, and we settled like a wallowing walrus. Just another little technique I was going to have to learn!

As soon as we were safely in the water, he lowered the water rudder and turned us round to head back to the beach, opening the canopy as he did so to let some fresh breeze into the steaming cockpit. Right at that moment, I am sure the youngsters in the rear were wishing they had chosen to take the ferry home, but a few minutes later, I know they

257

changed their minds. The three of us were in for yet another new — and for them — unique experience.

As we taxied in towards the beach, Peter reached for the gear handle and lowered the wheels while still in deep water. Once more, I looked at him with raised eyebrows and open mouth. But I was not game to ask if he was going to do what I thought he was going to do.

He was!

The wheels brushed the sandy bottom. He pushed the throttle almost all the way forward, the engine howled, and then we were up on the beach, sitting high and dry with dozens of curious and disbelieving spectators approaching the plane to get a closer look at this unusual phenomenon.

"WOW!" said the young man, in ecstatic disbelief, looking around to see if any of his new-found friends were there to witness his James Bondish arrival.

"Jesus" the young girl exclaimed profoundly, in awed amazement at her strange and somewhat different climax to her morning's adventures.

Peter left me sitting where I was, jumped out of the plane and threw the back of his seat forward to allow his passengers to disembark in grand style. He took the girl around her slender waist and lifted her bodily out of the aircraft to set her lightly on its nose for all the assembled crowd to admire. Now this was definitely what I called Public Relations!

We sat there for a few minutes while he answered questions from the crowd about the plane and where it goes and how much it costs. When he could not entice any other game customers to come forth for a ride, he grinned at the crowd, jumped back in beside me, yelled at them to clear away from the propeller, started the engine, and amid bellowing noise and flying sand, turned her nose towards the water with rudder and brake. Moments later, she was back in her second element, lean and low in the clear blue sea, bobbing gently from float to float as we taxied out for the takeoff. Pete raised the gear handle, the hydraulic pump whined as it sucked up the wheels, she sniffed the wind, roared as he hit the throttle, then leapt out of the water and onto the planing hull, apparently as relieved as we were to be able to get up and go so quickly once more.

We bumped across the languid swells for a short distance, then we were airborne and heading for home, a three minute flight across the straits to Shute Harbor. The terminal was deserted when we landed and taxied up.

"Thanks, Pete. That was great," I said sincerely. "I can't wait to start doing it myself. I am really looking forward to it."

"No worries, Hoppy. You'll be a veteran before you know it. Meanwhile, any time there is a spare seat, I'll tell the girls to let you know, if you like."

"You bet! It is quite obvious that I have a lot to learn."

"O.K. Well, I'm going to dash home for a break and a bite to eat before the tide goes out again this afternoon. I'll see you later."

"All right. Thanks again."

He waved as he crawled through the fence into the trailer park next to the airstrip where he and his wife and family lived.

I wandered up to the office trailer and sat with the girls for most of the afternoon, learning the ropes with the paperwork side of the operation. They informed me that Kevin and Rod had indeed left on time and caught the morning jet from Proserpine to Brisbane, where they would spend the rest of the week at Archerfield Airport assisting with the assembly of their two brand new Lake Buccaneers.

That evening, Annie and Di offered to take me out on the town and show me around. We had a marvelous time, and I learned the location and reputation of every bar and restaurant in Airlie Beach. The week passed quickly as I settled comfortably into my new home, and managed to score several more trips to the reef with Peter.

Ten days after my accidental arrival in Airlie, I was standing down at the terminal hoping to bum yet another trip with Peter, who was still holding the fort on his own, when Sue came down from the house with the news that the local flight service station had called to advise that two UFOs (ugly flying objects) to the air traffic controllers, had been sighted in the vicinity and should be appearing at any time.

A few minutes later, the unmistakable sound of double chainsaws came faintly to our ears. Then, from out of nowhere, two brilliantly white Buccaneers decorated with narrow, red and black pinstripes roared down the middle of the airstrip at zero feet, their keels barely twelve inches above the grassy surface. They had remained hidden from sight by flying round the hill to the north, low over the water until they had to rise over the palm trees and power line at the far end of the strip. In line astern, they zoomed up into a climbing left turn just past the terminal. The passengers and staff who were gathered outside the tiny building watched in awe as the two gleaming amphibians climbed back over the top of the strip and returned to land.

Moments later, they descended from the north again, this time with their wheels down, landed gracefully one behind the other, and taxied up to the terminal. As Kevin and Rod shut down the engines, the assembled crowd, including a number of people from the trailer park who had come out to see what the commotion was about, clapped and cheered at the impromptu air show.

Kevin and Rod patiently answered questions for a few minutes, then they made off to the safety of their homes to spend the rest of the day with their families.

I did not speak to Kevin until the following afternoon, when he summoned me to the house to give me a briefing on my forthcoming training sessions, which were to begin the next day.

The next afternoon, Kevin and I took off in the old red Buccaneer, Alpha Whiskey India.

"No point in punishing one of the new birds," he reflected with a grin.

We alighted in the same passage between Long Island and the mainland which we had used before. The wind was light and the sea was calm. We practiced displacement taxiing, step taxiing, turning on the step in and out of wind. We took off and flew at zero feet round to Palm Bay, a small cove on the same island with a few self-contained bungalows hidden in a grove of coconut palms. It had a good beach which dropped off to a gravelly bottom. We practiced what Peter had shown me the other day, lowering the gear in the water to run up onto the beach, turning to parallel the water at the same time, to make return to it less difficult.

Over the next few days, Kevin took himself off the flying schedule and spent all his time with me, patiently teaching me all the things he had learned by hard experience over the last few years since he had established Air Whitsunday. He taught me how to read the wind direction and strength from the condition of the sea. He taught me the very different methods of taking off and landing in calm and rough water; how to approach mooring buoys and boats at just the right speed, and when to shut-down the engine with varying wind and tide strengths, so that I would neither ram the object, nor stop short of it, necessitating another engine start.

It became painfully obvious that there was much more involved in getting an airplane safely on and off the water — even protected water — than there was in simply taking off and landing on a nice long piece of concrete runway. There were frustrating days, particularly in high wave and wind conditions, when neither of us thought that I would ever get the hang of holding the nose down and the keel level to prevent us from being thrown high into the air in a stalled condition, then to come crashing back down onto the heaving surface; a painful, spine-jarring experience which was not good for either aircraft or crew.

During these frightening episodes, I did discover to my immense delight that there were distinct advantages to possessing a steel spine. While Kevin, and later my passengers, suffered severe distress and back discomfort under these horrendous conditions, I felt no pain whatsoever. Good ol' Doc Yeoman! My bionic back was worth its weight in gold now.

After several days of rugged, non-stop training, Kevin pronounced me fit to fly his aeroplanes with a reasonable chance of survival. He reserved me for scenic flights and land-to-land charters for the first few weeks, to allow me to become completely familiar with the handling and feel and performance of the aircraft, before I was finally permitted to venture forth to the reef with a load of unsuspecting passengers.

Kevin, Rod and Peter all escorted me out on that first day in their own aircraft. Naturally, I had the old bucket (which now leaked substantially more than it did before we began training), just in case, through some dreadful error of judgment, I accidentally put her up on the reef. I was rather dismayed to learn that each of the other three aircraft had only two passengers on board, allowing them to pick up my three if I did have a problem of some kind. Consolation for them, I was sure, but that still left me standing on the reef with the tide coming in, fifty miles from the nearest landfall.

Despite these melancholy precautions, however, I still looked forward to my first reef trip with eager, excited anticipation. Naturally, I did not inform my passengers that this was my — and therefore their own — baptism of fire.

For most passengers, this was their first trip to the Great Barrier Reef. Also for most of them, it was their first experience with a light aircraft, and particularly an amphibian. Some did not even realize that they were, in fact, going to land in the water, and had to be briefed accordingly. With this in mind, I carefully and thoroughly explained to my three reef-trippers, as I had heard the other fellows do, that the plane was actually a flying boat, and that although we were taking off from land, we would be landing in the water out at the reef.

Kevin had selected passengers for me who were all reasonably light in weight, to prevent my having any problems when it came time to get off the water. I had a young married couple, and an older woman, possibly in her sixties. The young man was around my own weight, so I asked him to sit in the front right seat to assist in keeping the bulk of the load, and therefore the center of gravity, forward. We climbed aboard, started our noisy engines, and trundled in single file up to the south end of the strip to take off in the customary direction, down the slight grade and into the prevailing northerly breeze. Kevin led the way, I came second, followed by Peter, then Rod. What a magnificent convoy!

I was supremely happy that bright, clear morning. At last I was about to embark on my own first real flight to the reef with a load of excited passengers. Kevin reached up and closed his canopy; it was the signal that he was about to go. Seconds later, his engine bellowed and Alpha Whiskey Yankee, one of the two new planes, rolled down the strip toward the mountain at the far end of it. As he climbed away from the hill in a right turn out over the bay, I reached up, closed my own canopy and pushed my throttle fully forward.

The deafening roar, muffled for me by my headset, again reverberated around the valley, and then we were running down the slope, feeling the air with our wings. As the airspeed indicator quivered on sixty knots, she came away and we were finished with the ground, climbing in a gentle right turn over the secluded beach. Several nude bathers, no doubt sure that their privacy would be secure on that isolated beach, ran for the cover of the palm trees for the second time in a matter of minutes. They obviously did not know that there was an airfield just on the other side of the scrub which isolated them. I laughed aloud at the thought that they would be ducking for cover twice more as the remainder of the aerial convoy roared low over their heads, shattering their illusion of tranquility.

We circled out over the deep, blue Whitsunday Passage, waiting for the others to catch up, then we formed up in line abreast, so all the passengers could see the sleek, graceful lines of the Buccaneers in flight, and take pictures if they so desired. Then we headed out over the passage, pointing out the wondrous features of the islands and resorts as we winged our way out to sea.

The radio crackled in my headset, and I heard Rod, the last in the convoy, relaying to Townsville Flight Center the details of our aircraft.

"Townsville, Townsville, good morning. This is Waterbird Four. Alpha Oscar Whiskey, Alpha Whiskey India, Alpha Whiskey Yankee and Alpha Whiskey Zulu. Total persons on board, one three. Endurance of each is ninety minutes. Destination, Hardy Lagoon."

"Roger Waterbird Four," came the distant reply a few moments later. "This is Townsville. Report at Pinnacle Point. Have a good flight."

"Is that Captain Stubby?" Peter's voice came in through the headset.

"Sure is. G'day, Pete. I'll probably be down on the weekend."

Before I realized what I had done, my thumb mashed the mike button.

"Pardon my ignorance," I asked the ethereal world in general, "but who or what is Captain Stubby?"

A sound disturbingly akin to muffled laughter filled the airwaves, and Rod replied, "You will find out. Let's just say the title has no bearing on the brand of shorts he wears. More likely to reflect the number of containers in which his generous self-imposed daily allowance of hops and barley is stored!"

"Oh. I see," I replied, not really seeing at all, and silently cursing my regrettable habit of opening my mouth before engaging my brain.

"Is this the new jock?" the same, slightly lisping voice came back.

"Uh . . . yes," I stammered self-consciously, very aware of having aroused the curiosity of a member of bureaucratic officialdom. "This is Rod."

"Rod?" repeated the distant voice suspiciously.

"Hereafter known as 'Hoppy,'" replied my better-known namesake.

I could not believe the idle chit-chat that these guys engaged in over the radio, especially that of an air traffic controller. Things were certainly much more casual up here in the bush than they were in the big cities.

The conversation petered out and we each got back to shouting at our respective passengers, pointing out the various features on the islands to them. The young fellow sitting next to me suddenly tapped me on the shoulder, and pointed down to a large, dark area on the surface of the sea. He then gave me the dubious privilege of hearing for the first time one of several questions which I would hear over and over again during the course of the next few years.

"Is that the coral down there?" he shouted, grinning and nodding in hopeful anticipation.

"No," I shouted back. I pointed up through the perspex canopy to a small, puffy white cloud which was passing in front of the sun.

"It's a cloud shadow," I yelled, barely able to conceal my amusement at his naivete.

"Oh," he replied in embarrassed dismay, hoping his new bride had not witnessed his ignorance.

As we continued on our way to the reef, following the same loop that Peter had shown me on my first trip out, I shouted continuously and excitedly to my equally enthralled passengers, sharing my new-found knowledge of the surrounding area with them. We gradually left the land and the islands behind, and before us lay the vast, empty, silent Pacific Ocean.

After several minutes of flight beyond the last point of land on Hayman Island, a curious silence fell over the group, who had previously been shouting and pointing and asking non-stop questions. Oddly enough, this strange phenomenon occurred on almost every subsequent flight I made to the reef. It must have been that the people, not quite understanding that the place we were taking them to was not landlocked, expected to see more islands — or coral atolls at the very least. I know they did not expect to encounter what they did; an empty horizon, where burnished sky met copper sea — the beginning of eight thousand miles of Pacific Ocean where, apart from small group of islands here and there, the next stop was South America.

No matter how I tried to arouse their interest, nothing seemed to work until I could shout "There's the reef! See the lighter colored water up ahead? We'll be there in a few minutes."

Then they became excited again, craning their necks and straining their eyes through the glare on the water, trying to make out something which looked in some way familiar to them.

What they saw however, was so totally different from what they expected, so wonderfully unique, that it literally took their breath away. With no warning at all, the deep, dark ocean was miraculously transformed into a vast, shallow, turquoise and emerald, coral-studded sea.

There was no mistaking this for cloud shadow on the water! What a simply incredible manifestation of nature!

We flew over Hook Reef and Hardy Lagoon at a thousand feet, to give them a good view of the magnificent spectacle, then zoomed lower and lower as I showed them the different formations of coral surrounding and within the lagoon itself. As we roared past the 'Reef Encounter' at deck height, waving to those on board, I explained her presence there. I passed over the one narrow break in the entire coral wall of the lagoon, which allowed the huge vessel to pass through only at certain very high tides, and even then with extreme danger of ripping her hull from end to end.

Then we were outside the lagoon again, lining up over the deep channel separating it from Hook Reef, in preparation for landing. I put the flaps down, remembered to leave the wheels up, and came in for a long, low approach over the top of the already exposed coral wall. One tiny error of judgment here, and we would be sliced open like a knife passing through warm butter! Too low and we would strike the coral at the approach end of the lagoon; too high, and we would be running too fast to stop before we rammed into the coral at the other end of our landing area. No brakes here! No way to stop her except for her own inertia and drag in the water!

I watched Kevin land in front of me, picked out the exact spot on the water where his wake began when his keel cut the surface, and made that my aiming point. He had come to a stop in a flurry of spray about a hundred feet from the barrier at the far end of the run. No worries! We passed low over the channel, our keel barely inches above the treacherous coral wall separating it from the lagoon. I flared just inside the lagoon, and held her off.

It looked like a perfect approach . . . until, just at the absolute critical moment — of any landing, but particularly this one — the woman in the seat behind me discovered to her horror that there was no runway beneath us, despite my meticulous briefing before we departed.

"Aaahhh! My God! We're crashing! We're crashing!!" she screeched, at the same time seizing my throat in a vice-like grip from behind.

This unexpected outburst, not to mention the deathgrip on my windpipe, scared the living daylights out of me and threw me completely off balance. We hit the water hard, bounced once, lurched sideways as I tried desperately to regain control with one hand, while attempting to release the mad woman's clutch with the other, then we were skidding along the surface at breakneck speed toward the rapidly approaching coral barrier.

The young girl screamed. Her brainless companion, lacking something of substance to cling to, immediately and unerringly found the right hand control yoke, and gripped it tightly with whitening knuckles. Now I had to fight his panic-stricken grip on the aircraft, as well as the frenzied grip on my own person!

Definitely not a good way to begin my career as a reef pilot!

The reef loomed ahead, reaching out for us with deadly coral fingers. In sheer desperation, I knocked the fellow's hands away with a karate chop to both his wrists, twisted myself free from the maniacal woman behind me, pulled full back on the yoke, and shoved a big footful of left rudder in at the same time. The result was instantaneous and even more terrifying. I closed my eyes and prayed; there was nothing more I could do.

The plane's nose came out of the water, the tail went under, the left wing float dug in, and we slewed around to the left in a deliberate and ungainly water loop which probably saved our lives. A huge wall of white water engulfed us in a blinding sheet of spray. We came to rest, rocking and rolling, a bare twenty feet from the coral barrier wall. The engine was still ticking over with a comforting burble. The right wing was pointing toward the reef as a result of my desperate attempt to stop, so I kept my left foot hard on the rudder and continued the turn away from the coral.

"You O.K., Hoppy?" came Kevin's justifiably concerned voice over my radio headset.

"Ye . . . Yeah. I . . . I think so," I gulped. "It could have been worse, I guess."

"Not much," Peter chimed in with a chuckle, apparently amused by my almost fatal near-miss with the reef.

"What happened?" Kevin asked diplomatically.

"You don't want to know," I replied through clenched teeth as I tried to hold down my anger and rapidly rising aftershock.

"I'll tell you when we get over to the reef," I added, deciding that Kevin would indeed want to know what had happened.

By now we were safely taxiing back to the mooring area. I turned on the bilge pump, just in case. She pumped a bit of water overboard, but no more than normal for her age and the punishment she suffered during training sessions. I took a good look at the left float, but it seemed undamaged. At least, it was not slipping under the surface, a sure sign that it had popped some rivets and was taking water.

I turned with a very angry and frightening red countenance to the woman sitting behind me. She was shriveled up in her seat, kneading her hands in anguish, and her own face was positively ashen.

"Oh dear. Oh dear," she was mumbling to nobody in particular.

"MADAM!" I shouted, trying to keep myself as calm as possible. "I told you quite clearly before take off that we would be landing in the water. Don't you remember?"

"I . . . I forgot. I've never landed in the water before. When we took off, I thought we would be landing on an island . . . or something. I'm very sorry," she added meekly.

"She's sorry," I muttered to myself. Then I remembered the brainless galah beside me!

"And as for you," I snarled at him, unable to control my anger, "I also distinctly remember telling you not to touch the controls under any circumstances. Or did you just forget, too?"

"There was nothing to hold on to when we bounced. It was just there, so I grabbed it," he said brilliantly.

I shook my head in mute disbelief. Obviously, I had a lot to learn about human nature, too; and I had better learn it fast! I also made a mental note to remove the right side control yoke as soon as I got back to the airstrip.

Taxiing back to the mooring area, just near where we had all initially touched down, I shut down the engine and came to a drifting stop almost exactly beside my buoy, which I reached for and picked up with ease, and secured it to the nose cleat. A few very silent minutes later, Kevin backed the glass-bottomed boat up to us, and I was relieved to hand my three errant passengers off the plane and into the boat, under the watchful supervision of Kevin, Rod and Peter.

We reached the surface of the exposed reef shortly after, where Peter briefed the group once more on the perils of the coral, and how and where to walk, to prevent injury to themselves and the thousands of tiny life forms on the reef. They all donned their canvas tennis shoes and stumbled onto the sharp, craggy surface, to assemble in a rough circle around Peter, who was to give them his customary knowledgeable spiel about how and why the reef was formed, and pick up and show them some of the beautiful creatures that live on and in the coral. I never ceased to be astounded at his uncanny ability to answer almost any question put to him with the authority and confidence of an experienced marine biologist.

Kevin stoked up his pipe, remained on the boat, and signaled to me to do likewise. Here it comes, I thought. He peered at me through dense clouds of blue smoke, the only pollution for thousands of miles, and scratched his thick, black beard.

"Well? What happened?" he asked gently. "You appeared to be set up for a perfect approach, then you went haywire."

I explained to him in complete and embarrassing detail the circumstances of my near disaster.

"Hmmmm!" was his thoughtful reply, still scratching his whiskers. "Well, at least you had the presence of mind to stall and waterloop. It was a good save, under the circumstances," he said after a few moments silence.

"You'll know for next time that you can't tell these loopies often enough just what to expect when they get out here. Although it was just bad luck that you happened to get a crazy one! I have never known that to happen before. Not even to Pete. Don't worry about it. I'll take her back with me, and leave you to cope with the kid. I gave you three to get you used to a full load water take off, but you have plenty of time for that."

"Thanks, Kev. I appreciate your patience. It won't happen again."

21

Nothing further happened on the journey home to shatter my own —
or Kevin's — confidence. The lighter load allowed the Buccaneer to
leap out of the water, as if sensing it was time to get out of this
dangerous place. Fortunately for us both, I did not see my former
murder-prone passenger again.

Over the following weeks, I had several near-disasters as I learned
to cope with varying sea and wind conditions, which were impossible
to duplicate in a training environment. However, I managed, with a
little acquired skill and a lot of plain old good luck, to extricate myself
and my aircraft from these potentially deadly situations, getting away
without putting so much as a scratch on whatever plane I happened to
be flying at the time of the incident.

As my experience grew, I was assigned one of the new Buccaneers.
Alpha Whiskey Yankee became my personal toy and hobby, and I
treated her like my very own. Each afternoon at the end of the flying
day, I hosed her down with fresh water and greased all her movable

parts and bearings, particularly the wheels and brakes which were constantly in the salt water, to try to delay the inevitable corrosion.

Peter had recently been forced to demonstrate a wheels-up landing on the airstrip as a result of his gear seizing in a partially retracted position. The bearings in the gear legs had finally become so corroded that one day, they simply refused to come back down. However, as Kevin had assured me, there was no damage except for some paint loss on the keel and a slightly buckled left float when the weight of the plane came to rest on it.

There was other work to be done apart from the reef trips. Many times, we had to drop into sheltered — and sometimes not so sheltered — bays and coves to pick up or drop off people on boats for one reason or another. Some of these trips turned out to be far more dangerous than merely landing and taking off amid coral reefs.

On one of my first trips to a supposedly sheltered bay on the southeast side of Whitsunday Island, I realized far too late in my final approach that a huge swell, much bigger than I had at first imagined, was rolling into the beach; Landing towards the beach and across the swell, I broke the cardinal rule of seaplane operations, which is to always land along a swell wherever possible. The first bounce threw me fifty feet back into the air, with no flying speed left. The plane stalled back into the water with a horrible, jarring impact, and bounced again. This terrifying routine continued almost all the way to the beach. About twenty or thirty yards from the beach, I finally got her under some measure of control with a full stall landing which submerged the entire rear end of the aircraft.

The swell carried us into the shore, where my horrified would-be passengers stared aghast at the frightening performance. I shut down the engine and managed to jump out in time to prevent her nose gear doors from receiving a terrible pounding as she came crashing down on the rocky shoreline. Hobbling around to the nose, I just barely managed, using all my strength, to hold her off against the force of the huge waves, while my passengers stood there watching me struggle against the powerful elements of nature.

"Come on, you lot!" I shouted at them. "Don't just stand there. You!" I yelled, pointing to the largest of the party of two men and a girl, "Help me hold the plane off while you other two get in. Both of you in the back seat. Quickly now!"

When they were seated in the back, my reluctant assistant and I managed to turn the plane around to face the swell. I told him to get in while I held the nose into the waves and tried to hold her tail off the beach.

Standing there in waist-deep surf, I held her cockpit coaming in my left hand and reached in to start the engine with my right. Fortunately, she fired instantly and began to motor out into the waves, dragging me alongside. Against the combined pressure of the swells and the forward motion of the aircraft, I struggled to get my left foot on the fuselage step, found it, and heaved myself up and over the coaming into the cockpit, sloshing a generous amount of cold seawater in with me. Panting heavily with the effort, I got my feet on the rudders and held the plane into the waves.

My troubles were just beginning! I knew that there was no way that I was going to get off the water with this load in these conditions; we would all be killed if I attempted it. So we taxied! Each time her nose dipped into a wave, huge plumes of white spray came washing over us, so I closed both halves of the canopy, not only to prevent us from being totally drenched, but also to prevent the plane from filling with water and sinking! We taxied far out from shore, her bow sometimes plunging completely under the surface as she dipped into another swell. My passengers spoke not at all. I knew from previous experience that they were terrified! But they were not half as frightened as I was. I knew what was still to come!

Several hundred yards out from the beach, I turned to parallel the rocky coast. The wind was blowing from the direction of the shoreline I had just left, but to attempt a take-off in that direction — the same direction I had landed — would be suicidal. Bouncing across that swell with this heavy load on board, we would crash into the beach long before the plane had reached flying speed. The only alternative was to take off with a direct crosswind, along the swell, which was about four feet high, out in the open sea where I was now. I could not take off to the west, as that would be downwind and would lengthen my run through these ocean waves even more.

No! I had to make my run to the east. The only problem here was that a spit of land running roughly north and south projected from the east side of the beach. I would have to take off towards it. If I taxied any further out into the open water to clear the spit, the swell grew proportionately larger, and there was a very real chance that we would be swamped before we even attempted a takeoff.

I briefed my inert passengers to fasten their seat belts VERY securely! The right-hand control yoke was now removed so that no other mentally disturbed front seat passenger could attempt to kill me in a moment of panic. Reaching down between the seats, I pulled up the water rudder. She slowly swung around to face the east. I lowered it again to prevent her from swinging all the way through to northeast, into the wind. I locked down the canopy. Then I prayed. Fervently!

Gulping with fear at what I was about to attempt, I drew a deep breath, rammed the overhead throttle fully forward, then grabbed the yoke with both hands and pulled it back hard into my stomach. The engine bellowed, the nose came up, and a veritable wall of green-white water engulfed us.

She lumbered sluggishly through the waves, the swells from our right threatening to turn us over before we could get onto the step. I pumped the yoke back and forth, lifting and dropping her nose to try to get some momentum. Slowly, slowly, she lifted her bulbous snout out of the heaving sea, struggling to overcome the incredible drag created by her half-submerged hull. Then we were up and running, her keel slicing the windswept surface.

Her right wing and float took the brunt of the punishment from the huge swells, jarring the whole aircraft as they smashed over us. I ran down the trough of one, then up onto the crest of another, where I kept her finely balanced as she readied herself for flight. The spit of land rushed inexorably towards us. With the heavy load on board, we had taken too long to get out of the water and onto the step. We were running out of distance!

I tried lifting her off. She came out, then fell heavily back into the clutches of the swell. The land drew closer and closer! Finally, finally, the airspeed indicator quivered on sixty knots. She HAD to come away!

Reaching for the flap lever, I threw it into the down position. The extra lift catapulted her out of the water, where she hovered just a few precious feet above the surface. The airspeed remained steady because of the increased drag. We had to CLIMB! The spit of land was now only seconds away! And it was higher than I had at first estimated!

I raised the nose slightly, reached for the flap handle once more, and slammed it up. We sank immediately back towards the sea as the extra lift was stolen from her. Strictly no go! We were not going to make it!

"DO something, you fool!" my own snivelling organism shouted at me, not prepared for this terrifying experience.

Then the airspeed was climbing, and so were we. I inched the nose up further, aiming at the lowest point in the land which now filled the windshield. We roared over a barren, rocky slope, and through a shallow saddle in the terrain, barely inches above certain death. Then we were across the other side and climbing steadily away from the open sea below us once more. I let out a long, slow breath, which I just realized I had been holding since the beginning of the takeoff run.

Nobody spoke for the entire trip back to the airstrip, which was mercifully only about ten minutes. We landed uneventfully — although a crash landing which took off both wings would have been uneventful after that takeoff. Three ashen-faced, wild-eyed passengers stumbled out of the plane and tottered, on very wobbly legs, towards their car in the parking lot. They did not speak to me, but I heard the woman say to the man who had been sitting next to me, "Never again, Frank! Don't you EVER ask me to go up in a plane again. I'm telling you, Frank . . . " she was still yabbering at him as they got in their car and drove away.

I sagged onto the bench outside the terminal and tried to stop my hands from trembling, eternally grateful that neither Kevin nor the other fellows were present at that time to ask me how the trip went. Basking in the hot, balmy sunshine, I let the peace and quiet of this beautiful place seep into me, and reflected on how good it was to be alive.

I resolved that I would have to be much more careful about inspecting the sea conditions BEFORE I committed myself to a landing. Especially when I was picking up passengers rather than dropping them off. It would have been much less traumatic had I been taking off empty, when the plane would have come out of the water quickly and cleanly!

That night, I treated myself to an excellent dinner and a bottle of fine Australian wine at Romeo's Italian Courtyard restaurant, to celebrate my continued existence in the mortal world. Yet, sitting there under the ancient mango tree in the courtyard, watching young and old couples coming and going, I realized that I was still very lonely. This feeling had been creeping up on me for some time. I had been living and flying here for several months now, but I knew that despite my miraculous come-back from being a paraplegic, I was still not completely happy.

Oh, I had a lot of new friends, all right. I had been out with Annie and Di on several occasions, but they were just very good friends and workmates. I had taken out one or two of the local girls from time to time, and even had a regular girlfriend for a while. However, the gnawing discontent and loneliness continued to build, deep inside me. I knew that I would never go back to Sydney now. I had finally admitted to myself that my life there was past history; gone, but never forgotten. With that melancholy thought in mind, I bought another bottle of wine and left Romeo's on legs more unsteady than usual, to drive the short distance to my apartment; a journey which was probably, considering my inebriated condition, much more dangerous than the life-threatening situation in which I had placed myself earlier that day.

On reaching the safe haven of my apartment, I curled up with the second bottle and played some of my favorite record albums. The wine and the music made me even more melancholy, and I finally stumbled up the stairs to bed. Next morning dawned bright and clear, and so did my spirits. Parrots shrieked and crows cawed outside my window, calling me to get out of bed and enjoy the new day in this tropical land of peace and beauty.

Finished with breakfast, I donned my cleanest uniform shirt, shorts and salt-stained cap, trotted out to the car, and drove the short distance through Airlie Beach to the airstrip for another hard day at the office.

Time passed and I found myself coping much better with my ability to extricate myself from dangerous situations at sea in small aircraft not really designed for the work we were doing with them. As my experience level grew, both Kevin and I became more confident in my capability to handle increasingly difficult missions. I flew several medical evacuations, plucking injured people, some of whom would probably have died, off the decks of boats to fly them to Proserpine Airport, for transfer to the hospital.

This work was tremendously satisfying, both in the challenge and danger of getting the plane in and out of very hazardous waters, and the reward of gratitude by the injured patients and their shipmates.

However, my restless loneliness remained. The very fact that I was living in a virtual paradise, and had not found the ideal mate with whom to share it, was what was ailing me most. I had often spoken to Nellie by phone, and sometimes to Barb if she happened to be there when I rang. This only made matters worse, though, knowing that our lives were so far apart now, but still hoping that someday we would be together again.

Then one night, the phone rang and the bottom fell out of my world.

❖

22

"Hello," I answered morosely as I picked up the receiver.

"Rod, this is Nellie."

I knew instantly that she was crying and that something was terribly wrong.

"What . . . what is it, Nellie? What's happened? It's Barb, isn't it?"

There was silence on the line for a long time.

"She's dead, Rod. Oh Dear God, she's dead!! Our Barby's gone!"

She began sobbing uncontrollably.

So did I!

When the horrible, sickening initial shock had passed, I managed to speak.

"God, Nellie," I cried, wiping the flood of tears from my eyes, "what happened to her? Oh Lord, I can't believe it. I won't believe it, dammit!"

"It's true, Rod. She . . . she and Chris. They got married, you know. I didn't have the heart to tell you. I wish to God I had! Anyway, she had been drinking a lot lately. They were driving home from a party. Both of them had been drinking. They . . . they hit a . . . a telephone pole. Both killed instantly. Not a mark on Barb's body. The shoulder strap of her seat belt crushed her windpipe. Oh Rod, I am so sorry. So terribly sorry. I always hoped you two would get back together again one day, but now . . . "

"So did I, Nellie," I sobbed. "I dreamed constantly of the day she would come to me here, and never want to leave."

We cried and consoled each other for a long time.

When I finally put down the phone, my life was more empty than it had ever been in the two years since finding this perfect place. I sat for a long time in the silent darkness of the apartment, and wept for things that could never be. Days passed and I gradually picked up the pieces of my broken dreams, and put them away in the back of my mind as treasured memories.

I took to spending much more time with the pilots, particularly the new guys, Paul, Dick and Glenn, who had joined the company about the same time I did. I found myself drinking more than I had been accustomed to. The daily sessions at Kevin's place became almost a ritual to me. One day, though, I decided that enough was enough. While a long way from becoming an alcoholic, I did not want to go the rest of the way towards finding out before, like Barbara, it was too late to turn back. I had to either give up flying, or give up drinking; or one day when I needed all of my faculties functioning perfectly to save myself and my passengers from another accident, I would not be capable of doing so. So, I gave up drinking. A good thing, too.

One day after I had come to the brilliantly perspicacious conclusion that drinking and flying don't mix, I was assigned to pick up three passengers off a boat moored in a cove on the north shore of Hook Island, about two miles across from the resort on Hayman. I landed in a moderate swell of about two feet, taxied up behind the boat and, though both yacht and plane were rolling heavily in the on-shore swell, managed to transfer all of them into the aircraft without any of us taking an involuntary swim.

Pushing back from the stern of the yacht, I started the engine and taxied to the most favorable place for takeoff, abeam that rocky and inhospitable shore. We were not terribly heavy and the takeoff was more or less normal, considering the sea that was running.

We roared past their boat at low level so that my passengers could wave good-bye to their comrades still on board. As we banked into a steep left turn away from the boat at about two hundred feet above the waves, I sensed that something was not right with the aircraft. I turned the yoke to the right to level the wings. Nothing happened! There was absolutely no response by the ailerons to the pressure I tried to bring to bear on them via their cables connected to the control yoke. It was sloppy and useless under my hand! The aileron cables had parted! Oh my God! Here we go again!

I immediately kicked in full right rudder to stop the aircraft from rolling over and spinning into the sea. She sideslipped down towards the water for a few seconds, until I drew gently back on the yoke. I still had rudder and elevator control, but it was plainly obvious that there was no way I could make it back to the airstrip and pull off a successful landing with no ailerons to counter the strong, gusty downdrafts that were a constant danger on either approach to the strip. In fact, I could not be sure just how long I could remain airborne at all, with only the use of rudder to steer her and keep her level. The only safe option I had was to get back down into the sea. And quickly!

We were more or less straight and level now, heading downwind at about one hundred feet above the white-capped waves. There was no way I could try to turn back into wind at this altitude, and to attempt a climb would be to increase the chance of spinning if a wing went down in a gust and I put in too much, or not enough rudder to counter it. There was no way around it. I was going to have to attempt a downwind landing into a rolling, two feet swell with no ailerons to prevent a wing from dropping into the sea, which would in turn initiate a high speed water loop. Not a pleasant prospect!

I shouted to my passengers that we had a slight problem and that I was going to set her down in the water again, just to be on the safe side. Ha! The less they knew, the better. Besides, I was too busy to tell them that they were seconds away from death!

I pulled the power all the way back, got the flaps out, raised the nose and let the airspeed bleed off to about sixty knots and eased her down into a gentle descent. The waves rose up to greet us. The rocky shore to our left seemed to be beckoning us over to be pounded to pieces on its granite ramparts. Then we were just a foot above the swells, holding off to let the airspeed come off. We were flashing over the surface at a much faster than normal approach speed, despite what the airspeed indicator read, because of the wind behind us. I guessed it must be still about eighty knots. Much too fast, and there was nothing I could do about it.

Inches above the waves . . . slight pressure on the right rudder bar to bring her nose to bear more or less along the swell.

Right wing dropping! Pick it up! Pick it UP, for Christ's sake!

Left rudder!

Steady, steady now. Hold her off! Keep her straight!

Left wing dropping now!

Right rudder again. Quickly now!

Nose dropping! More back pressure! More back . . .

The keel sliced the top of the first swell. I pushed forward gently on the yoke now, to keep her keel down in the sea. A bounce at this point would finish us.

Still too fast! Skipping along the swells; the frightening sound of the waves battering against her thin bottom.

Slowing now. Keep the nose down . . . Keep the nose down . . . Looking good . . . Might just get away with it!

Just as I was thinking it was going to be all right, a huge swell rose out of the sea immediately ahead of us. We hit it and bounced! The nose came up and the left wing went down. Strictly no go! We were going to break up! In sheer desperation, I yanked back on the stick and put the tail in the water, at the same time kicking in right rudder. We stalled into the sea, the right wing float went under, we rotated around it, then slowed and came to a heaving, spray-splattered stop and sat rolling in the heavy swells.

I took off my headset and wiped the streaming perspiration from my face and forehead with hands that were none too steady.

I had gotten away with it again! I did not deserve this much luck! How many more times was I going to have to tempt fate like this?

"What happened?" asked the fellow sitting next to me, blissfully unaware that he was very lucky to be alive.

"Oh, just a slight malfunction of the controls. I thought it would be safer to get us down than to try to press on. I am going to call up our base and have them send over another aircraft to take you home. Should not be too long. In the meantime, if you would like to get out and sit on the wings or the top of the cabin and soak up a bit of sun, you're more than welcome to do so."

They did not seem particularly perturbed by our ungainly return to the sea, which was by no means as bad as when that crazy woman had been clutching at my throat. I opened the canopy on the right side and my passengers took me at my word, climbed out and up onto the roof of the cabin to sit with their back to the engine pod, dangling their feet over the side of the fuselage. Using the company channel on the high-frequency radio, I called Annie and told her about my difficulty, then turned us towards Langford Reef where I could nose up to the sandy beach and let my people off so they could be transferred to another aircraft.

Fifteen minutes later, I put them all ashore at Langford just as Alpha Oscar Whiskey touched down in the calmer water beside us. Peter nosed her into the beach and jumped out with his usual wide grin, and we stood holding our aircraft in waist deep water as we discussed the problem. We decided the best thing to do would be to taxi over to Hayman Island, where I could run the plane up on the firm, sandy beach above the high tide mark. Pete could take the passengers back to the airstrip, bring a mechanic and tools over to Hayman, and then take me back with him.

Late that afternoon, back at Kevin's house, it did not take much to talk me into falling off the wagon again — but only to celebrate yet another miraculous escape from almost certain disaster.

So I had just a couple of beers, then went home to ponder my future.

23

On a warm October morning, I was standing on the reef at Hardy Lagoon, showing my passengers a few of the thousands of colorful specimens of marine life which made their homes in the coral. There were perhaps a dozen people standing around on the top of the exposed reef, and several more snorkeling in the clear, deep blue channel off its outer edge. Six Buccaneers rode gently at their moorings in the turquoise water of the calm lagoon.

I was squatting down pointing out a bright red feather starfish to one of my people, when I happened to glance toward the channel just as one of the snorkelers was climbing out of the water. She was wearing a light blue, one piece bathing suit. Her long, dark hair was braided into pigtails. Her legs were long, brown and slender and her feet were only partially protected from the razor-sharp coral by a pair of old, worn, battered canvas tennis shoes which had more holes than covering, and which were about three sizes too big for her.

For some reason, I could not take my eyes off her. I became conscious of the fact that I was staring at her, and that my passengers were becoming restless at my sudden lack of attention to them. I reluctantly returned my attention to the starfish which had wrapped its spikey, but harmless, tentacles around my fingers.

Shortly after, when my people had wandered off to explore on their own, Peter came up to me and pointed out the girl, who was now hunkered down near the outer edge, exploring the coral and its denizens with her fingers.

"Hey, Hoppy. Two of my passengers have never snorkeled before, and want me to teach them. My third one is over there. She has already been in the water and I think she's O.K., but keep an eye on her for me anyhow, will you? She's a photographer from the States."

I couldn't tell whether he had noticed that I was already keeping both eyes on her, and was just pulling my leg.

"O.K., I'll see if I can manage to squeeze her into my busy schedule," I wisecracked.

I tried several times to approach her, but each time, I turned away with confused thoughts running around in my head. Finally, I gave up and returned to the glass-bottomed boat, where I stood with my steel spine resting against the central hand-rail and my face to the breeze, staring towards South America and wishing I was there.

My mind was literally eight thousand miles away, when the back end of the boat dipped slightly as somebody stepped aboard. I turned to see her sit on the bench behind me. She reached into an old, faded blue nylon camera bag and brought out an ancient brown floppy-brimmed straw hat which had almost as many holes in it as her shoes. She jammed it down on her head and looked up at me, squinting against the glare.

"Don't move," she said. "You make a nice windbreak. I am absolutely freezing. I spent too long in the water. It's really beautiful!"

"It . . . it certainly is," I stammered in reply. "I'll be more than happy to be your windbreak. Where are you from?"

"Dallas, Texas," she replied.

"Oh really," I replied with quickened interest. "One of my favorite parts of the world, Texas. Although I haven't actually been to Dallas."

Those few magic moments were shattered by the return to the boat of some of the other passengers. We continued to chat, but she was much more reserved with the others present. She did take a few pictures of me with a well-worn old Leica she took from her bag. When all the reef-trippers and their pilots were back on the boat, we motored off to our respective aircraft.

As I sat on the bow of Alpha Whiskey Yankee, dangling my feet in the water and waiting for the other planes to be loaded, I watched her board Peter's plane. She squatted on its nose and aimed the camera at me. On a mad and irrational impulse, I rose to my feet and deliberately threw myself backwards over the bow of the plane and into the cool, clear water of the lagoon, badly jarring my steel spine as I landed flat on my back with a huge splash. She got the shot, despite the fact that she was laughing uncontrollably at my ridiculous and impromptu clowning.

My own passengers, for their part, quite rightly believed that I had taken leave of my doubtful senses, and stared at me from inside the cockpit with mouths agape as I swam back to the side of the plane and heaved myself aboard, dousing them all with water as I did so.

I sat in my soaking seat, completely befuddled by my own highly irregular behavior. It was not normally in my nature to carry on like an adolescent schoolboy!

"Are you all right?" she shouted to me across the fifty feet or so which separated our aircraft.

"I'm fine," I called back. "Never better, in fact," I lied as my spine throbbed with the aftershock of impact.

She spoke again, but her voice was drowned out by the roar of Peter's engine starting up. She waved as she jumped down into the cockpit and they taxied away towards the beginning of the take-off run.

It was then that I realized I did not even know her name. Great going, Romeo. Right on the ball! She'll probably disappear as soon as she gets back to the strip and you will never see her again. So? What else is new?

To my great surprise and delight, however, I was wrong — as usual. When I taxied up to the terminal, she was there, squatting with one knee on the grass, her old camera balanced on the other one, as she photographed my arrival.

I got rid of my passengers as quickly as courtesy allowed, then walked up to her, trying hard to hide my limp, as she stood to get another shot of the plane.

"By the way, my name's Rod," I said with a grin and an outstretched hand.

"But we call him 'Hoppy,' " chuckled my namesake, who was relaxing on the verandah with the inevitable dangling cigarette and a cup of coffee. "Just so there won't be any confusion," he added with a broad grin under his bushy moustache.

"Hi. I'm Cindy," she said, briefly shaking my hand, and waving to Rod.

"I have to drop off some of the other passengers in town," I remarked casually. "If . . . you're not doing anything, perhaps you would like to come with me. Maybe we can get a bite to eat."

"Thanks anyway," she replied, "but I'd like to get some more shots before I leave the area today."

"Oh," I said dejectedly. "Well, maybe I'll see you before you go then."

"Maybe."

I turned and walked over to the Air Whitsunday mini-bus parked outside the terminal. It was already full of recently returned passengers who were anxious to get back to Airlie Beach for some lunch themselves. As I climbed into the driver's seat and started the engine, the front passenger door opened. She stood there in her floppy straw hat, over-sized canvas shoes and a pair of scraggly blue shorts and an equally nondescript T-shirt.

"On second thought, I do need to go into town. I have to get some postcards and more film before I leave."

"Hop in," I said, grinning and pushing my old salt-encrusted red cap onto the back of my head.

She didn't speak again on the way into town, except to make a remark to the effect that she hoped my flying was better than my driving, clutching desperately to a hand-grip as we rounded the curve at the bottom of the mountain slope.

I made several stops at the various hotels in Airlie, and finally disposed of the last of my passengers.

"Sure you wouldn't like to have some lunch?" I asked hopefully.

"I guess I am a little hungry," she replied coyly.

"O.K. Let's go back to the Terrace coffee shop at the edge of town. They have excellent sandwiches and snacks there."

I could not believe she was actually going to have lunch with me. Maybe my luck was changing at last. We parked at The Terrace and ambled past the tables and chairs placed in front of the coffee shop. Inside at the refrigerated display of deli meats, cheeses and tempting cakes and pastries, she pondered a while, then ordered a plain roast beef roll with mustard, and a small bottle of fresh orange juice. I had the same kind of roll and a large chocolate milkshake. We went back outside to sit in the cool breeze at one of the sidewalk tables.

"So how did you like the reef?" I asked, not quite knowing how to strike up an intelligent conversation with this tom-boyish young girl.

"It was great! That was the second time I've been out there. Peter took me out yesterday. It really is beautiful. Do they actually pay you to do that?"

"They better!" I replied emphatically. "It's not all beer and skittles, you know."

"Not what?"

"It's not all fun. Sometimes it can be extremely dangerous. I guess I can say that, now that you have your two feet firmly planted on the ground," I grinned.

"Well, I thought it was fantastic. If I was not heading north tomorrow, I'd do it again."

"Can't you stay a bit longer?" I asked, trying not to be too obvious.

"Nope. I've got a real tight schedule. I have to be in Townsville tomorrow afternoon to catch a flight out to Alice Springs. Then I rent another car and drive to Ayers Rock, and on down to South Australia."

"I see. Sounds like a great trip. Where do you go from there?"

"Well, I drive back across through Victoria and New South Wales to Sydney. Then I fly down to Tasmania for a few days, then over to New Zealand for a week's hiking trip around the South Island."

"Sounds wonderful!" I said, genuinely excited for her. "When do you get back home?"

"Well, I have promised my parents that I will be back in Dallas for Christmas. So I will probably leave to go back from New Zealand when I have finished there."

"How long have you been away?"

"Oh, about three weeks so far. I intend to be gone for around three months altogether."

"Are you going to sell your pictures to somebody when you get back?"

"Maybe. If I can. I don't have a buyer right now. I am just going to put them together with a story and hope some magazine will buy them."

"I'm sure they will," I said, confident that she could do excellent work.

I was having such a great time just being in the company of this fascinating girl and talking to her about her trip, that I had completely forgotten I had to get back to the airstrip for a couple of scenic flights.

On an impulse, I looked at my watch and realized that I had ten minutes to get back to the strip and ready my plane for the next trip.

"Something wrong?" Cindy asked, a trifle miffed that she had caught me clock-watching.

"No. Not at all. I do have to get back though. I have a couple of scenic flights to do. Would you like to come?"

"Well, it would be a long walk back," she said.

"No, no. I mean, would you like to come on one of the flights with me? I didn't mean would you like to ride back in the bus . . . "

Her grin gave her away. I realized that I was going to have to be very careful how I worded my sentences from now on.

"Just kidding," she smiled, rising to her feet. "Let's go, then!"

We jumped into the van and rode back to the airstrip in silence, admiring the beauty of the surrounding bush, and the silence broken only by the screeching of wild parrots and the constant drone of cicadas in the trees.

The short time I had spent with Cindy already had me convinced that I must see her again before she left town. I knew in a few hours she would be gone from my life before I could know her a little better, and the thought saddened me greatly. To find someone like her, only to lose her again almost immediately . . .

The story of my life!

As we pulled in beside the terminal, I asked her again if she would like to go on a scenic flight with me if there was room.

"Sure. That would be fun. Maybe I can get some more shots of the islands before I leave," she said.

With that, I dashed inside to ask Di how many passengers I had on each trip. My heart sank as she checked the schedule and told me that all the seats were full on both flights. The first three people were waiting outside already, and I had not even refueled the plane yet.

I went back outside to find Cindy shooting some beautiful poincianas growing alongside the terminal building.

"I'm sorry," I said ruefully. "All the seats are taken. Are you sure you have to leave tomorrow? Maybe I can take you up on a special flight."

"That's O.K. No. I have to leave, but thanks anyway for trying."

"What about later this evening, then," I persisted. "Perhaps we can grab a pizza or something for dinner."

"Maybe," she said noncommittally.

"Well, I have to go and fuel the plane. I'll see you later, I hope."

She raised her hand in a half wave, but did not reply.

I turned and limped dejectedly over to the fueling tractor, jumped on and drove it and the trailer holding six drums of aviation gasoline over to where Alpha Whiskey Yankee was parked in front of the terminal.

"Won't be long, folks," I called to my curious passengers as I hauled the long black hose up to the central fuel tank, the filler cap of which was on top of the fuselage to the left of the engine pylon. Jumping up onto the left wing, I perched there and pumped the gas into the tank. I looked up to see Cindy in front of the plane, squatting in her familiar crouch to steady the camera, taking several shots of me sitting down on the job.

"Don't move," she called, squinting at me around the viewfinder. "That's great, just like you are. Except, push your cap back a bit, so your eyes aren't in shadow. There!"

Several minutes and a dozen shots later, she seemed satisfied, and backed off to await further developments. I cleared away the fueling equipment, then beckoned to my people that we were ready to go. As they climbed awkwardly aboard through the front canopy hatches, Cindy recorded it all on film for posterity.

I started up and taxied down to the north end of the strip, turned around and applied takeoff power. As we roared past the terminal, I kept her low to the ground and saw Cindy waving as we zoomed up into a steep climb. When I returned about thirty minutes later, she was gone.

My next three passengers were waiting as I taxied up, so I did not have time to try to find her. I took off again with a knot of anxiety hardening in my stomach. I could not get her out of my mind and the thought of her leaving without my seeing her again was almost unbearable.

I fretted during the entire thirty minute flight, answering my passengers' questions with short, terse, almost rude shouts. When one of them asked me THE question, I practically chewed his head off.

"Is that coral under the water down there?" he asked, pointing at the cloud shadow on the surface below.

"NO! It's cloud shadow."

"Oh," he said meekly, not to be heard from again.

Then I was suddenly sorry that I was being such a boor. After all, it was these people who paid my wages and allowed me to live this wonderful life-style. I realized that I was simply impatient to get back on the ground and find HER. So for the rest of the flight, I tried to be tolerant with their repetitive and ridiculous questions, and was less surly with them.

We finally landed, taxied back in and I off-loaded them and wished them well for the rest of their stay. As that was the last trip for me for the day, I took the Buccaneer up to the wash-bay near the hangar, where I hosed her down and began greasing her bearings. As I crouched under the right wing with the nipple of the grease gun firmly attached to the right wheel brake assembly, a pair of tanned feet sparsely protected by brown, cracked leather sandals, approached the plane and stopped before it. I looked up and my heart skipped a beat as I saw her standing there. She had showered, as she no longer had beads of salt sticking to her fine bronze skin. Her hair was still in pig-tails, and she had changed into a dark blue skirt with little white flower patterns on it, and a white blouse with a square-cut navy style collar.

"Hi," she said, squatting down in her apparently customary crouch to see what I was doing.

"Hello again," I replied calmly, although my pulse was racing.

It was almost impossible to believe that she was still here. I was beginning to think it had all been a dream, brought on by my self-imposed solitude.

"Did you decide about dinner, yet?" I asked casually.

She flashed me that broad white grin.

"Pizza's fine. And orange juice."

"Don't you drink anything else?"

"If you mean, do I drink, the answer is no. And I don't like any of your other soft drinks. They're too sweet. And that colored candy water you people drink! Green death! Yuck!!"

I chuckled at her reference to the 'cordial' based drinks so common in the stores.

"Any other complaints?"

"Sorry. It really IS awful. But the orange juice is the best I have ever tasted."

"Orange juice it is, then," I said, awkwardly crawling out from under the wing. I stood and arched my back, rubbing at my steel spine to ease the pain generated from bending and crouching like that.

"Are you all right?" she inquired gently, impulsively placing her hand on my arm and sending an electric shock of warm pleasure surging all through my body.

"Yeah. I'm fine. Just an old war wound," I joked.

"Really? Where does it hurt?"

"It's my spine. But I was just kidding about the war wound. Actually, I crashed a plane a couple of years ago, and they had to remove half my spine, which was smashed beyond repair, and replace it with a steel one. I was left a paraplegic, and they told me I would never walk again, but I fooled 'em."

"Oh, I am so sorry!" she said with genuine sympathy and concern. "Is it O.K. now?"

"Hurts like blazes! But only when I move," I smiled. "No, seriously, it aches a bit when I bend or crouch like I was just doing, or if I sit in the same position for too long, the steel pulls on what is left of my own spine causing it to hurt after a while. Apart from that, I am as good as new except for my legs, of course. You can see the left one is thinner than the right. That's because my right one became un-paralyzed first and I began to favor it. Still do, causing me to limp. That's why my mates call me 'Hoppy.' ''

"I wondered about that," she said.

"Anyway, I'm finished here," I grinned, changing the subject.

"I have to go home and shower to get this salt off me. Would you like me to come back and take you into town to eat, or if you prefer, I can bring it back here to you."

"I have quite a bit of packing and tidying up to do. Why don't you bring it back here. I am in a cream camper under a gum tree just inside the airport boundary fence. You can see it from the terminal."

"I'll find it," I said with confidence. What do you like on your pizza? The works?"

"Everything but anchovies and olives!"

"That's O.K. I don't like them either."

"What time?" she asked.

"Oh, around seven. It'll take me an hour to get home and cleaned up. Another half hour to get back to the pizza factory and wait while they burn — I mean, cook it."

"O.K., I'll see you then," she grinned. Then she waved, turned and wandered back down towards the trailer park.

I stood there watching her until she disappeared behind the trees at the edge of the airstrip, still not believing that this was happening to me. My heart was lighter and happier than I could ever remember. I did not want to admit that I was falling in love. After all, I had only known her a few short hours. Any fool knew that love at first sight only happened in the movies.

Yet here I was, trembling all over with anticipation and excitement at the very thought of just seeing her again. Could it be? Could it really be that I had actually found HER? The mate with whom to share this tropical Paradise? The soul-mate I had dreamed about for so long? No! It was impossible. She was leaving tomorrow morning, and I would never see her again.

Why then am I punishing myself like this? Why grow to like her, only to have to say good-bye yet again? It could never work, for a thousand reasons; not the least of which was the minor detail that she lived about ten thousand miles away. She might as well live on the moon! Why was I even thinking these thoughts? After all, I had only just met her!

While my head was thinking one thing, my feet were doing quite another. Before I was consciously aware of it, I was in the car and throwing gravel as I spun the wheels, hurled the 240Z out of the parking lot and up the short, narrow street and turned into Shute Harbor Road.

Kevin and the boys would be wondering why I was not in attendance at the pit for the afternoon's briefing session. No doubt, Pete would put them straight! You could always count on good ol' Pete!

Fifty minutes after returning to shower and make myself a bit more presentable to my new-found friend, I was again in my 240, her rakish snout aimed towards Airlie Beach. The setting sun was a crimson ball of fire, painting the summer clouds scarlet and grey and pink as it sank into the heart of the great 'Outback' of Australia.

I pulled up outside the pizza parlor in Airlie, went in and picked up their largest 'special,' ordered by phone a few minutes before I left the house. Opening the self-serve refrigerator, I extracted a large plastic bottle of freshly squeezed orange juice, then went to the counter and paid for both items.

The handling qualities of my sports car were severely tested on the way to the airstrip, where I arrived in record-breaking time. I turned in at the entrance to the "Flametree Caravan Park," ignoring the sign which plainly indicated the visitors' car parking area a the left of the entrance. I did slow to the posted five miles per hour, so as not to attract attention, and idled through the park, searching for the cream camper while there was still enough twilight to find it without flashing my headlights all over the place.

My stomach was curling in a familiar knot as I located the camper, though this time the tension was caused not by trauma but by sweet anticipation of seeing Cindy again. There was light in the pop-top as I parked the car, got out lugging my huge, flat cardboard box and my bottle of O.J., and knocked on the sliding side door.

She opened it immediately, and welcomed me in with a shy smile.

"One large Mexicana Pizza and one large O.J., special delivery, ma'am."

She took the proffered food, slid into the forward side of the small

291

foldaway dinette facing the rear of the vehicle, and waited while I struggled up the high step to slide in across from her.

"Hi! I'm starving," she said, lifting the lid of the box to peek inside.

"Hi. I'm Rod," I quipped.

She grinned politely at the old joke.

"It smells delicious."

"Best pizza in town!" I remarked.

"Only pizza in town," we said together, laughing at our identical thoughts.

Soon we were chomping down as if it was our first meal in weeks. In her case, it was. She poured a glass of orange juice for herself, and was appropriately horrified as I took a swig from the bottle I had brought for her.

"Yuuuck!" she gasped. "Didn't you bring your own drink?"

"No," I replied, surprised at her concern. "I thought we would share it. That's why I got a big one!"

"Uh-huh," she said doubtfully, staring from me to the bottle and back, as if I had suddenly grown two heads.

"Don't worry. I'm not completely uncivilized," I said. "I bathed and washed my lips just before I came," I added reassuringly.

She stared at me again, then her hunger overcame her disgust, and soon we had gobbled that giant pizza down in about five minutes flat.

The rest of the evening passed so quickly, I don't know where it went. We sat talking about anything and everything in her country and mine, until I happened to glance at my watch and discover that it was almost one a.m.; and I had to be up early to fly.

I didn't want to leave, as I knew there was a very real chance I might never see her again.

"What time are you going in the morning?" I asked nonchalantly.

"As soon as I can get my stuff together. I want to hit the road early, before it gets too hot. You people also don't seem to believe in air-conditioning in cars," she smiled.

"Or buildings either, for that matter. People up here think it's wimpy to have canned air. The most they'll tolerate is ceiling fans, to circulate the heat. Life's tough in the bush," I said, only half joking. I have to fly at eight. "I'll come early, say around seven, to say good-bye, if that's O.K."

"You don't have to do that," she said. "I'll drop you a postcard, or something."

"I'll be here," I replied with determination.

"O.K. then. I'll see you in the morning," she agreed, sliding over to the edge of her seat to open the door.

Something told me it was definitely time to go. I took the hint and stepped out of the camper, not wanting to do anything which might offend this girl. Our new-found friendship was too important to me.

For a few moments I stood looking up at her, not quite knowing how to end the evening.

"Thanks for the pizza," she smiled knowing I did not want to go. "It was really nice talking to you. I'll see you in the morning."

"O.K.," I replied, still reluctant to go.

She was bending down half out of the doorway. On an impulse, I stretched up and kissed her lightly on the lips, then turned and opened the car door.

"I'll see you in a few hours, then," I said as I slid down into the seat of the 240.

"Night," she replied, raising her hand in that little half wave that seemed to say so much.

My heart was pounding. I did not want to leave, yet I knew that if I made one unwelcome move, I would lose any chance of seeing her again. Some things she had said during the course of the evening made it quite obvious that she had her own strong convictions. Indeed, it was plain that she was embarrassed by her impulsive suggestion that I join her here in the camper for dinner. No. Any move I made now, other than to get in my car and drive away, would be the wrong one. I found I already cared too much to do anything else. So I drove away!

❖

24

At seven a.m. the same morning, I was knocking on her door. There was no answer. I knocked again, thinking she may be asleep. Still no answer! Perhaps she was over at the facilities block taking a shower. I waited. At seven thirty-five, I was about to give up and head on over to the airstrip to start getting my plane ready. Where could she be? Was she deliberately avoiding me? Did she not want to see me again after all? Had I done something, despite my concerted effort at self-restraint, to offend her?

I started the car and was just backing out of the narrow space between her camper and a tall old gum tree, when I spotted her climbing through the fence between the airstrip and the trailer park. She was dressed in the same white square-cut top, a pair of almost tidy but faded blue shorts and the old leather sandals. Her hair was again in pig-tails, although it was no longer stiff with salt. She came loping up to the car, waving and smiling at me.

"I didn't really think you would come," she panted as she slowed to a walk. "I went for an early walk along the airstrip. It's so peaceful and pretty. No sound except the wind and the wild parrots in the trees."

"It sure is," I replied, a little miffed that she did not expect me to turn up. "I was getting worried myself. I thought you were trying to avoid me. I thought I must have done something last night to upset you."

"No, no. Nothing like that. It's just that I am so used to people not doing anything they say they are going to do. I . . . just didn't expect you to show up, that's all."

"Not a very trusting soul, are you?" I said with a grin.

"No. Not any more. I have been hurt and disappointed too many times before by people who have lied to me."

"Well, I am here. I could not wait to see you again. Who knows when the next time might be? I will be wondering every minute you are in this country, where you are and what you are doing."

"Thanks. That's nice. I really will write to you."

"I'll be looking forward to it. Where do you go from here? Townsville, did you say?"

"Yes. I have to catch a plane from there to Mount Isa this afternoon. Then on to Alice Springs."

We were both standing beside the car under the gum tree.

I turned and took her hands in mine.

"I don't suppose there is any chance of your coming back this way before you head on home, is there?"

"I'm afraid not," she answered almost sadly. "My ticket is already written to leave from New Zealand back to the States. It would cost me more than I can afford to return to Australia after I have been there."

"What about before you leave for New Zealand?"

"I . . . don't know. I don't think so. Let me think about it. Look, I have to leave now. It's a long drive to Townsville, and I don't want to miss that plane. Thanks for coming to see me and say good-bye. I really do appreciate it; more than you know."

I lowered my head, deeply disappointed that she did not seem to want to see me again.

"It's mah pleasure, l'il lady," I said in my best — but still atrocious impression of John Wayne — trying to hide my sadness.

"Well, I guess I better run along as well," I added. "I have to get my plane ready for a reef trip in about half an hour."

I was still holding her hands firmly in my own, and shuffling my bare feet nervously on the dusty ground. I hesitated for a moment longer, then let go her hands, put my arms around her waist, and kissed her gently on

· the lips. She was warm and responsive in my arms, yet cool and predictably aloof at the same time. She did return my kiss, though, and at that moment I knew I simply must see her again before she left the country for good.

She drew away from me, taking my hands once more.

"I really do have to go now, Rod."

"I know. So do I. Keep in touch, please. I am very glad we met. I had a good time yesterday and last night."

"So did I," she smiled demurely.

I bent forward and once more kissed her lightly on the lips, then got back in the car. She leaned through the window and planted a return kiss on my right cheek.

"Please write," I pleaded. "I'll be waiting to hear from you."

"Don't worry, I will."

As she let go of the side of the car, I eased away from her, down the narrow driveway to the entrance of the park.

"Thanks again for dinner," she called after me, waving as I drove away.

As I returned the wave, a deep depression settled on me. I did not want to simply drive away from this girl, yet there was nothing else I could do.

She was determined to leave town and continue with her adventure tour around this huge country of mine. I could not blame her a bit for that! After all, Australia is as big as the continental U.S.A. and she had a lot of territory to explore in a very short time. But something had to be done to let her know that I was thinking about her.

When I got to the airstrip, I went directly into the terminal and rummaged through the reservations desk until I found what I was looking for — a Trans Australia Airlines schedule. Scanning through the pages, I found the correct flight number. Her flight left at one-forty this afternoon for Mount Isa, with continuing service onto Alice Springs.

She was right! She was already pushing for time. It was eight a.m. now, and she had at least a four hour drive to Townsville, find an unfamiliar airport, check her baggage, and dispose of her rented camper. I knew what I was going to do, though; I was going to call her at every airport where I knew she was going to be, until she got the message that I was not about to forget her.

Whistling with happy anticipation of hearing her voice again, if only on the phone, I went to prepare my aircraft for flight. The morning passed slowly. My usual enjoyment of the flight to the reef was tainted by concern that I may not make it back to the airstrip in time to page her at the Townsville airport before she left. We were due to get back at about twelve-thirty, but anything could — and often did — delay our return to the mainland.

Fortunately, today my fears were groundless, and I touched down outside the tiny terminal just slightly late at twelve forty-five. I taxied back and came to a rolling stop, shutting down my engine even before the plane had come to rest. I jumped out, remembered to assist my passengers to do the same, and excused myself, telling them nothing short of the truth, for a change.

"Sorry to rush off, folks, but I have a very important long-distance phone call to make. I hope you enjoyed your trip. The girls inside will be only too happy to help you with any souvenir purchases you would like to make."

With that, I did indeed dash off, up to the main administration office. In the more than two years that I had been there now, several improvements had been made to the facilities at Air Whitsunday, not the least of which was the replacement of the old trailer with a brand new, made to order administration building under some shady gum trees just next to the trailer. This building was connected to the house by a narrow, wooded path through the bush. It housed the telex machine, all the accounts, pilots' briefing and coffee break room and all the essentials for the day-to-day running of the company. It was also much more private for making phone calls to new friends.

At twelve fifty-two, I put a call through to T.A.A. at Townsville Airport, paging one of their passengers on the Mount Isa flight. I heard the loudspeakers over the background noise in the terminal.

"Paging T.A.A. passenger, Miss Cindy Harmon. Telephone call for Miss Cindy Harmon. Please pick up the nearest white courtesy phone."

I waited; and waited.

"I'm sorry sir. She doesn't seem to be answering the . . . "

"Hullo?" a breathless voice suddenly gasped.

There was a 'click' as the operator hung up.

"Hi. Just wanted to say good-bye. Again. I could hardly wait to get back from the reef to talk to you before you left. Hope you don't mind."

"Mind? I'm so glad you called. I have been thinking about you. I just wish there was some way . . . "

"So do I. But I want you to see as much as possible of the country before you go home. Have a good time, and be careful driving alone in the bush."

"I will. Don't worry. I'll send you a postcard from Ayers Rock."

"If you get a chance to call me," I said hopefully, "well . . . you have my number here and at home. If you have any kind of problem anywhere on the trip, please call me. I will try to help, even if I have to commandeer a Buccaneer to do it!"

"Thanks, Hoppy. I appreciate that. It's nice to know that there is someone in a strange country I can contact if I need to."

"You called me Hoppy."

"I know. It does kind of suit you. Listen, I have to go. They're boarding the flight. It's full and I don't want to have my seat taken by a standby. I'll try to call you. Take care. Bye."

"O.K. Bye. Don't forget to write."

"I won't. And Hop, thanks for calling me here. It was a nice surprise. The second one I have had today."

I grinned into the phone and uttered a typical Aussie reply in parting.

"No worries, mate! I'll see ya later."

"Bye. Got to go."

Click!

She was gone. For the second time that day, I felt disturbed, depressed and lonely when I lost contact with her. I thought I had learned what real loneliness was all about over the last couple of years — especially since Barbara's death — but nothing I had known before matched the deep feeling of despair I now harbored inside me at the loss of this girl.

I hung up and wandered back down to the airstrip to refuel Alpha Whiskey Yankee. Neither I, nor the red and white Buccaneer, was scheduled to fly again that day, so I taxied her up to the wash bay, gave her a good hose down and spent the rest of the afternoon drying, polishing and servicing her. I cleaned her inside and out, vacuumed about twenty cubic yards of sand out of her carpet ad seats, and finished up by sitting in my seat wiping all the grubby fingerprints off the vinyl headliner and side panels, and coating the instrument panel with half a bottle of Armorall.

Then I went up to the office and called Alice Springs Airport. I had already checked the schedule, and had been glancing at my watch every two minutes for the last three and a half hours.

"Hullo?"

"It's me again."

"Don't you ever give up?"

"Funny. You're not the first person to ask me that. My answer is still the same. If I did, I wouldn't be here."

"How did you know I would be here?"

"Pretty amazing, actually. I looked up your E.T.A. in the schedule, added about twenty minutes to allow for delays and for you to get inside the terminal, and there you were. Worked out rather well, didn't it?"

"Very clever. I'm glad it did."

"Me too. How was the flight?"

"Just fine. A bit bumpy for the last part. The pilot said it was the heat coming off the desert."

"That'll do it. Must be over a hundred degrees out there. Well, have a good time. Give my regards to Uluru."

"To who?"

"The Rock. That's the Aboriginal name."

"Oh. Well, I'll try to phone you from Adelaide, maybe. Thanks for calling again."

"No problem. Just wanted you to know I'm thinking about you."

"I can tell. Anyway, I had better go. I have to see if someone here knows anything about a rental car for me."

"O.K. Take care. I'll look forward to hearing from you. Bye."

"Bye Hoppy. I'll call when I can."

As the phone went dead, that almost nauseous feeling hit me in the pit of the stomach once more. This time, it was worse. Now I had no way of contacting her again. A desperate feeling of loss came over me.

What if she did not call or write? What if she just drove off into the Northern Territory sunset, never to be heard from again? It had happened before. Many times. No! I HAD to see her again, dammit. She must call. She MUST!

She didn't.

For the first few days after I lost contact with her, I nearly drove myself and everybody else at Air Whitsunday crazy. I sat at home by my phone every night, waiting for her to call. I went to work early every morning and waited for her to call there. Every time I landed after a trip, I would ask the girls if there had been any calls or mail for me. I took to going into town myself whenever I could to pick up the mail from the company box at the post office. Nothing! On the fifth day, however, just when I did not think I could take another minute of this torture, Annie arrived back at the strip with the mail. I was sitting in my Buccaneer, just about to start up.

"Hoppy! Hoppy wait! There are some postcards for you from Cindy."

I leapt out of the plane with more speed and agility than I was aware my legs would allow.

"Thanks Annie," I said, taking the cards from her with trembling hand. "You're a bloody lifesaver!"

"Boy! You've got it bad, haven't you?" she laughed, striding into the terminal.

My first flight was empty, so as to pick up passengers on one of the islands. I told myself they could wait a few minutes. I sat in the sun outside on the verandah, turned the cards over and carefully placed them in order of the dates she had written on them. There were four altogether; two were from Alice Springs and two from Ayers Rock.

They all had brief, newsy comments about the weather and the wonders of the Outback. Nothing sentimental. Not the slightest indication that she missed me or wanted to see me again. Just fulfilling a promise to write. But she HAD written! Four times on four different dates. At least, she had put different dates on them. It didn't matter. I was on Cloud Nine! She had written to me. I stuffed the cards in the back pocket of my shorts and jumped back in my plane. For the rest of the day, I was the most co-operative and friendly pilot and tour guide in the islands. Nothing was too much trouble for me. It was like my first day at work. I even answered the 'cloud shadow' question with a civil reply!

The days that followed were the same. I was euphoric. Almost every day now, I received at least one card from her. The concise messages gradually became less clipped and formal and more indicative of her bright, life-loving personality. She began drawing little animals and birds and footprints all over the cards. She made me laugh and cry with joy when I read them — over and over again.

Two weeks after I got the first card, I was sitting in the pilots' room having a cup of coffee with the boys when the phone in the outer office rang. Di answered it as usual.

"Good morning. Air Whitsunday. May I help you? Uh . . . I think so. Hang on a minute, please. Hoppy? Telephone. I think it's Cindy."

I leapt off the bench, throwing hot coffee all over Paul as I did so.

"Hey! Watch it, Hop!" he shouted indignantly, reaching for a damp cloth to dab at the stains on his already dirty T-shirt.

"Sorry mate," I shouted back at him from the other room, "Emergency."

"Emergency my . . . " he returned quite disgusted. "Bloody women," I heard him muttering to the fellows in the other room as I picked up the phone.

"Hello?"

"Hi Hoppy. It's me. I can't talk long. I am using a private phone."

"G'day, mate! Boy, is it good to hear your voice. Where are you?"

"I am still in Adelaide, staying with some very nice people who own a ranch — I mean, a sheep property — down here. I just met them."

"That's wonderful! Hey, thanks for all the cards. I have been driving everyone around here nutty waiting for the mail every day."

"Good. I want to ask you something. Don't feel you have to say yes. Just think about it. I want to see you again, but the only way is if you can meet me in Sydney next weekend, before I fly to Tasmania. Is . . . is there any chance? I . . . I mean, would it be possible for you to get down there?"

"Are you kidding?"

"I'm sorry. I guess it's not very nice of me to ask you to fly a thousand miles to see someone you have only known for one whole day."

"No, no. What I meant was, I would love to come. I'll be there!" I replied, excitement rising in my voice. I could not believe what I was hearing

"Seriously?" she said. "You never cease to amaze me. Where can I meet you, then?"

I had to calm down and think for a moment. My pulse was racing and my heart was pounding. I still could not comprehend that this was happening to me.

"Do you know the Wentworth Hotel?" I asked hopefully.

"No. Where is it?"

"It's one of the most famous landmarks in Sydney. It's just up from Circular Quay, in Bligh Street. Just ask anyone, once you get downtown. Put your car in the underground car park and meet me in the main lobby at three o'clock on Saturday afternoon. How's that sound?"

"Wonderful! I'll be there! Are . . . are you sure it's O.K.?"

"Don't worry! I'll be there too. I can't wait to see you again."

"Me too! Saturday afternoon, then. In Sydney. I'll have to leave right away. It's about a four or five day drive from here, isn't it?"

"At least. You will be pushing it. What's today? Tuesday. You should be able to make it O.K. It's only about twelve hundred miles, I think."

"Well, better go. I am glad I caught you in the office. I will be on the road from now on, but I'll try to call if I get a chance. See you on Saturday, then?"

"Looking forward to it. Thanks for asking."

"Thank you — for saying you will come. Bye."

I put down the phone, wondering how the hell I was going to get to Sydney on Saturday. Well, she was expecting me in Sydney on Saturday afternoon, and by God I would be in Sydney on Saturday afternoon!

I walked back into the pilots' room in a complete daze, ignoring the rude comments from my colleagues about young — and not so young — love. Assuming I could talk Kevin into giving me the weekend off when it was not my turn, I still had to get on one of only two commercial jet flights from Proserpine to Sydney. I knew those flights were usually booked solid at least a week in advance.

Down at the terminal a little while later, I checked the schedules for Ansett and T.A.A. flights leaving Proserpine on Saturday. Both departed within thirty minutes of each other; one at nine thirty-five and the other at nine fifty. I called reservations and got the dreaded answer twice. Both flights were oversold. There was not even a chance that I could get on the standby list. But I HAD to get on, dammit!

Well, first things first. I tracked Kevin down at the house, told him my predicament, and asked him if I could have from Saturday to Monday off — just in case I could not get back on Sunday. He agreed, for the usual blackmail price of a carton of beer.

The following Saturday morning, I was at Proserpine Airport even before the airline staff had arrived. At this large municipal airport, the modern terminal building which housed both airlines was generally deserted except from about two hours before to an hour after the scheduled flights had come and gone.

The agents of both airlines knew me well enough, as I had often had passengers charter a Buccaneer from Shute Harbor to Proserpine to catch their commercial flights out. I told the airline agents my plight, but the situation was still the same; no hope of getting on board! There were already more than enough standby passengers to take care of any no-shows. I waited in utter dejection as time wore on and the first jet came and went. When the second had closed its doors, turning away dozens of others as well as myself, I despondently trudged back to the T.A.A. ticket desk.

"Nothing else going out today, I suppose?" I asked hopefully.

"Not to Sydney, I'm afraid," the girl replied, punching her computer keys. "But wait! There is a flight to Brisbane departing at eleven ten. You could connect with a Sydney flight from there."

My hopes soared.

"How does it look?"

"It's full, too. But so far there are no standbys. Do you want me to put you down?"

"Yes. Thanks. I'll try anything at this point."

I waited nervously for another hour.

The DC-9 landed, unloaded its passengers, and almost immediately began taking on the southbound people. I stood by the desk and looked hopefully at the traffic agent.

"It doesn't look good, I'm afraid. Every seat has been accounted for."

"Oh. Well, thanks anyway for trying," I said as I sadly shrugged and turned to walk away. Just as I did so, however, the captain of the DC-9 came out of the operations office behind the ticket counter.

"Hey, Rod!"

I turned to be confronted by Hal Anderson, the only T.A.A. pilot I knew in the whole damn airline. I had met him a couple of times before, both here and in Mackay, when I was standing around waiting for my own passengers.

"Hal! How are you?" I greeted him, genuinely happy to see him.

"Fine. How about yourself?"

"I'd be better if I could get on that plane of yours. I'm trying desperately to get to Sydney today, but everything is full."

"Are you kidding? You can ride on our jump seat! Turn your ticket back in. I can get you as far as Brisbane. When we get there, I will check the pilot list and ask whoever is flying that trip to take you on the jump seat there, too. How's that sound?"

"Hal, you have just done your good deed for the year. I owe you a big one!"

"Forget it," he smiled, looking at me quizzically, but not deigning to ask what I had meant by my comment. "Come on," he added, striding away towards his big silver bird, "I'll show you my office."

An hour and forty-five minutes later we were on the ground in Brisbane. True to his word, Hal organized a jump seat for me on the next Airbus bound for Sydney. Unfortunately, it was not due to arrive there until two forty. I was going to be late!

My cab pulled up outside the grand front entrance of the Sydney Wentworth Hotel at three twenty-five. I overpaid the driver, generously compensating him for risking both our lives on the half hour breakneck speed journey from Kingsford-Smith Airport into town.

The magnificent lobby was, as usual, full of people milling around waiting and watching for their guests or friends to arrive. It was one of the most famous meeting places in Sydney. I looked around frantically. I did not see her anywhere. Surely she would not have left already! Oh please, let her be here somewhere. Suddenly Cindy's tanned, smiling face appeared through the crowd. She rushed up to me and put her arm around my waist. I did likewise, and we turned to walk back outside where we could breath and talk more easily.

"I didn't think you were coming," she said. "I thought for sure you had changed your mind and decided that this was crazy."

"It is," I chuckled. "That's why I'm here. I love doing crazy things. I'm sorry I am late, though. I almost didn't make it at all. The only connection I could get did not land until about half an hour ago. So, how was your long drive?"

"I want you to know that I have driven non-stop for five days to get here this afternoon. I slept in the car every night, and passed up a lot of sight-seeing of some beautiful country. I think I would have been mad if you had not shown up."

"Wouldn't blame you a bit. I don't think I would like to see you mad," I replied, only half joking.

"Well, where do we go from here?"

"I don't suppose you're hungry?"

"Starving!"

"What do you feel like?"

"Do you know what I would really like?"

"Name it!"

"A cheese, lettuce and mustard sandwich — on whole wheat bread."

"Ah, a girl of simple tastes," I laughed. "That's what I like. Well, let's go for a walk through Kings Cross and see the sights. There are lots of good restaurants there, so if you change your mind and want a real meal, just say so."

So we walked. She picked a little deli bar tucked in a niche between two much nicer restaurants, and ordered her sandwich. She was certainly different. I had to admit, she was wonderfully, refreshingly different!

"Where to now?" she asked as she finished her customary orange juice, carefully guarding it so that I was not able to take a swig of it in public.

"How about we take a stroll around the Opera House?" I suggested.

"Great idea! I love that place; the harbor and the wind blowing off the water. I went to a concert there the first night I arrived here from the States."

"O.K, let's go."

"Do you mind driving? I'd kind of like to be a passenger for a change, so I can see the sights."

"Not at all. It's only five minutes drive from here, anyway."

The Sydney Opera House was remarkably uncrowded for a Saturday afternoon. We wandered hand in hand around the acres of concrete surrounding the famous and unusual building. We leaned over the rail on the harbor side, facing the stiff wind and breathing deeply of the salty air.

"I love this!" she said. "I love being outside in the wind. No people around to bother us either. The boats on the harbor, the blue sea and sky. It's great!"

Suddenly she trotted off towards a kiosk — one of several food bars set into the base of the building.

"Let's get an ice cream," she said mischievously.

"O.K.," I laughed, following her lead.

She ordered a huge double scoop of chocolate ice cream. A single was quite big enough for me.

We went back outside and sat on the railing, licking at our ice cream cones like a couple of big kids. She got me to hold hers while she took a couple of pictures of me with her ever-present Leica. Then she rested the camera on the side of a concrete flower box, squatted to aim and focus it, pressed the button and came running over to put her arm around my waist before the timer released the shutter.

We finished our ice creams and then strolled down to the famous "Man-O-War" steps beside the Opera House. She sat and listened with genuine pleasure and awe as I repeated my father's story that this was where he — and thousands of other sailors over the last two centuries — used to jump ashore from the Navy lighters when they arrived in Sydney on Liberty. He had spent the duration of World War Two on the cruiser 'Hobart' and many times skipped up these very same convict-carved steps to enjoy the sights and sounds of war-time Sydney.

There was a concrete and steel pontoon tied alongside the steps now, and I jumped on to it to pose for Cindy as she took some more pictures.

From there, we strolled around the quayside and up the hill overlooking the Naval Base at Garden Island. We entered the same gates of the Botanical Gardens which I had stumbled through nearly three years ago, when I had ventured into Sydney for the first time since my release from hospital.

As we ambled along, I reflected that I was a much happier man today than I was on that previous visit to these beautiful gardens.

Cindy tugged at my hand and pulled me over to the sandstone seawall. We jumped up and sat on top of it in almost the same spot I had sat so long ago. We kicked our heels against the wall — so easy to do, now that my legs were virtually back to their full strength again.

We spent the rest of the afternoon wandering happily around those hundreds of green acres of shady trees and sweet-smelling summer shrubs and flowers. By the time the sun was beginning to set, I knew I had found my mate.

As we found our way back to her car, I asked her if she had any special accomodation organized.

"No. Do you know a nice place to stay? Somewhere around here on the harbor?"

"Let's drive around to Rose Bay. It's a pretty suburb. There are a couple of good hotels near the old flying boat base; right on the water."

Twenty minutes later, we were checking into the Cameo Inn, a circular building overlooking the entire harbor. From our rooms on the seventh floor, we could gaze out across the sparkling, moonlit water at the lights of the north and south downtown areas, connected by the single span of the 'Coathanger' — the famous Sydney Harbor Bridge.

We ate downstairs in the hotel Chinese Restaurant. The food proved to be superb. Later, we wandered along the fine sandy beach which flanked the harbor in front of the hotel. We walked ankle deep in cool, clear water gently lapping at the shore.

The sand was soft and cool and inviting, so we sat and admired the brilliant stars. The Southern Cross glittered down from a cloudless sky. For the first time in my life, I was truly, supremely happy, and contented in the company of another human being. I had at last found someone with whom to share all the wonderful things in life that I had learned to appreciate much more since recovering from my paralysis. The moon and stars, the sea and sky and wind; a sunny day, a rainy night. They all spelled Cindy now. But more than that. I was in love!

The following morning, we drove the short distance back to the neighboring suburb of Double Bay, where we had breakfast at George's coffee house. Cindy was a connoisseur of tea, and she was really sold on the fine Australian blend, which she said was excellent.

The morning passed far too quickly, and soon it was time for me to get back to the airport. I had taken the precaution of buying a ticket home before I left the airport yesterday, while there were still a few seats. There was no way I would be lucky enough to land myself a jump seat again.

We were both miserable as we sat in the T.A.A. lounge waiting for the inevitable boarding call.

"I don't know when or if I will ever see you again," she said, "but I will be thinking about you. All the way through Tasmania and New Zealand — and all the way home. Is . . . is there any chance that you might be able to come to Dallas . . . sometime?"

"I just happen to have six weeks vacation due in January. And I haven't been to the States for years. What a great idea! When is the best time to come?"

"It will probably too cold for your tropical blood in January. April-May is springtime. It is pretty then, with all the wildflowers blooming."

"I'll be there. You can count on it!"

The speakers blared that this was the last call for flight 469 to Brisbane and Proserpine. It was the only flight to Proserpine that afternoon, so I had to be on it. We stood and hugged tightly, embarrassed though she was at this public display, then I was carried off in the last wave of boarding passengers.

I did not see her again for nearly four months.

The next few weeks were filled with expectant joy every day. Cards and letters streamed in from all her ports of call; even a newspaper clipping with a photograph of her feeding a baby wallaby, taken somewhere in Tasmania. Cindy hiked and drove all around Tasmania and both islands of New Zealand, keeping in constant touch by phone or card or lengthy, newsy letter.

No matter where I was or what I was doing, I could not for one minute of the day or night get her out of my mind. Even when I was flying, which was usually my favorite part of any day, I found my mind replaying a mental videotape of how she looked in all her rag-tag clothes, her pigtails, her old leather sandals and even older canvas tennis shoes and floppy straw hat. Her love of everything in nature — every bird and animal, every tree and flower and insect, was something I had never known in any other person before. I looked at the world with freshly inspired eyes, and wished that she could be with me again to share my life, and the ordinary things I would have taken for granted before she came along.

Now, every time I saw an unusual shell or pebble on a beach, or a brightly colored fish or coral or bird, or a giant turtle or even a tiger shark,

I wished she was there to see it, too; to laugh and cry for joy; to simply love life and all things in life as she did so fervently.

As Christmas approached, her time in the South Pacific drew to an end.

Finally, she called to say the next time I heard from her, she would be home in Dallas. But somehow, ten thousand miles did not seem so far any more. I resolved that I would indeed spend my vacation in Texas.

On Christmas Day, Kevin and Sue let everyone take the day off to spend with their families. All flights, except for emergency charters were cancelled. All they required was one person to man the office and the phones. The pilots drew straws. With my inimitable skill and cunning, I selected the short one. So I spent Christmas Day sitting in un-air-conditioned one hundred and five humid degrees, waiting for someone to book a flight to the Great Barrier Reef!

The day was not entirely wasted, however. At about three p.m., I was sitting there literally fuming, since nobody had even thought to bring me a bloody beer, when the phone rang — for the first time since I had been there.

"Hi Hoppy! Merry Christmas! I tried to get you at home, but you weren't there. I miss you terribly!"

"G'day, mate! Merry Christmas to you, too. No! I am not at home. I am the only sucker on duty, while the rest of the gang are living it up. Shrimp on the barbie, ice cold tinnies in the fridge, and all that. Paul is throwing his customary party. He even said somebody should bring a ham this year, since I was not coming. Very bloody funny!"

"I am so sorry, Hoppy. I wish you were here. It's so cold! Even the creek behind my folk's place is frozen over. I can't remember that ever happening before. Did you get the pictures I sent you?"

"I sure did! It looks great! I wish I could be there, too."

"Do you think you can come over in April, then?"

"Nope. I don't think so."

"Oh," she said in a tiny, disappointed voice. "Later, then?"

"No." I paused for effect.

There was a long silence on the other end.

"How about February?" I asked quietly.

"That would be wonderful. I . . . I thought you were going to say that you weren't coming at all now. But February? Can you do it?"

"Of course I can do it. Let's say February fourteenth, just for the heck of it."

"But that's . . . that's Valentine's Day."

"Can't think of a better day to arrive, can you?"

"It's perfect! I can't wait to see you, Hop."

We talked for what seemed like hours. When she said she could not talk any longer because her phone bill would be astronomical, I told her to hang up and I would call her back. I gave us both a Christmas present, compliments of Air Whitsunday, and returned her call. We spoke for at least another thirty minutes.

The next six weeks could not pass quickly enough for either of us. We ran up huge bills on both our phones. We called each other at all hours of the day and night. More often than not, we found each other's lines busy, only to discover that we had been trying to call at the same time. We had a very strong mental bond and seemed to be able to reach out to each other's mind.

The weeks dragged on ever so slowly, and I asked Kevin and Sue for my six weeks leave well in advance. Not only did they grant it, but they helped me get tickets on QANTAS at airline discount rates, which saved me over a thousand dollars.

I decided that I would leave from Brisbane so I could spend a few days with my parents before I took off for the States. My folks were delighted to see me, of course. They still could not believe that I was walking and flying again after being crippled as I had been. Finally the day came for me to leave. They drove me to the airport and sat patiently waiting for me to board the 747. My Mother cried profusely, as always.

The boarding call came. I hugged them both, shook hands with Dad and kissed Mum's salty cheeks

"Have a good time," she said through her sniffles. "And be careful. Call us when you get there."

I smiled patiently. "'Bye folks. Don't worry. I've done it all before, you know. After all, I WAS a flight attendant for eight years. I'll be fine."

Ten minutes later, I watched through my window as they waved furiously from the glassed-in observation deck. I knew they could not see me. They were just hoping I could see them.

The muffled whine of four mighty Rolls Royce turbofans winding up in their start sequences flowed through my entire body. It felt good to be on the move again. The last time I had been on one of these giant ships, I was on duty as a flight attendant. The huge Boeing trundled down to the end of the runway and seconds later we were rolling, the engines now screaming at full power. The deck angle was suddenly at twenty degrees nose up and we were climbing away. When those eighteen wheels again touched the ground, we would be in Honolulu!

I discovered that I knew several of the cabin crew members from my previous years with the airline. Talking about old times with them, and filling them in on what I was doing now, helped to pass the time much more quickly than normal on this long, nine hour flight.

I had decided not to stop over in Hawaii, wanting to see Cindy too badly to waste any time lying on Waikiki Beach alone. So for fourteen hours I ate and slept and talked and read and fidgeted and thought about Cindy and what I was going to say to her when I got to Dallas.

In Los Angeles, I checked in at the American Airlines counter, got my boarding pass, then fidgeted for another two hours until my flight was ready for departure.

I did not mind admitting to myself that I was nervous. In fact, I think I was terrified! I was going to be meeting Cindy's parents and living in their home for the best part of a month. I sure hoped that we would get along! I need not have worried, though.

Another two hours passed and I walked out the gate at the American Airlines terminal of the massive Dallas/Fort Worth International Airport. Cindy spotted me immediately and pushed through the crowd towards me. She practically leapt into my arms and we hugged tightly. She cried, just as my mother had done on the other side of the world.

She introduced me to her parents, who were so like my own, it was almost unbelievable. Cindy and I had told each other all about our parents, but I still could not believe that they had the same first names.

Almost an hour later, her father's huge Lincoln Town Car cruised silently down the quiet, old, pecan lined street to their beautiful home in east Dallas. They knew I was dead on my feet, so Cindy led me straight to the room they had prepared for me. We sat talking until we both realized that I was falling asleep in the chair. She took my arm and led me to the bed, on which I immediately collapsed.

"Get some sleep," she said. "Whenever you wake up, we'll decide what you want to do about dinner tonight. O.K.?"

I did not hear the end of her sentence. When I woke, it was dark. A royal blue down comforter had been tucked around me and my shoes had been removed. I looked at the luminous dials of my watch. It was only six p.m. How could it be dark? Then I remembered it was the middle of winter here. I struggled out of bed, went to the bathroom and threw cold water on my face to bring myself back to a reasonable state of consciousness, then found my way out to the living room of the huge house.

Cindy heard me and intercepted me halfway, took my arm and escorted me down the hall.

"Mom and Dad want to know if you feel like going out to dinner with them tonight," she said, clinging tightly to my arm and resting her head on my shoulder. "Do you feel up to it?"

"I feel up to it," I replied. "But if they don't mind, I'd kind of like the two of us to go out alone. If that's O.K. with you?"

"That's exactly what I already told them. Great minds think alike!"

"Do you have a favorite restaurant? It's your town."

"I sure do. I have taken the liberty of making a reservation, hoping you would not be too tired to go out."

"Sounds great to me. What kind of food?"

"Definitely not what you're used to, from what I have seen of your eating habits," she laughed. "Mostly good, fresh seafood. But you can get other stuff as well. And they have a dessert called Chocolate Satin Pie which is out of this world!"

I greeted her parents once more as we entered their huge living room. They understood completely that we wanted to be alone with each other for the first time in months.

After taking a long, hot, sudsy shower to rinse away the fatigue and grime of a ten thousand mile, non-stop trip, I dressed in my only suit, which was remarkably uncrushed, and let Cindy lead me out to her old 1970 orange Cutlass coupe. I had absolutely no idea where we were going, so I sat back and enjoyed the drive, trying to calm my knotting stomach at the same time. The old familiar tension was building, but this time for a totally different reason.

We were seated at a table for two in the restaurant decorated with lots of shiny brass rails and dark wood and black and white marble floor tiles. After perusing our menus, we gave our orders to a hovering waiter whose moustache was as starched as his snow white jacket, then sat back enjoying each other's company again. By the end of the main course, I was as nervous as a cat on hot bricks and Cindy was feeling the tension, too.

"What's the matter, Hoppy?" she asked shyly, knowing very well what the matter was. She did not have to be as bright as she was to realize that there was a very special reason why I had chosen February fourteenth to arrive in her country and go out to a romantic dinner the same evening.

"I . . . uh, that is," I stammered foolishly, reaching across the table for her hands again.

"Cindy, I love you, you know."

"I know. I love you, too," she replied softly, gripping my hands tightly.

"Will . . . will you marry me," I finally managed to blurt out.

Her grip tightened on my hands and as she gazed across at me, her eyes filled with tears.

"Hoppy, I do love you. Very much. But there are so many things I have to think about before I give you an answer. It's not just a case of our different countries and backgrounds, either. I . . . wanted to do so many things before I got married. Australia was to be just the beginning of many trips I had planned to take, places I wanted to see. I still want to do all those things. But then I met you and as I got to know you better, I realized that I wanted to share all those things with you. I am very confused right now. Please let me think about it before I give you an answer. O.K.?"

I was, of course, devastated! It had never once occurred to me that she might not want to marry me. All our phone calls over the last few months, the long, loving letters, her reaction to my wanting to come to America so soon after I had last seen her, had indicated to me that she wanted to marry me as much as I wanted to marry her.

Now she was telling me that she had other more important things to do before she thought about getting married!

"I . . . I'm sorry," I began, tears beginning to well in my own eyes. "I thought . . . I mean, I don't know what I thought. I guess I just assumed that you wanted to get married as much as I did. I have given this a lot of thought too, you know, over the last few months. It's not something I just decided on the spur of the moment."

"I know, Hoppy. And I am proud and honored that you asked me. I just need some time, that's all."

"O.K.," I replied sulkily, calming down a little as the built-up tension seeped away. "I won't push you. I won't mention it again. I am going to be here for a month, so let's just enjoy the time we have together and get to know each other better. Maybe you will be able to give us both an answer before I go home."

"Thanks, Hop. Don't be mad at me. I do love you. I am just very confused, that's all."

Of course, I did not keep my word about not pushing her into making a decision. At least once a day, every day for five weeks, I asked her if she had made up her mind yet. I knew it was bothering her tremendously, but I simply could not help myself.

We did have a wonderful time, though. She took me skiing in Colorado. It was only the second time I had ever seen snow, much less tried to ski on the stuff! Cindy taught me how to ski. She had been doing it herself since she was about ten years old, so she was quite an accomplished skier. I was terrified that I would twist myself around my thinner, weaker, left leg and either break it or some other part of my body again. However, I managed to survive without injuring anything except my pride, which was already severely dented by Cindy's continuing refusal to give me an answer to my proposal.

The days and weeks passed incredibly quickly. When we got back from Colorado, she took me, at my request, to San Antonio to see the Alamo, one of my favorite pieces of American history. Much to the astonishment of Cindy and her family, I knew more about that particular legend, and the lead-up to those 'thirteen days of glory' than they did. By the time we finally returned to Dallas, we knew we were very much in love, and knew deep down that it was our destiny to be together. However, Cindy was still unable to give me a definite answer. She wanted to visit me again in Australia and meet my parents and sisters, since I had come all this way to meet her parents and brothers.

On the day I left Dallas, we agreed that she would come to see me in May, about eight weeks away, to spend some time with my family. Those weeks were the longest I had known in my entire life; even longer than the weeks I had lain on my back in hospital, desperately awaiting the day I could get out of bed. We ran up another two incredible phone bills during the intervening period.

I was quite impossible to live with a far as my mates at Air Whitsunday were concerned. They gave me up for hopelessly lost. I asked Kevin for some more time off to spend with my family in Brisbane. He jokingly agreed that I was useless to him until I got my love life sorted out, so he let me go for another two weeks.

The day before Cindy was due to arrive, I flew to Brisbane. I could not wait for her to get off that QANTAS 747. Finally the hour arrived, and so did the giant aircraft — on time — incredibly enough. My folks and I waited outside the Customs gate; and waited. And waited. Three hundred and sixty people came through that barrier, but Cindy was not among them. I grew more panic-stricken with every passing moment. After a very long time, the cabin crew came through the gate. I stopped the Flight Service Director and asked him if there was anybody left inside. He said that he did not see anyone. The crew was usually the last out.

She had not come! After all this painful anticipation and waiting, she had not been on the plane. Oh God! What was I going to do without her? I could not stand the thought of going through this again. My parents and I sadly turned and walked away from the gate. My mother began to cry—as usual. My Dad put his arm around me and the three of us headed towards the front door of the terminal.

Cindy was not coming.

As we were about to step outside the terminal, the Customs gate slid open one last time. I turned as I heard the sound, and there she was! I ran to her and we embraced tightly and did not let go of each other for a long time. Cindy was crying. My mother was crying. We all hugged together, and I knew instantly that the three of them were going to get along just fine.

"What happened to you?" I asked as the excitement of the moment wore off.

"You wouldn't believe it," she replied, not at all amused. "They lost my bag. Only MINE! Of the hundreds of people on that plane, they lost my bag! The thing is halfway to New Guinea by now, apparently. They took your address and said they would send it to me there, as soon as they retrieve it."

We walked hand-in -hand out to the car and sat happily in the back as Dad drove us home. The three of them chatted continuously all the way, laughing and joking as if they had known each other forever.

We spent the first week at home. Cindy met my sister Sandy and her husband, John. Cindy and Sandy hit it off immediately, as they both loved animals — horses in particular. Then Cindy and I drove out to see my other sister Wendy and her husband, Leith and their three great kids, Tanya, Jo-Anne and Duncan, who live on a cattle station three hundred miles west of Brisbane. They took Cindy riding and chased up some kangaroos for her to photograph in the wild.

By the time we got home from that trip, she had at last agreed that our being together was more important than any of her previous plans. She said her mind had been made up by my family, who had opened their hearts and homes to her so warmly. Her family and mine were so similar that we both knew our relationship was going to join two families and two cultures across ten thousand miles.

We spent several days searching Brisbane for the perfect engagement ring, but Cindy could not find one single ring that appealed to her. Then one day at home, she noticed my mother's ring.

"That's IT! That's what I would like. A ring just like that!"

She already had my mother's firm approval and friendship, but this absolutely sealed it. We found a young jeweler in downtown Brisbane who enjoyed a challenge. He crafted an exact duplicate of that forty-five year old ring, and was justifiably proud of the result.

We took a long time discussing the pros and cons of where we would live. In the end, we decided that it would be easier for me to move to Dallas, as Cindy was still living at home and was very close to her family. My folks were quite accustomed to not seeing me for long periods. I had been a transient aviator for many years now. They understood that to me, home was wherever I happened to hang my hat. They also understood the strong bond between Cindy's parents and their only daughter, and their natural desire to have her married in Dallas. We therefore decided, much to her folks' relief, to marry and settle in Texas. Australia would always be our other home.

Now that Cindy had finally let herself make the big decision, we were both supremely happy. She left to go back home and begin making preparations for our new life together, not the least of which was the long and tedious process with the U.S. Immigration Department about my permanent entry into the country.

I gave notice of my intention to resign from Paradise as from the last week in August. Kevin and Sue had been, without a doubt, the best employers I ever had, and I was very sorry to leave them. Even now, I look back fondly on those wonderful days on the Great Barrier Reef, and often think about the possibility of returning.

I sold my faithful car, gave away all my other worldly possessions, filled one suitcase with my favorite clothes (reminiscent of the day I left Sydney for the aviation academy all those years ago) and said goodbye to my family and my country for the last time on the first day of September.

My Dad was proud and honored when I asked him to be my Best Man at our wedding.

Six weeks later, on the nineteenth of October, exactly six years and one month to the day since my near-fatal airplane crash, Cindy and I were married in Dallas with our fathers from opposite shores of the Pacific Ocean standing proudly by our sides.

We are still living happily ever after!

———————————— ❖ ————————————

EPILOGUE

The following January, after three months of study and frustrating job-hunting, I was hired by a company which operated a fleet of fifty year old DC-3s on cargo flights throughout Texas and the neighboring states.

I flew as co-pilot for the next six months, learning all there was to know about the tricky handling characteristics of these ancient machines. Finally my big day came and I was tested and promoted to captain.

For two years, I flew through some of the worst weather I had so far encountered in my flying career. I began to think that the terrifying ordeals with which I had been confronted on the Great Barrier Reef were nothing compared to flying through Spring and Fall thunderstorms and Winter ice-storms — especially in airplanes that were half a century old and had already been flown far beyond the normally accepted limits of wear and tear. After all, some of these same planes had flak and bullet holes in their sides, still there from World War Two! Only God knew what punishment they had endured by three generations of pilots since then!

I could not decide which was worse; getting tossed around by Nature gone berserk during the Spring thunderstorms, or watching the layers of deadly, lift-destroying ice build up on the wings while flying through sleet and snow in the dead of winter.

Well, I tolerated this madness for two years while I searched for a job flying aircraft with such modern amenities as anti-ice equipment and weather radar. During this time, I defied death on numerous occasions which were solely related to the age of the aircraft and their components. In one period of about four months, the airplanes I was flying suffered no fewer than six engine failures! Naturally, they all occurred in the middle of winter when fog, rain, snow and low visibility made blind landings under instrument conditions difficult enough on two engines. On one engine, these approaches became positively mortifying! The DC-3s never did give up attempting to kill me, right up to my last trip with the company. But that is another story, to be included in a future book devoted to my adventures as a DC-3 freight dog.

Next, I was offered a position with a larger freight airline which operated Boeing 727s. Of course, I had to begin the new job as a flight engineer, and I flew 'sidesaddle' with this company for nearly two years.

Finally, my big break came and I was offered a job as a first officer with one of the largest regional airlines in the country, flying brand new, state-of-the-art aircraft. After another two years, I made captain again.

It was just one more challenge on the long, hard road from wheelchair to wings!